The Violinist.com
Interviews: Volume 1

LAURIE NILES

ISBN: 978-0-9838130-7-1

ACKNOWLEDGEMENTS

This book involved the efforts of many people, and I'm grateful for all their help in making it happen. My thanks to all the musicians I've interviewed over the years for Violinist.com, and especially to those featured in this book: Hilary Hahn; the late Ruggiero Ricci; Anne Akiko Meyers; Rachel Barton Pine; Joshua Bell; Anne-Sophie Mutter; James Ehnes; Janine Jansen; Tasmin Little; Philip Setzer; Philippe Quint; Gil Shaham and Adele Anthony; Augustin Hadelich; Sarah Chang; Zachary DePue; Simon Fischer; Clara-Jumi Kang; Lara St. John; Nicola Benedetti; Nadja Salerno-Sonnenberg; Judy Kang; David Garrett; Leila Josefowicz and Esa-Pekka Salonen; Stanley Ritchie; Maxim Vengerov; and Elmar Oliveira. Thank you to the publicists who provide so much information and also navigate some very complex schedules to make these interviews happen, especially Amanda Ameer, Rebecca Davis, Jane Covner, Melanne Mueller, Laura Grant, Jaime Campbell Morton, Elena Gisler, Olga Makrias, Louise Barder, Isabelle Ligot and Lisa White.

Thank you to the readers of Violinist.com, from whom I've learned so much.

Thank you to my mentors in arts journalism, especially to Peter Jacobi and to the late Tom Willis. Thank you to my mentors in violin, especially Jim Maurer, Gerardo Ribeiro, Victor Yampolsky and Henryk Kowalski. Thank you to my first writing coaches and supporters in my earliest violin endeavors, my parents, Pat and Tom Noonan. And the biggest thanks to my husband, Robert Niles, without whom "Violinist.com" would likely have become a spam-robot website instead of the thriving community that it is today. His vision, encouragement and technical know-how made it all happen!

CONTENTS

FOREWORD

For a performer, musical communication with an audience involves never-ending sequences of decisions, most indescribable and imperceptible. Some elements are settled almost subconsciously, while others are worked out over hours of practice. This produces infinite combinations of details that add up to a unique big picture.

There are equally infinite ways to conduct an interview. Many journalists focus on asking the right questions, but that is only the basis, the scales and arpeggios. Other people do lots of research and arrive at an interview prepared for anything. (Some don't. How could I forget being asked, "What instrument do you play?") While background knowledge is helpful in conducting an interview and appreciated by the interviewee, research does not a great interview make. The sizzle that will keep readers engaged comes from the rapport and the trust that is conveyed not only during the interview but also in the "writing up" of the encounter before publication. You can think of it this way: Inaccurate reporting is like clamming up onstage, while clarity of writing lets the phrases flow and the emotions speak.

The single most important factor in an interview with a performer, however, is a genuine curiosity from the reporter about what happens inside the artistic experience. Musicians check in with their playing and their minds multiple times per day, ruminating alone, comparing ideas with colleagues, translating inner emotion into outward physicality, and challenging their comfort zones. They tend to know their process rather well. Sometimes too well! If a journalist can highlight that knowledge, and that depth of thought, that exploration is exciting to read.

Laurie Niles has interviewed me many times over the years. Every time we talk, I am impressed by the balance she strikes between understanding and curiosity. I never feel hurried — in fact, I wind up saying more than I intend to at times, because she listens well and asks interesting follow-up questions. Laurie addresses topics that are comfortable but all-consuming, such as current projects, and delves into the delicate nuances of creativity. She captures specific moments in time.

I love that. In this collection, you can observe her at work, but you will also travel along with her interview subjects.

The violinists in this book remind me of my history as a student, concertgoer and touring musician. I met many of these performers when I was little, introduced to them by mutual friends or backstage after concerts. I had the opportunity to ask them questions myself, but I mostly stuck to the facts. It's illuminating to read what they have to say about other aspects of their work. On tour lately, I've bumped into some of them at festivals and hotel breakfasts, or in airports or radio stations. In between chance meetings, I enjoy reading about their activities and passions — the music world is so rich with possibility. I'm sure you will find something new in every one of these conversations. Don't forget to check in to Violinist.com to share your thoughts and your favorite quotes. Happy reading!

Hilary Hahn
New York
December 2013

INTRODUCTION

In a day when any kind of music is available at the push of the button, why would anyone take up the arduous task of learning to play the violin, one of the most fiendishly difficult instruments to play well? And if this music is so easily available, why would one aspire to the risk-laden career of a concert soloist, who makes great personal sacrifices for a life that involves traveling the world to play live concerts and leaves time for little else?

The answer: It's an inexplicable kind of love, for music, for excellence, for moments of the sublime. I know about it myself: I took up the violin at age 9, when a little girl visited my public-school classroom and played a jig on her violin as part of a recruiting mission for the music teacher. Despite coming from a non-musical family (or so I thought), I looked at the instrument in her hand and recognized it with excitement: Mine! It was love at first sight; I had to play it. Many years later, I learned that my family history did indeed include some musicians; my grandmother's maiden name had been "Geiger" — "Violinist" in German.

My non-musical parents both were writers, and I'd caught that bug as well, scribbling every day in a journal from fifth grade on. I earned my Bachelor of Music degree from Northwestern University, while also taking courses in the Medill School of Journalism, then went on to a Master's in Journalism at Indiana University, while also studying violin at what is now the Jacobs School of Music. I worked for five years as a newspaper reporter, moonlighting as a symphony musician, and had started studying Suzuki pedagogy when my husband, Robert, bought me the domain name "Violinist.com" as a Christmas present, back in 1996. Neither of us knew then what we'd do with it.

Trained as a violinist, violin teacher and a journalist, I set about creating a website that would help my professional musician friends further their careers, help my students further their knowledge, and also provide an outlet for creative writing about music, from the creative people who were attracted to the site. My husband not only encouraged me, but he also made these ideas happen on the technical end of things.

With a growing sense of responsibility, I watched as our handful of Violinist.com members grew to tens of thousands of members from all over the globe. Could it be, that this many people shared the same passion for the violin? With so many media outlets bemoaning the so-called death of classical music, this was good news. Classical music, and violin music, was not so dead, after all. And these readers coming to Violinist.com included a huge contingent of young people and students, banging at the door, wanting to make the violin theirs as I'd wanted to make it mine as a child.

What would happen, if I could use the website to encourage this desire with more knowledge, more passion, more excellence?

If I could sum up what people are seeking, when they look to make the violin their own, it might be that they are looking for the answer to this question: How do the best violinists in the world reach that level of accomplishment?

Over the four centuries since the Italian violin maker Antonio Stradivari perfected the violin into its current form, people have come up with many theories about the finest of violinists. For example, in the early 19th century, critics offered an interesting explanation for the astonishing abilities of the legendary Italian violinist Niccolò Paganini: He (or perhaps his mother) had made a deal with Satan. (*The Devil Went Down to Georgia* proffers the same idea.) Another popular notion is that the best among us are simply "born with talent." Maybe, but none was born with the 10,000+ hours of practice required to cultivate that talent!

In speaking with the violinists featured in this book, I would say the answer lies in an almost monastic devotion to practice. It lies in an unquenchable thirst for excellence in playing, for meaning and eloquence in music and for quality in the instrument itself, which in many cases means acquiring an irreplaceable antique, valued at millions of dollars. Their accomplishment lies in their enormous courage: to first put their talents before the critical eyes and ears of the finest teachers, then before a general public that is a mix of supporters, detractors, adoring fans, and green-eyed nit-pickers.

And these artists are absolutely human, which makes their feats all the more admirable. Many have had to conquer physical injuries, or to cope with exhaustion from sustaining such a high level of playing while constantly traveling and putting their heart, soul and self out on stage some 100 times a year. Some violinists find that the quest for an excellent instrument leaves them as heartbroken as a bride who was jilted at the altar. Some break the mold of the child prodigy or career classical soloist, and find themselves on the defensive, despite their popularity.

In thinking about how to arrange these stories, I realized fairly immediately that they simply had to go in chronological order. Each violinist's story affects another violinist's story, from the specific instruments that they play to the projects they do. Despite the sometimes-competitive nature of violin-playing, violinists mentor one another, support one another and look to one another for inspiration. The common thread of devotion and love for the violin and its music runs throughout all these stories.

In deciding which interviews to include in this book, I chose a mix of violinists whose various careers and philosophies together take the reader on a broad and interesting adventure. I certainly was not able to include every violinist who would be worthy of inclusion in such a volume, and that's why I've called it "Volume 1." This volume includes only a couple dozen of the 75+ interviews I've posted on Violinist.com, and I'm certainly not through posting interviews! I anticipate a "Volume 2" and maybe more. Until then, I hope you'll visit me and the Violinist.com community for interviews and stories both old and new, and that you'll help us make the case to a broader public for furthering the art of violin, music education and live music performance for the 21st century. As Hilary said, happy reading!

Hilary Hahn. Photo: Mathias Bothor for Deustche Grammophon

HILARY HAHN

Originally published on October 23, 2007

For our original interview with Hilary Hahn, readers of Violinist.com were given the opportunity to submit questions for her. Our conversation covered questions about her set-up, physical conditioning, her Vuillaume violin, and her recording of the Schoenberg and the Sibelius concertos, which came out after the interview, in 2008.

Hilary Hahn, at age 27, is living the dream — if you dream of being a concert violinist and well-respected performing artist. She's won a Grammy, and she's recorded most of the major repertoire, between her current contract with Deutsche Grammophon and her previous one with Sony. A graduate of the Curtis Institute of Music, she began playing at the age of three and started concertizing at age 15. She has played with major orchestras the world over and recorded nine albums that include many of the major concertos of the violin repertoire.

I spoke with her the night before her LA-area recital, an early stop in her current recital tour. She had just spent the afternoon answering questions and talking with local music students and faculty members at Occidental College.

Hilary has been exceptionally busy this year; her summer vacation, normally a time for decompressing, visiting family and studying things other than violin, was broken up by a recital tour with singer/songwriter Josh Ritter. It was a project that she enjoyed, but nonetheless it gave her less down time before a demanding fall season. Though she said she normally limits her time on the road to five weeks, her current tour will keep her hopping across North America for two and a half-months, returning her to home in Baltimore Dec. 21.

Laurie: It sounds like you are going straight from a summer where you did do musical things to a very busy fall.

Hilary: I did have some time off, and I went white water rafting. I went to British Columbia and spent a week on a couple of rivers and just kind of camped. It was really fun! That was my change of pace. And then I came back and started getting back into the season.

Laurie: Did you take your violin white-water rafting with you?!

Hilary: No...I was going to take my sort of junky violin, but then I realized I didn't have any junky bows! (laughing). I didn't want to lose the bows I have, going down the river. Even the bows I have that aren't expensive, I really like them. Then, I was going to take one of my mandolins, but it turned out I didn't have my mandolins in the city I was departing from, they were all in my apartment in Baltimore. I needed to do something to keep my callouses up, so I bought a junior-sized Martin guitar. I took the indestructible Martin on river with me and it turned out nothing happened to the instrument.

Laurie: What did you learn to play on it?

Hilary: I learned a few chords, learned a few sequences, and then came back and madly started practicing violin again!

Laurie: Well, our Violinist.com members had a lot of good questions for you. First I have to ask you: do you use a shoulder rest?

Hilary: Yes!

You use the one that's right for you; it really doesn't matter what so-and-so uses. People are so physically different; a shoulder rest is a physical aid for playing the violin. A certain kind of shoulder rest is something you either feel comfortable with, or you don't, and if someone important in your mind uses this particular shoulder rest, it might not work for you!

It won't make you play like them, it won't make you have the same posture when you're playing, because you're built differently.

You can become so injured doing the wrong thing with a shoulder rest — and if you have the wrong posture when you're playing. You really have to look at yourself in the mirror and stop what you're playing, keep the same position, feel the straightness of your spine with your right hand, check that your neck is straight. You fall into these habits when you're younger, when you're not quite fitted to the instrument. You're still growing and the instrument is still all different sizes on you. You're not going to injure yourself when you're young; your body's more pliable. But you don't realize what you're doing to yourself. 'What's comfortable' is not always the same thing as 'doing it right.' It has to be comfortable, but it has to work for your body. When you wind up being able to do it right well, then that becomes comfortable, and then that's your frame of reference for what works for you.

Laurie: How do you keep yourself from being injured?

Hilary: I just try to be aware of my body. If something feels strange, I stop, I figure out what's going on. I have no problem icing muscles after a concert and I don't mind doing stuff at the gym to build up my strength. You have to make sure to have a strong core, make sure your lower back is strong and your abs are strong. If you don't do that, there's nothing to support the awkwardness of playing. If you're not strengthening the middle of your body, all the burden comes from either your hips or your upper back, and those aren't necessarily the strongest areas to balance yourself from. I have done some yoga, I have taken ballet, I've worked out at gyms.

I'm not a fiend for exercise, although I really enjoy it. What I like most is going out and rowing on the water — I have a rowing shell. But I can't really do that on the road. I don't do things I hate to stay in shape, but every now and then I'll be watching T.V. and just start doing some crunches or stretching.

Laurie: Another V.com member asked, what is the technical detail that troubles first, if you don't work on it all the time?

Hilary: It's the same as anyone else! It's intonation, bow control, cleanliness of playing...those are the technical aspects. What people don't think about is the technique of expression. Being technically accurate in itself isn't the goal, because that excludes the thought of phrasing. You have to practice playing the technical sections so that the technique is not important in what the audience is hearing. And you have to practice the bow technique of phrasing. You can't practice technique just to practice it, you have to actually apply it for it to work.

The more you learn to do, the more you have to maintain. You don't just have to never work on the basics again. You have to work on the basics plus all the refinements you've built up over the years, plus the expression, plus the concept of the piece. You have to practice the concept, too, and see if it's going to work. There's a lot to work on. People might think that it gets easier as you do more, but in fact, what you're working with is much more specific and much more conceptual, even within technique. And sometimes that's even harder to pinpoint. It's harder to know when you're doing it right.

You can do all that from when you start, too. You don't have to wait a number of years. The earlier you start thinking about how to apply that to your playing, the easier it will be to apply it later on.

Laurie: One of our members was wondering if you would ever see yourself on the faculty of a music school or conservatory. Is teaching something that you enjoy, or would consider doing in the future?

Hilary: I would think about it, but I don't think my schedule would allow me to be a very responsible teacher right now and I'm not really looking at a big schedule change at the moment. The time that I take off is important for me to keep off so I have a bit of a break, so I can prepare my season's repertoire, or visit my family.

Laurie: Another member wanted to hear your favorite Jascha Brodsky story...

Hilary: I actually have some good stories from when I wasn't studying with him. He apparently was much more feisty when he was younger; by the time I started studying with him he'd mellowed out. He used to teach a lot of chamber music at Curtis, and he was giving a chamber coaching. The quartet he was coaching was not doing at all what he wanted. They hadn't prepared, and they'd just thrown things together at the last minute. He knew that they'd done this, so he was really peeved at them. He started yelling at them, swearing, and giving them a real piece of his mind. They knew he was bound to do this, so they taped it for everyone's amusement. After the coaching, they gathered outside the studio and started playing back the tape they'd made of their coaching. All these students started to gather around and were listening...He walked out of his studio and right into the middle of this gathering! They all kind of turned and looked at him, and he just laughed and walked away.

I like that story because it's hard for me to imagine him doing that; this is a part of him I never saw. As far as I knew, he called everyone sweetheart and darling and sweetiepie. He was very meek in a sense, but I always knew he had this strong personality and very strong preferences.

I think he respected when people were really trying, and he got really frustrated when he felt that his time was not being used to its best advantage.

Laurie: Another member asked, what has caused you to keep your Jean-Baptiste Vuillaume violin for all these years?

Hilary: I've had it for about 13 years, and I don't see any reason to change, I find that the violin just keeps responding really well. It changes itself every year; it ages, it goes through all these different environmental changes, and of course, the traveling...It develops on its own, just as any performer does. It's a very stable instrument, so I can rely on it, but at the same time it always shows me a different side of things than I expect.

Laurie: Do you feel that the player shapes the instrument a little bit?

Hilary: Yes, I'm sure they do. They say that after someone stops playing on an instrument for a certain number of years, you can still hear them in the instrument. I don't know if that has anything to do with the karma of an instrument; I think it has more to do with the fact that, when you physically play an instrument, you encourage certain sounds out of it. That sound is produced in a very physical way from the instrument. So certain elements of the instruments get used to being vibrated in a certain way, and those elements are extremely developed when that instrument passes on to the next player. I think there probably is a very scientific reason for it. It's nice to think, though, that there's a personal connection there.

This instrument is really good for everything that I do. I've played it in blind tests, because people tell me that I should. They say, hey, let's do a blind test of your Vuillaume and this Strad and this Guarneri and this Amati. I dutifully go into the hall and give them all a fair try, and people who hear the test say, "I really liked that one, what was that one?" — and it was the Vuillaume. They inevitably like me playing this instrument better than me playing any of these other instruments.

You get to a point where it's not productive to keep trying other things, and it's not helping you to switch. In order to develop as a player, I think you need to spend a certain amount of time with an instrument that really works for you. When you keep switching it, you're having to start over from scratch. You get only to the same point, over and over again with the new violin. You don't push yourself further. You don't really necessarily find out what the instrument has to offer you that is really unique to that instrument because you don't necessarily give yourself the reason to explore it further.

Laurie: Do you think you'll ever switch instruments?

Hilary: No...it's probably like a marriage. You could always imagine yourself married to maybe someone else, maybe there is someone where it looks like the grass is greener, but really, in the end, you're quite happy where you are. So why go and look? It just makes you more unhappy with where you are, in a sense. I imagine it's very much like that because it's a match that you commit to, long-term, and if you're always looking somewhere else for what you want out of an instrument, even if you've committed to this particular instrument or you really like it, then you're not giving that instrument a chance to really work for you.

Laurie: Unless it's really not that great.

Hilary: If it's not working, then you move on. I'm mean there's no point in staying with an instrument that's not working for you. That's just weird. Even if it's a famous instrument, even if it's made by a great maker, it may not be right for you. So why keep clubbing yourself over the head? It's kind of demoralizing, when you have a certain sound in your mind and you can't get it. But at the same time, if have a lot yet to learn about an instrument, or if you have a lot yet to learn about playing, it's not going to do it for you. You have to give each instrument a fair shot. You need to play it in, give it a chance to live, too, and then really see how it turns out. And if it's not working, you move on.

Laurie: Here's another question from a Violinist.com member: besides classical music, what types of music and artists do you listen to?

Hilary: I like a lot of kinds of music. For me, it's more a matter of how much work I can tell the person has put into it and how much they are expressing themselves, rather than a certain genre. There's nothing I like absolutely across the board. I like a variety of things. I don't tend to do well just picking a favorite of anything, because I'll listen to it nonstop, and then I'll want to hear something else. It's not a short attention span, it's more that I really like hearing the place of things in a broader context. I appreciate it more if it's part of something rather than if it's just completely on its own all the time for me.

Laurie: In your blog, you wrote that one thing you can do when you are bored in a hotel is to act out your own video. I was wondering, what would be the tune these days that you would want to act out?

Hilary: Oh, I did the total violin geek thing and I choreographed Paganini *Concerto No. 1*, third movement!

Laurie: Did you get it on video?

Hilary: I wanted to, but I didn't quite, no. I didn't manage to find anyone to capture that...

Laurie: How did this come about?

Hilary: I was doing all this editing of that Paganini concerto, listening to edit after edit after edit in the process of producing the album. You're listening for balance, or extra noises. So there are a lot of times when you are listening to the music, but it's not really about the music. So what are you going to do during that time? Are you going to just sit there, bored? It's fun music! So I would just get up and sort of start dancing around to the Paganini, and then I'd sit down quickly at my desk in front of the score when the moment came up to listen for, and take notes, and then stand up and dance some more. Otherwise you get so caught up in all the details, you don't think about how the movement is flowing and all. You don't really enjoy it. So it's nice to be able to kind of get into the groove while you're still getting some work done, too.

Laurie: Tell me about this new CD that you just recorded for Deutsche Grammophon. I understand you recorded the Schoenberg and the Sibelius concertos, can you tell me a little about the thinking behind this pairing?

Hilary: The idea behind the pairing was that I really wanted to record Schoenberg, and I was looking for something that was a major stabilizing work. I like to show any unusual piece that people aren't used to listening to with a piece that they're more familiar with. I thought, what haven't I recorded that could be more familiar for this album?

I think both concertos have this innate lyrical element that's completely glossed over most of the time, not necessarily in the performance, but in the perception, in the definition of the work. The Sibelius is defined as this cold, Nordic music, with dark undertones, and Schoenberg is thought of as academic. I don't think that either one is done justice by those definitions. So I wanted to try to bring out the lyrical element of both and also stick as much as possible to what was written in the scores. I think that both of those factors are sometimes a little bit thrown to the wayside.

As the content of the music itself, I think both composers' connection to the visual art world is really unusual, at least by today's standards. Schoenberg was a visual artist, and he was part of this huge scene in Vienna. He had connections to all these different artists and different genres of expression. Sibelius lived in an artists colony, so he was surrounded by this as well. I feel like the visual plays into their music, as composers, and I don't think there's anything is academic about either one of them. I think they're both romantics. Granted there's a dark side to both works, but there's this overarching sort of idealism I hear in both pieces, too.

Laurie: I don't really know of that many recordings of the Schoenberg ...

Hilary: No, there aren't that many. There aren't many major label releases that are current. The recordings I heard weren't quite what I wanted to do with the piece. So that gave me a starting point.

Laurie: What was your approach to the Schoenberg?

Hilary: I listened to recordings (of various works) when I was deciding what to do next, and when I heard the Schoenberg recording, I thought, hmmm, that's interesting, it's not at all how I would play it, though. I wonder if anyone else has a more similar take on it? So I start listening to a bunch of recordings of the Schoenberg. I probably didn't hear everything, but a lot of the ones that I heard where sort of a different approach than what I imagined for the piece. Then I looked at the music and I started to take it apart in that sense.

Laurie: So this was a new piece for you?

Hilary: Yes, I learned it with the purpose of recording it at some point, which is unusual for me.

Laurie: Did that change your approach at all?

Hilary: It made it so that I wanted to define to myself immediately how I wanted to play it. Knowing that I eventually would record it, I had to have certain ideas in mind by the time that I got to the sessions — of how exactly I did want to get this down on record.

Laurie: It sort of sets it in stone, to record it.

Hilary: Yes, but it's also fluid. I mean, people don't expect you to play it like the recording for the rest of your life. But when you're in the sessions, you have to know what you want to do with it. You have to play differently in sessions. You have to get everything exactly right; you have to be able to do it the same, technically, time after time, but also experiment with the musicality throughout the course of the sessions and keep that fresh. Knowing that I would eventually have to go through that process was a good incentive for me to actually do it all right from the start, so I wouldn't have to un-do anything later.

Laurie: With whom did you record the new album?

Hilary: I recorded it with conductor Esa-Pekka Salonen, with the Swedish Radio Symphony Orchestra, the same orchestra I recorded the Paganini and Spohr with.

Laurie: I think people are going to like it. One of our members said he heard you play it live, and he loved it.

Hilary: It's been a surprise audience favorite! I thought that it had potential, that it would have great effect, and people are constantly surprised, they're like wow, they really liked the Schoenberg! And I'm standing there, thinking, well, yeah! Of course they do!

The Schoenberg has been new for every orchestra and almost every conductor I've worked with. You have to give them enough time in rehearsal...I usually specify there has to be six hours of rehearsal time before the first concert. It's the only way to even start to get the Schoenberg together, not to mention start working on the music. It's so unfamiliar to people, just because it's not played live much.

I think when you spend time on anything, then people have this attitude of, okay, we're going to get this. We're going to bring this across and we're going to do our best. And when you have that attitude, people really appreciate it, no matter what it is. But I think that piece particularly benefits from that.

Laurie: With such an unfamiliar piece, the orchestra would need extra time. You can't be doing it in your sleep...

Hilary: You can't do anything in your sleep, you just think you can.

Laurie: People try to do it in their sleep, unfortunately!

Hilary: Once I was booking the Tchaikovsky concerto and they asked for a certain amount of rehearsal time and I said, 'I don't know if that's quite enough rehearsal time...' I think it was time enough for one play-through in the regular working rehearsal and then just enough time to play it through again in the dress rehearsal. And I said, 'Is there any chance I could have a little more time in the working rehearsal ?' I got a note back from the administrators saying, 'But, aren't you afraid that, since everyone knows this piece already, if we rehearse it any more than that everyone will go on automatic pilot?'

I thought, are you proposing that we do less rehearsals for it to be better? Even if people know the piece, you have to start over like you don't know it, because someone might have a different approach to it or you might actually want to turn the piece on its head for once and try to do a whole different approach. How are you going to be able to do that if you don't have the time? No, I don't think automatic pilot is a problem. Everything is hard, no matter how easy you think it is.

In Schoenberg, I find the first step is just getting people familiar with the notes. That takes time, and it's a lot of work. It's tricky for everyone. Then it's really important to take the 'academic' out of it. You're supposed to do that from the start, but it's kind of scary to try to do all of that at once. A lot of people prefer, in the rehearsal process, to tackle one thing at a time. Then you really try to sort of make it be almost Brahmsian in some ways, like Stravinsky or Shostakovich in others. Not that it is that music, every composer stands on his or her own. But it's not acceptable to play any composers in an academic way, including Schoenberg.

Laurie: Is the Schoenberg a piece that's built on tone rows?

Hilary: I don't care. I really don't look at things from that perspective. It doesn't matter how a melody is constructed, it's still a melody. It doesn't matter whether a structural element is there because a composer woke up with it from a dream, or they sat down and mapped it out. It doesn't really matter. That's all in the music, and it's all there to be interpreted. People draw their inspiration from different areas, and whatever helps them express what they want to express musically should not be the determining factor for how it's interpreted.

Our idea of melody is really quite random. Just because we've been trained from birth to think of some things as melodies doesn't mean that they have any more right to be called a melody than anything else we're less familiar with. If you played tone rows for little kids, they would start humming them. The first things they hum are very structural elements that go into the traditional melodies.

If you take all emotional bias out, everything has equal musical importance.

Ruggiero Ricci. Photo courtesy Julia Ricci

RUGGIERO RICCI

Originally published on December 1, 2007

Ruggiero Ricci was one of the most famous child violin prodigies of the early 20th century, with a career that spanned more than 75 years. Born in 1918, he died at the age of 94, in 2012. I spoke to him at his home in Palm Springs, California in 2007, shortly after the release of his book about violin technique, called Ricci on Glissando. *We talked about his career, about Paganini, Ricci's influences, and his then-new book.*

"All that great violinists do, he did," a New York critic wrote of a 1929 performance by Ruggiero Ricci.

High praise for an 11-year-old "wunderkind." Too bad it reads like a career epitaph. Indeed, a career as a prodigy is doomed to end: Grow up and it's done.

"When I was nine-, 10-years-old, they said I was a genius," said Ricci, now 89, sitting at the round kitchen table in his Palm Springs, Calif., home. His wife of 32 years, Julia, sits near. "When I was 12, 13, I was a has-been. In my teens, I was nothing. I wasn't a grown-up artist, and I wasn't a prodigy. Those were bad years. No matter what I did, they criticized me."

But a prodigy can grow into an artist, and that is what Ricci did.

At 89, Ricci sits atop a mountain of achievement. And though he has retired (at age 85) from performing, he still teaches privately, gives master

21

classes and has recently published a new violin technique book called *Ricci on Glissando.*

Ricci began playing the violin at age six, with Louis Persinger. Later teachers included Michel Piastro, Paul Stassevitch and Georg Kulenkampf.

It was during his difficult teen-age years, neither still a prodigy nor yet an artist, when Ricci plowed into the Paganini *Caprices,* territory largely unexplored at the time.

"I decided that the only thing I could do was to play more than the other guy, so I did," Ricci said. "To get a lot of technique, it's rather unpleasant. You don't get technique practicing the pleasant. You get it from practicing the unpleasant. So I forced myself to play the most difficult music."

For the *Caprices,* Ricci went to the source of this fiendishly difficult music: the urtext, Paganini's unedited version. And while the 21st-century violinist has the benefit of a wealth of editions, recordings, and experts in the field of Paganini, Ricci did not. He dissected these works himself, and fit them into his own hands.

In fact, Ricci was the first violinist to record all 24 Paganini Caprices, in 1947. He went on to record all the available violin works of the composer, including five more recordings of the 24 Caprices, one on Paganini's own Guarneri, which by the way, Ricci said "was the loudest fiddle I ever played on.

"It has a very strong sound," Ricci said. "It was very weird. They just take you to a little room, they take it out, and the guard is standing there, and you can't practice on it," he said. "It was a very difficult fiddle to play. It's quite a large fiddle, it has high ribs. It's a hard violin to play."

Ricci's recording of the *Caprices* on the violin known as the "Cannon" is not his favorite. "I don't recommend recording on a fiddle that you've never played on, I don't care what the fiddle is," Ricci said.

Ricci also performed the U.S. premieres of both Paganini's Fourth and Sixth Concerti, and his repertoire included about 50 of the major violin concertos. He premiered the violin concertos of modern composers Alberto Ginastera (1963) and Gottfried von Einem (1970), and throughout his long life he performed more than 5,000 concerts in

65 countries. His discography is staggering, with more than 500 recordings on more than a dozen record labels.

Does he have a favorite, of his own recordings?

"That's a little bit hard to say," Ricci said. "There's a difference in your style when you were 20 years old or when you were 40 years old. There should be a change. If you're the same, that's a bad sign. Your basic style doesn't change, because everyone has his own characteristics. You shouldn't push your style, shouldn't try to exhibit your style, because if you have one, it's going to come out anyway. You shouldn't feature it.

"For instance, (Fritz) Kreisler, when he was young, had some great recordings," Ricci said. "When he got older, there's much more sugar in his playing. He was a very sweet guy, and it comes out in his playing. He's still a great violinist, but I prefer the young Kreisler."

In fact, Ricci played for Kreisler in 1929. "He came to hear me with Jacques Thibaud. The two of them came together and I played them the A major Mozart Concerto. Kreisler liked me, he picked me up in his arms. I was 11, but they used to lie about my age, I was supposed to be nine.

"You can always add two years to any prodigy's age, from the time of Mozart. They always took two years off. Even (Jascha) Heifetz, only he never admitted it. Heifetz said he was born in 1901. But I talked to (Mischa) Mishakof, who was the concertmaster with (conductor Arturo) Toscanini, and he knew Heifetz. He said Heifetz was born in 1899, not '01, like he said."

Kreisler and Heifetz were the violinists Ricci most emulated during his formative years, he said.

"There are many great violinists. But I would say Kreisler was representative, and Heifetz was representative. They're both different, but they both have a stamp, or a style," Ricci said. "I don't care what anyone tells you, when you learn anything, you copy. If you didn't copy, then you wouldn't learn to speak Chinese. You hear Chinese, you speak Chinese. If a gypsy hears another gypsy, he's going to play in a gypsy manner. You can't help being influenced by whatever you hear. So sometimes we're a composite of different influences. I'm a composite of Kreisler influence, Heifetz influence. Those two. I think people recognize my style, that it's not a copy of Heifetz, or of Kreisler. But they did influence me."

Of the more modern violinists, Ricci says he likes Vadim Repin, Hilary Hahn, Gil Shaham and Leonidas Kavakos.

"In style, (Hilary Hahn) is the closest to Henryk Szeryng," Ricci said. "They both played according to the urtext. They both play very correctly. Not an over-stylistic, not a terribly strong stamp. Because a strong stamp is, in a way, sort of a distortion. If it weren't a distortion it wouldn't be a stamp.

"Kavakos, he's a very good violinist," Ricci said. "He has an architectural kind of style — a strong structure, a pulse. The structure has its sharp, focal points. He's not slithering around; it's a definite viewpoint, but it's architectural in character."

His new book, *Ricci on Glissando*, is an elegant explanation of advanced lefthand technique, with exercises and advice on how to cultivate a fixed-thumb position by practicing various glissando scales in single notes and double-stops. Ricci compares modern fingerings with suggestions about what fingering would look like using the glissando technique he describes. There are also some wonderful and random pearls of wisdom assembled in the back of the book. Editor Gregory H. Zayia, a PhD in chemistry from the University of Chicago and amateur violinist, performed the difficult task of organizing Ruggiero's lifetime of violin wisdom into this book, Julia Ricci said.

"With the invention of the chinrest, we lost one of the best features of the old system, the glissando technique — which must be studied if one is to ever acquire true mastery of the fingerboard," Ricci says in the preface to the book. (A "glissando" is simply sliding the lefthand fingers, instead of putting down one finger after another.)

"To be able to play a scale with one finger, a glissando, that's difficult. So you should practice glissando scales — you don't need to practice the other ones, that's easy," Ricci said to me. "You don't have to practice the easy ones, you practice the hard ones."

"You need to learn the art of shifting," Ricci said. "When the thumb and first finger go [down the fingerboard] together, that's a shift. When the first finger goes [down the fingerboard] and the thumb remains [against the ribs], that's not a shift. The shortcut is the glissando."

This assumes one has made friends — good friends — with the traditional scales that require shifting. The book is not a wholesale rejection of modern technique, nor of modern inventions such as the chinrest and shoulder rest, Ricci said.

"These are conclusions I came to over a lifetime of study," Ricci said of the glissando and fixed-thumb techniques described in his book. "Ideally, you would first learn the old system, which was glissando and the fixed thumb. In reality, however, most will learn shifting, which is entrenched, and then glissando and the fixed thumb."

The invention of the chinrest was unfortunate for the way it did away with a certain approach to the violin, he said. Ricci's book describes the different fingerboard mentality of the pre-chinrest violinist.

"This was a terrible invention," said Ricci, pointing to the chinrest on my violin, which he held throughout our interview. "Before the chinrest, they held the violin with the left hand. If you didn't hold it, it would fall on the floor, right? But when the chinrest was invented, it became chin-held, and consequently you lost contact. When it became chin-held then you started playing the trombone [sliding the left hand up and down]."

"Before the chinrest, there was no such thing as position change. There was no first-, second-, third-position," Ricci said. "When Paganini said, 'There's only one scale, and one position,' he meant that the position was here [by the ribs], not here [by the scroll]. This is no-man's-land, out here [by the scroll]. They stayed here [by the ribs]. When you make a jump, I keep my thumb [by the ribs]; I've got one foot on the ground. I make a jump, and I'm making an arc [with the left hand]. If I do this, I don't lose track."

I asked Ricci, should people go throw their chinrests and shoulder rests in a lake?

"No," he said. "You can't make a general rule. Some people have a very short neck, some people have a very long neck. What are they going to do? But the lift should be on the top," with a higher chinrest rather than a higher shoulder rest. "If you put the lift on the bottom, you are raising the violin. The higher you raise the violin, the higher you have to raise your bow arm. And the higher you have to hold your bow arm, it becomes that much more difficult. Theoretically, it would be better to hold the violin here," Ricci said, holding the violin down on his chest. "But we have nothing to hold it way down here."

A Violinist.com member asked what two exercises Ricci would recommend for sustaining technique, one exercise for the right hand and one for the left. For the left hand, Ricci said, "if I could only practice one type of technique, which one would I choose? I would choose thirds. The quickest way to improve your technique would be with scales and thirds."

For the right hand, he said it's very difficult to break it down to one exercise, as the right hand must produce a variety of strokes: legato, stopped strokes and spiccato. He did recommend playing ricochet: two up and two down, then three up and three down, four up and four down.

Both hands have very different tasks in violin playing, and it's quite a feat just to pull it off:

The lefthand techniques Ricci suggests are truly quite different from the way most modern violinists play, and putting these suggestions into practice takes some experimentation, said violinist David Yonan, who has known Ricci for 20 years, since playing for him as a 12-year-old at his first international master class in 1987 Berlin.

More recently, Yonan took his own students from Chicago to play for Ricci in Palm Springs. While preparing them for the trip, he tried showing them how to do the glissando technique. In all honesty, "it was hard for the kids to accept his approach," Yonan said.

Yonan, who has played all the Paganini Caprices since age 13 and has studied them with several different mentors, including Roland and Almita Vamos, feels that what Ricci says about the lefthand thumb is invaluable. "I really think Paganini played it that way," Yonan said.

The Ricci approach comes best into focus when it is applied to the most advanced violin repertoire and employed by the most advanced violinists. This means that for most violinists, it is an understanding that will require work, experience and practice — but in time, he said he hopes its advantages will be recognized for teaching beginners.

As Ricci told me, "To improve your technique, you have to try for the impossible, in order to make the possible possible."

Anne Akiko Meyers. Photo: Lisa Marie Mazzucco

ANNE AKIKO MEYERS

Originally published on February 12, 2008

Since this interview with Anne Akiko Meyers, she has gone on to acquire some of the most sought-after instruments in the world, in 2010 buying the 1697 ex-Molitor/Napolean Strad for a then-record-breaking price of $3.6 million and also receiving lifetime use in 2013 of the Vieuxtemps Guarneri del Gesu, which at one point was valued at $18 million. She also married, and now has two children. In 2009, she released an entire album, called Smile, named after the Charlie Chaplin song.

When the composer Joseph Schwantner wrote a fantasy for amplified violin and orchestra for violinist Anne Akiko Meyers, he called the piece *Angelfire*.

"He says he entitled that after knowing me," Meyers said, laughing. "Supposedly I was an angel off stage, but like a tigress on stage."

Recently I interviewed Anne in Los Angeles, and I also saw her play an intimate recital for L'Ermitage Foundation, with pianist Kevin Fitz-Gerald. She was in the area to also play the Mendelssohn Violin Concerto for series of concerts with the New West Symphony (which were met with great enthusiasm).

Schwantner does have a point.

Onstage, she wore an all-black, simple sleeveless gown, her dark hair slicked back, her wide smile punctuated with dimples. She began with selections from *Pulcinella* by Stravinsky, and after three notes from her 1730 *Royal Spanish* Strad, the luthier sitting next to me whispered to no one in particular, "WOW."

Meyers has an ease with her powerful instrument. She wears her technique like she wears her nose — it's simply a part of her. There's nothing tortured in Meyers' violin playing, nothing to distance the listener from it. She hasn't pasted something artificial to its surface, like a perma-vibrato or pressed sound; her sound is fluid and changeable.

During a passage of fast spiccato (a jumping-bow stroke), I jotted down, "it's so solid — one gets the feeling she could do it hanging from her knees, upside-down in a tree."

"I just had to take this out of the dusty vault and shine some light on it," she explained to the audience before playing Respighi's *Poema Autunnale*, a piece I certainly was hearing for the first time. After a slow introduction, the piece revved up, giving way to some octaves and other passages that made me understand why the piece sleeps in silence — it's gnarly hard! Pretty soon she was playing attack chords — the musical equivalent of hitting a punching bag. It looked so satisfying. Go girl! Get it out! Give 'em hell! But then it dissolved into harmonic glissandos, circular-sounding, calming down, thinning out.

At the end of her recital, she played *Somewhere Over the Rainbow*, which she introduced as "one of the most beautiful tunes written in the American language."

"This kind of music just makes me so happy," she told me earlier in the day, speaking also of Charlie Chaplin's *Smile*. "It's so moving on such a deep level. It's the lyrics, but it's also the arrangements — such a simple melody can hold such deep feeling. I think that's what I absolutely crave and look for in any music."

Meyers, of Japanese and Caucasian descent, is wrought in the American language and culture as well. Born in San Diego, her father is a university president from Chicago and her mother is a painter from Tokyo. Anne started playing the violin at age four, and her journey as a violinist has taken her to concert stages from Carnegie Hall to Sydney, Australia. She has appeared on television shows and magazine covers all over the world. At age 11, she appeared twice on Johnny Carson's

"Tonight Show," and at age 23 she was awarded an Avery Fisher Career Grant.

"I remember the day that I got the violin," she said. "I was standing on the couch in the living room and I was trying to play it upside down. My father walked over and said, 'No, actually, to make a sound with it, you flip it up.'"

It didn't take her too long to figure it out. Her first teacher was Suzuki teacher Shirley Helmick.

"She was wonderful in that she found it necessary and important for my development, to read music," Meyers said, "She had me read the notes from the start, so I was very thankful for that. I was told that everybody was supposed to learn a piece for Suzuki class, and I was the only one who came the next day and really learned it and memorized it. It just was instant, natural talent with the violin — like some kind of strange happening."

At the time, her family lived in Ridgecrest, in California's Mojave Desert. When she was seven, they started driving to Pasadena for lessons with Alice Schoenfeld.

"My mom was making this trek, three hours each way, from the middle of the desert to take me to lessons until my father was able to secure another job," Anne said. " I just can't even imagine doing it without the support and dedication of my family."

"Alice had this way of really making a visual impact with sound, like imagining even the luster of a pearl, opening the first chord of the Mozart G Major Concerto," Meyers said. "To hear these kinds of things, that kind of sophistication, at such a young age, was incredible."

As a teenager, Meyers went to Indiana University, where she studied with Josef Gingold for what she called "a very short six months."

"I was way too young, 13 or 14 years old, and it seemed like everybody was a doctorate student," Meyers said. "They didn't have a pre-college division back then, and so I was going to normal high school in Bloomington."

"After that, I played for Dorothy DeLay in Aspen, and she offered me a full scholarship to Juilliard," she said. "So my mom and my sister and I got into the Audi again and drove across the country. We turned around and thought about coming back to California, and then decided, oh, okay, the daisies are pointing east, so we'll follow that."

The family finally made it to New York, and they settled in Bedford Hills, where Meyers went to Bedford Hills High School. On the weekends she went to Juilliard pre-college, and "I fit right in to the Juilliard scene; everybody was basically my age," she said. Among her peers were Gil Shaham, Midori and Matt Haimovitz.

"Everybody was incredibly talented — you just took it to be part of your air that you inhaled," she said. "Looking back, I realize how much talent was there."

Talent, and adolescent hi-jinx.

"I remember those guys were always playing practical jokes. I had to lead the quartet with Gil (Shaham) and Misha (Keylin) and I think it was Chee-Yun Kim, and we were playing at Carnegie Hall," Meyers said. "I opened up the music, and there's a photo of Sylvester Stallone, naked, in my part," she laughed. "It's like, thanks, guys."

Now in her mid-30s, Meyers is a veteran of the violin soloist lifestyle.

"It is definitely a very challenging life and lifestyle," Meyers said. "When I was about 23, it was at the height of a lot of things. I just was in the middle of a recording session with Andrew Litton and the Philharmonia Orchestra. We were recording the Mendelssohn concerto, and I had this exclusive contract with RCA. I was playing maybe about 80 to 90 days a year, and traveling alone as a single woman, which has its challenges. I started to feel a numbness in my pinkie, and then it was announced that I'd won the Avery Fisher prize. Career-wise, it was just wonderful, but I felt like my life was just out of control. There was just a deep loneliness, and feeling of being so isolated. Eight o'clock comes, watch the monkey play. There's that feeling, where you're almost like a one-trick pony. You wonder, what is there, really, to this life? To be playing the same repertoire over and over and over again got to be so fatiguing."

"That's when I learned about my body: stretching, massage therapy, becoming more holistic. Not having to say yes to everybody and everything, and being more in control of your projects," she said. "What really fascinates me is to have a project where I'm working with a music director or working with a composer to write something new and then to premiere it and record it. That, to me, is totally exciting."

And that is just what she has done: championed the works of modern and living composers. The list of new music she has premiered is long, including works by David Baker, John Corigliano, Nathan Currier, Roddy Ellias, Karl Amadeus Hartmann, Jennifer Higdon, Arvo Part, Manuel Maria Ponce, Somei Satoh, Teddy Shapiro, Joseph Schwantner, and Ezequiel Viñao.

Besides being the inspiration for Schwantner's *Angelfire*, Meyers also has inspired Japanese composer Satoh, who wrote his Violin Concerto for Meyers, "I'm a huge fan of his piece for violin and piano entitled *Birds in Warped Time II*." She gave the piece its premiere in Japan.

She also has worked with Argentinian composer Viñao.

"He wrote this piece, very difficult piece called *Saga* (check out the *Wanderer* movement) that I played with the Absolute Ensemble with Kristjan Jarvi — it was a straight-shot *Saga*."

She also feels strongly about *Concerto Funebre* by Karl Amadeus Hartmann.

"I just absolutely went bonkers playing that piece," Meyers said. "It's so beautiful and dark. It's almost like the sun when it just comes out from the clouds, finally, and you just feel bathed in light. The ending is so stunning. (Cellist Mstislav) Rostropovich had just died when I played that, and also a very good friend of mine who used to run my website — a young man who died tragically. I just kind of absorbed myself in that music, and it was just kind of very cathartic in a lot of ways." Meyers has yet to make a recording of the Hartmann.

"I'm always looking at composers — compositions they're sending me," Meyers said,

Meyers is now playing on a violin that she owns herself: the 1730 *Royal Spanish* Stradivarius, once owned by the king of Spain.

"I've had it couple of years now," Meyers said. "I was very lucky to find this violin, and this owner, who's passed away now. She was very particular about who she would sell her collection to, even though this violin belonged to her deceased husband. It went through a dealer in New York. She heard me play at Carnegie Hall, knew my music, and we just had to agree on the price."

"I've performed on Guarneris and other Strads — almost every album I've recorded is with a different violin," Meyers aid. "I never loved returning the instrument. It's like having your left arm amputated. You've just inserted your personality into this violin for two, three years, and they say, 'We want it back now.'"

"But now that I own this violin, no one can do this," Meyers said. "It's very powerful, knowing that you own your own equipment. It's not like *Sophie's Choice* anymore."

Meyers also uses a Peccatte bow. "You do flip out when you find a perfect bow," she said. "I would die without that Peccatte. It's my life blood. But I would love to find another bow, to alternate. It's been this crazy process, just try, try, try. You start to think, okay, I am just too picky? But nothing compares to my Peccatte, and to be able to buy it — there's my Mercedes 500 SL, right there."

It's funny, to think that a violin costs that much, but also a serious problem for young violinists.

"It's really a tough choice today for a lot of young artists," Meyers said. "Do I put a roof over my head, or do I buy a good violin?"

I asked Meyers how much she practices, and she said about two hours a day.

"When I have a lot going on, it will be three, but I just physically can't handle it," Meyers said. "I don't like sitting so much. I don't like staring at a stand. I'm very aware, on a beautiful day outside, you're inside in a dark room. It just feels wrong."

Though life can't be all violin, all the time, the discipline of practice can be calming.

"It does give you a centering feeling," Meyers said. "A lot of times, when there's just absolute chaos going in my life, then I finally sit down for half an hour — I can exhale."

Rachel Barton Pine. Photo: Lisa Marie Mazzucco

RACHEL BARTON PINE

Originally published on July 29, 2008

For this interview, I met Rachel Barton Pine at a hotel in Los Angeles while she was in town for a performance. She actually had asked to interview me for one of her podcasts; I naturally knew that she was the more interesting subject for an interview! Her husband, Greg Pine, who always travels with her, sat in the next room as we spoke. Since this interview, Rachel has published many books and recordings: The Rachel Barton Pine Collection (2009) *with cadenzas and arrangements she's written;* Maud Powell Favorites *(2010), a book with sheet music to go along with her 2007* American Virtuosa *recording; edited arrangements of the Wohlfahrt etude books; a heavy-metal album,* Earthen Grave: Dismal Times *(2009);* A German Bouquet *(2009);* Glazunov Violin Concerto and Meditation *(2011);* Capricho Latino *(2011); and* Violin Lullabies *(2013), inspired by the birth of her daughter, Sylvia, in 2011.*

After meeting Rachel Barton Pine and talking with her about her life and her projects, just one word comes to my mind to describe her:

Tireless.

This is a woman who practiced every single day, from her first violin lesson at age three until she was 13 — even if it was Christmas or her birthday, or she had the flu. As a teenager, she was practicing up to eight hours a day, learning the solo repertoire at a voracious pace and also playing in the Chicago Civic Orchestra.

She also endured a life disruption that few of us can imagine, when at age 20, her right foot was crushed and her left leg severed above the knee by a Metra train accident in Chicago. A March 30, 2008 *Chicago Tribune* story illustrates this episode vividly and with much detail. I'd have to dispute one thing about that article, though: reporter Howard Reich's dramatic statement that this accident "shattered" not only her legs but her career. It's just not the truth. Yes, it forced her into a period of physical recovery that has included more than 40 surgeries and undoubtedly put her career on hold. But "shattered"? Hardly!

Rachel has garnered more artistic respect, has come up with more creative projects, and has advocated more for our art than most violinists of her generation. Her musical and personal voice rings loud and clear, and it reaches many. In addition to performing as a soloist with orchestras around the world, playing radio broadcasts, recording CDs and giving the occasional masterclass, she also runs a foundation, serves on the board of four Chicago charities, posts weekly podcasts in which she interviews various musicians, and willingly takes time to answer those seeking her expert advise on the violin. If it's possible to have MORE of a successful career in music than Rachel has, I'd be hard-pressed to imagine it.

Laurie: I would think this traveling lifestyle would be really difficult. When do you practice? How do you manage that? Do you have a process for when you get to the new hotel room and you find the place?

Rachel: Actually I think the reason that I can get away with being less consistent these days is the fact that I was extraordinarily consistent when I was a kid. It's really the homeschooling that allowed me to be that consistent. Because I was able to do so much practicing so consistently when I was growing — during the "cartilage years" — my reflexes and my muscles are there. I obviously have to maintain, but I have such a strong foundation that I can get away with more that I might otherwise be able to. I'm very grateful for that.

These days, there are days that I don't get to practice despite my best efforts. The plane might have been late, then there's traffic, then I have to eat dinner because I haven't eaten lunch, then I have to go to rehearsal and then I have an interview...

Laurie: It must be a tremendous thing, to let go of the daily practice, actually.

Rachel: When I don't get to do as much personal practice, I'm usually playing the violin for many, many hours in rehearsals. But when I'm home, I make up for lost time. I'm very, very grateful to live in the apartment I live in because it has double walls and triple floors.

I can play fortissimo without my practice mute at any hour of the 24-hour period. This allows me to make up for lost time when I'm not on the road. In between each trip — when I'm home repacking the suitcase, doing my laundry, sorting through my mail — then I'll do five hours of practicing from 10:00 p.m. to 3:00 in the morning.

Laurie: How much did you practice when you were little?

Rachel: I really built it up. I was doing like five hours a day by the time I was seven. I think my maximum was eight hours a day, from the age of 11 to 17, when I completed my formal training. But that's a little misleading. You can only do so much on a certain piece in a day before you reach that saturation point and you have to get a good night's sleep and attack it again the next day. I used the hours that were available to me to practice a lot of different repertoire. No one piece was really practiced any more than your typical student would practice it, but I was able to do more pieces simultaneously and learn a larger chunk of the repertoire in fewer years with my eight hours a day. I always had a voracious appetite for repertoire.

I was doing period-instrument performance with Baroque violin from the age of 14 onwards. I was learning not only the works of major repertoire but I was learning all kinds of unusual stuff by unjustifiably neglected composers. I was doing a lot of chamber music. The Civic Orchestra of Chicago, of course, is one of the most intense orchestral training programs in the country. I joined just before my 12th birthday and I was in that ensemble until I was 17.

I have to say this, that I feel that my level of understanding as a performer of concertos was greatly enhanced by the years I spent in the

Civic Orchestra, playing all the Brahms symphonies with guys like (Daniel) Barenboim and Michael Morgan, and working with (Pierre) Boulez, working with (Sir Georg) Solti back in the day...

I also had the opportunity to play the symphonic works by the composers whose concertos I was learning. I had spent those hours in my practice room with the Brahms Concerto, but the hours I devoted to learning the Brahms Symphonies helped me know who Brahms was so much more deeply.

Also, sitting in orchestra when other people were soloing, I got to know exactly what kinds of rubatos simply didn't work. Sometimes when you're learning your concerto, experiencing it with a piano accompanist, you have a false sense of, "I can really do anything that I feel, and it's everybody else's job to follow me," but no. That's totally not right.

It's not just about the practical considerations: being respectful to your colleagues, who simply can't follow you through certain twists and turns because it doesn't work for their parts, even if they're fabulous instrumentalists. It's also about the music, because if it doesn't work, it probably means that it's musically not valid.

The solo part is only one component of the entire musical expression. It was in orchestra that I learned how to listen to all the other instruments, how to adjust my tone colors, whether I was playing with a clarinet, versus a bassoon, versus the double basses.

Laurie: Last year you came out with your CD, *American Virtuosa: Tribute to Maud Powell.* Can you tell me a little bit about this album and this American composer from a century ago?

Rachel: Favorite topic. Actually, the music on the CD falls into two distinct categories: Music arranged by Maud Powell and music dedicated to Maud Powell. When I do Maud Powell tribute recitals, I also include music from three additional categories: music premiered by Maud Powell, even if she was not the dedicatee; music recorded by Maud Powell; and music championed by Maud Powell.

Laurie: When you were following so closely in her footsteps and playing the things she played, did you get a sense of her musical personality?

Rachel: Not only have I spent a significant amount of time playing Maud Powell's repertoire, but also, I've been the primary collaborator with the Maud Powell Society on preparing a sheet music collection for publication. This is a collection of works dedicated to and arranged by Maud Powell. Most of these works were in manuscript only; or they were published during her lifetime, but they've been long out-of-print. Some of the works actually had to be transcribed from a recording of her playing them, because the manuscript had been lost.

That was an intense project. Because I was serving as the primary musical editor for all of the sheet music, I got to know her arranging style on a different level.

I feel a definite spiritual connection to Maud Powell because I've tried to emulate so many of the same values she had. There are the fun coincidences: we were both born in Illinois and had our earliest training in Chicago. She received her finishing training in Berlin with Joachim, and I received my finishing training in Berlin with a student-of-a-student of Joachim. Her husband traveled with her 100% of the time, and my husband travels with me 100% of the time.

She didn't have red hair, so it's not an exact parallel! But so many cool coincidences. She was a woman ahead of her time: She was the first to break the gender barrier by forming a string quartet with men, before the genders ever used to mix in an ensemble. She championed the works of living composers, women composers, composers of the African descent. Before I had ever even heard of Maud Powell, I was very involved in playing the music of black composers. I was so excited to learn that Maud Powell was really the first white artist to consciously bring this music before the public, before it was as socially acceptable.

Also, there were her activities that we now call would call "outreach," a century before that term was ever invented. She would play one recital in a big city, then a couple nights later another recital in a big city, and instead of resting, she would find some small town halfway in between and play that town's first-ever classical concert. She didn't have do this; she was one of the most renowned artists of her generation, and she was earning a fine living. She had plenty of concerts. She could've relaxed on that day off, but she believed that it was her mission in life to bring music to people. It was not to increase her audiences, not to sell more of her records, not to preserve her livelihood in years to come, but this is what she felt like she was put on this earth to do.

That's the sense that I had about the meaning of my life as a musician; then reading Karen Shaffer's biography of Maud Powell just reinforced all of my beliefs and made me realize that none of my ideas are new. I'm really just privileged to follow in the footsteps of the great artists of the past who also knew what it meant to have music be your calling.

As far as Maud Powell's actual playing is concerned, this was such an interesting journey for me. In a way, it was like period-instrument performance, playing music from the Victorian era. The playing, in some ways, was so different. Take for example, the use of shifting and expressive slides. I think it's great that we've removed the 1940's-style soundtrack slides out of Mozart. It used to be, when you listened to some of the recordings, they played Mozart like they played Strauss. That's a little questionable, now that we know better. But yet, now orchestras play Barber the way that they play Mozart. In other words, there's a certain sterility. They're trying to so hard not to sound schmaltzy. I always have to urge orchestras, in the Barber violin concerto and in the Korngold violin concerto: "Hey, wait a sec. This is music from the 1940's. Please, guys, I want to hear some shifts. That's the historically authentic performance practice of the time."

Laurie: Throw on the Cheez Whiz here.

Rachel: It's not cheesy. It's just what those artists were. These were their expressive tools. If you don't have those, then you're not playing the music that the guys wrote. It's funny. String players in orchestras almost seem to feel guilty about having too juicy of a slide. I'm like, "No, that's not enough." That's the 1940's, 1950's sound. But when you go back half a century farther — if you listen to the earliest examples of violin playing from the beginning of the recorded era, the sound of those kind of shifts was something quite different.

The question for me was: How do I approach playing this repertoire? Do I actually try to make it as authentic as possible and play those kind of shifts that would sound just bizarre to 21st century ears? When I say they would sound bizarre, certainly some people do listen to early recordings, but it's not what you'll normally hear on a classical radio station. They tend not to broadcast even with the remastered versions, because there's still so much extraneous sound.

(For example) there's a wonderful CD set, *The History of The Recorded Violin*, with a little bit of everybody — it's brilliant stuff. You can hear (Grigoras) Dinicu's own version of the *Hora Staccato*, and it makes Heifetz's sound so bland. There are so many more spicy harmonies. He goes about half again as fast (one and half times as fast!). Heifetz doesn't sound very gypsy or very technically impressive after you hear Dinicu doing the real thing! There's a violinist (Vasa Prihoda) who does part of "Nel cor più non mi sento," and of course, you know it's one, live take, no splices. It's an amazing series. Certainly some members of the public have heard that stuff, but we have never heard that style divorced from the recorded sound quality of that time.

The really clean, pure audiophile sound that we can get with today's technology, combined with slides from a century ago, is not something people have heard. They've only heard it with the cracks and pops and sort of white noise you get with the old recordings.

Laurie: So you are saying there is a kind of "period performance" to explore for Romantic violin music, just as people have explored authentic performance for Baroque music.

Rachel: I'm convinced that that within our lifetimes we're going to start to see a big change in performance of Brahms, Tchaikovsky and those composers. Maybe not to the degree that we don't like hearing it on the modern instruments, but definitely more, so that hearing the historic version will become something that we completely embrace as familiar.

Moving that up to the Victorian era, to the post-Romantic era: I know that guys like (the conductor Nikolaus) Harnoncourt have started to do period-instrument Schoenberg, with more historic uses of vibrato. Apparently with Schoenberg, continuous vibrato was not yet quite the norm. To me, hearing it, there were some pure moments that worked. There were some other moments that I wasn't convinced. Probably it's like when people were first starting to figure out how to play Baroque-style unaccompanied Bach; they were swelling every note, and it sounded (sea)sick. People said, "Oh, Baroque style is ugly." That's because people hadn't quite figured it out. So probably this (kind of period performance) will continue to be refined and explored, and it'll come to be something very natural to our performing and listening experience.

Still, I didn't want to be the first, and to have everybody think that my album sounded bizarre. Until a number of us start going back to Victorian-era slides, and having that be the way that we play Dvorak and so forth, until we start doing that as a conscious, historically important performance practice approach, I didn't want to do something that was just going to sound strange.

Laurie: You didn't lay it on real thick.

Rachel: I didn't want the strangeness of the approach to distract from the beauty of the music. So I chose a half-way approach, where I wanted to retain something of the flavor of the time, but also have it be understandable to my current listeners.

Laurie: To make it palatable for modern ears.

Rachel: There really hasn't been a lot of musicological research into this particular period of performance practice, so I kind of did what you would consider to be primary research, taking Maud Powell's recordings and marking my music with my own system of little symbols for exactly where she slides. Patterns started to emerge.

I could have done a whole treatise, but I don't have time for that. I hope somebody will — it's waiting to happen. Somebody needs to write a dissertation about not just Maud Powell, but take 10 different violinists and analyze this, and see what's Maud Powell specifically, and what is the style of the times that everybody does. Where is the individuality and where is the consensus?

I started to get a sense of the kinds of places where she would insert slides and how many times she tended to slide per phrase. Drawing upon the knowledge that I had gained from my analysis, I then would made my own choices within that framework.

Then the kinds of slides that I did wouldn't be exactly 1900's style. They would be what I would call a visible slide, expressive slide, but more of a 21st-century visible expressive slide; and appearing more frequently as in the 1900's. That's how I kind of balanced the past with the present.

Laurie: How do you differentiate between a 1900s-style visible expressive slide and a 21st-century visible expressive slide?

Rachel: The slides from the 1900s, to my ears, sound so slow and deliberate. It would take me awhile to get used to even playing that way and used to feeling like I could express myself with that tool. I'm so used to playing Baroque music and expressing myself with no vibrato.

I'm sure that if I worked on it long enough I could express myself with the slow deliberate slide, but that isn't yet one of my artistic personas or incarnations. What I did take away from my study of her slides was where to put them, and how often to insert them. Then I did my style of slides.

Laurie: It's sort of like, if you're not a native of Great Britain you really can't wear that accent effectively.

Rachel: But you can make sure that you use the right slang with your American accent.

Laurie: Right. Exactly.

Rachel: That's a very good analogy.

Laurie: I was wondering what is the next thing here for Rachel Barton Pine?

Rachel: The rebec.

Laurie: The what?

Rachel: The rebec, my new friend. You can buy a rebec with a bow and a case . The rebec is one of the medieval ancestors of the violin. It was tuned in fifths.

Laurie: Four strings?

Rachel: Three strings. It's thought to have developed from the Middle Eastern rabab, which was literally a hollowed out gourd with a piece of goat skin stretched across the top. When it came over to Europe, they made it out of wood, but with the same half-pear shaped body, flat top, and tuned in fifths with a curved bridge. Those are the elements that were once influences on the eventual violins. One of the other ancestors of the violins, of course, is the vielle, or the medieval fiddle, and that's an instrument with a flat bridge that was usually tuned to the arpeggio of whatever key you were playing that song in. You could only really play the melody line on the upper string and the rest were kind of drones, but that instrument had a body that was shaped much more like the violin.

Laurie: Right.

Rachel: This is just a superficial version but: To take the body of the lira da braccio, the tuning in fifths and curved bridge of the rebec, and suddenly, magic. You have the violin. Just like when a new species mutates, and all the other lesser good species....

Laurie: They die out.

Rachel: But does that mean that we shouldn't play the rebec? Not at all! Even though it died out, it was popular in the 900s to the 1500s. Actually the rebec was the most popular of the string instruments for about 500 years. The violin has yet to match that. There's some incredible, intricate art music written for rebec. It's played on the arm. One of the foremost medieval string instrumentalists in the world just happens to live in Chicago, David Douglass. He's artistic director of the King's Noyse which is the only renaissance string band in all of North America. They have a little set of violins, violas and cellos made out of the same tree, just like they would have for a household in the 1500s, when violins were first invented.

Laurie: Oh my gosh.

Rachel: In the middle 1500s, when (the violin family instruments) were a brand new kind of instrument, they would make them all out of them same tree: a whole set with big violins and little violins, small and large violas and cellos. Everybody had to stand to play in the presence of their employer. They would play tunes in the first position. It was very improvisatory. This little string band has re-created that. It's amazing. David Douglass also plays all those medieval instruments, and he's artistic director of the world renowned Newberry Consort. So I'm going to make my rebec debut as a guest artist with the Newberry Consort in the spring of 2009.

You see, I had to learn the viola d'amore so that playing the Baroque violin seemed less weird by comparison. I had to learn the rebec so that playing the viola d'amore seemed a lot more normal. I eventually want to own one of every possible bowed string instrument played this way on the arm or on the shoulder. People say, "Oh you play viola d'amore. Do you want to play guitar?" I'm like, "No way. I only play things with a bow this way, but I want to play all of them."

Laurie: So how many do you have so far?

Rachel: Well just the four. Regular violin, Baroque violin, viola d'amore and rebec. I want to own a Norwegian Hardangar fiddle — It's really a folk instrument. I want to own a crywth. I have a long wish list of funky fiddles, and I want one of each of them.

But the great thing about the violin is you can really play almost anything on the violin.

Laurie: What would you encourage a young violinist or a young musician to learn about, besides their instrument? If you're going to live a life as a musician, what are some of the things that would be good to look into?

Rachel: Well, it all comes down to communication. As artists, we're expressing the music that we play. We're communicating those feelings and emotions, the story that we're telling. The whole purpose of it isn't to recreate what the composer wrote in some kind of a glass bubble. Ultimately, it's to bring it to the concert stage and communicate that to the listeners. "Sharing" is another word that really captures what an artist's life is about.

That goes beyond your instrument. In order to fully draw people into this art, you have to break down those perceived barriers between the artist who's creating the music, and the listener who's absorbing the music, by doing some non-musical things. Michael Morgan, one my mentors from my teen years, always told me that any musician who wants to really make an impact in the world has to learn how to write and how to communicate. I didn't know what he was talking about at the time.

I thought, "Well, you're the conductor. I just go out on stage now and play my concerto. What do you mean I have to know how to write?" As it turns out he was absolutely on the money.

The interesting thing that I've found is that communicating with the public — whether it's speaking to them from the stage, participating in pre-concert talks, posting podcasts and YouTube videos, writing blogs and e-zines and my liner notes for CDs — all of those things actually have helped me to grow as an artist. It's made me clarify a lot of things that I might never have bothered to or thought needed clarification.

If I go out a half hour before I'm about to perform a Tchaikovsky concerto, and an audience member asks me, "What's your favorite spot," or, "Why do you do this phrase the way you do it," suddenly I have to think, "Well wait a sec. What is my favorite spot, and why?" Then I'm that much more inspired when I actually perform the piece. So I've found that all these things I do benefit myself. It's a never ending circle: the more I grow as an artist, the more I can give to the public.

Laurie: It's a positive cycle.

Rachel: Absolutely.

Laurie: What would you say to somebody who's in a negative cycle, who's thinking, "Hey, that's not my job. Come on, I didn't go to music school for this." How does a person break out of that?

Rachel: Midori expresses it so well: we talk about "outreach" and now the new term is "community engagement." We need to be able to buy our groceries and pay our rent, but that's not why we're in this particular profession. Outreach is not about filling the halls. It's about our mission as musicians: to share our music with as many people as possible. Even if we're earning as much money as we could possibly want and all our concerts are sold out, we still need to do that. It brings us back to that pure place of why we make music. If you can think of it in that way, it becomes a very organic part of your life; it's all part of the same life mission.

Each of us is where we are in life because we have reaped the benefit of having been taught by various mentors along the way. The only way to return that favor is to pass along the knowledge to people who don't yet have that information.

Laurie: Do you teach these days?

Rachel: I did have a studio in the mid-90's. I completed my formal training when I was 17. My music education had been expedited because of the fact that I homeschooled from 3rd grade to the end of high school. I did all of my college/conservatory level work, orchestra, chamber music, music history and all of that during my teen years and finished my formal training at the age of 17. Of course one never stops learning. If I'm doing a piece by a particular composer, I'll go to a specialist in that composer or in that particular style of playing. When I was doing my Scottish Fantasies album, I consulted with Scottish fiddler Alasdair Fraser to make sure that I had all the right inflections in the original fiddle tunes that appeared in the Bruch and other concertos. But as far as the formal weekly lessons where my teacher assigned me an etude and all of that, I did finish that when I was 17.

That same year I joined the faculty of the Music Institute of Chicago. I had already been teaching for a few years prior to that, had built up a studio so it was a very natural thing at that point to join the faculty even though on paper it looked kind of unusual.

I loved having a studio. I loved the excitement of seeing my students' progress, of forming lifelong relationships with the students and their parents. But ultimately, I won my international competitions, had my recording debut in '95, and my touring schedule just simply got to be too intense to maintain a studio.

I know that a number of my colleagues do combine the traveling lifestyle with a professorship. That can work for students, especially at the graduate level, for their teacher to kind of drop in and out. But having taught so intensely for those years — seeing my students every seven days, going with them to their competitions, having weekly studio performance classes and extra lessons if an audition was coming up — I just feel like I personally wouldn't want to teach in any other way. I wouldn't want to drop by every three weeks and then disappear. If I'm going to teach, I want to do it in what I consider to be the ideal circumstances. Therefore I don't have a studio.

I do give master classes in almost every city I visit, and I give a lot of supplemental lessons on the road and at home. People who might be working on a particular piece or preparing for a particular competition or performance will come for some extra advice. But I don't have my own permanent students who see me on a regular basis as their primary teacher. I miss that. I also miss sitting in the back of the section and playing a Mozart symphony. You can't do everything simultaneously. I miss being a concertmaster. You can't be a permanent member of the string quartet and be a soloist. Just can't do it.

I thought about all these different things I did and loved, and I thought, "Which one, if I didn't do it, would I miss the most?" and it was soloing. For me, that's how I feel I can best express my personal voice as a musician and give the most to my audiences. That's the genre in which I feel most personally creative.

But back to the teaching question: My life plan is — if I have a hopefully long life — that I will retire gracefully from the stage when I start to lose my edge rather than lingering on embarrassingly. My husband's going to be the first one to say, 'Wait a sec. You're vibrato's starting to get wobbly there. I think we're entering old-lady territory. Your form isn't quite in control anymore.' Even if I'm not self-aware enough to pick up on the signs that I'm losing my edge, I know my husband will be the first to point it out. I'll probably be annoyed, yet I'll also be grateful.

Laurie: That's when you'll snap up your 50 students.

Rachel: Hopefully it won't be till my 80's. But then I'm going to have a professorship and teach till I'm in my 90's, like Gingold.

Laurie: That sounds like a good plan.

Rachel: Why should a musician ever retire?

Laurie: No. I can't imagine it.

Rachel: Unless you're senile, unless you have some kind of brain issue where your thought processes are no longer functioning...

Laurie: Even then.

Rachel: You can contribute to the world of music research, the world of music education, supporting young artists, promoting the cause of music before the public, promoting the cause of music education, music charities. There's so much work to be done and I plan to keep doing as much as I possibly can until the day I die.

Joshua Bell. Photo: Lisa Marie Mazzucco

JOSHUA BELL

Originally published on August 29, 2008

Many people know Joshua Bell as the famous violinist who played in the Washington D.C. subway for an experiment by Washington Post *writer Gene Weingarten. Long before that, I knew him as one of the finest violinists of my generation, for he is the same age as I am. I spoke to Joshua Bell the day after seeing him perform with the Los Angeles Philharmonic at the Hollywood Bowl. After this interview, in 2011, Joshua Bell was named Music Director of the Academy of St Martin in the Fields in London, the first person to hold the title since Sir Neville Marriner, who founded the Orchestra in 1958. When he isn't touring, he lives in New York, near his three children. His two-story Manhattan apartment was specially re-designed and rebuilt to provide space for holding house soirées with music.*

Can I bring you to the Hollywood Bowl for a moment? Imagine perfect weather (this is Los Angeles, after all): a pink sky, at dusk, and the Los Angeles Philharmonic warming up under a clean white arch. The audience stretches up a Hollywood hillside, with much of it organized into terraced cubicles for eating dinner. People sit in on green canvas lawn chairs, with little foldout tables on which they've placed wine bottles and glasses, colored table cloths, cheese and grapes, food from baskets, Tupperware and tins. They chat and giggle and generally get rather squirrelly as they drain those bottles.

The sunset brings mild chill, and as darkness falls I look at my $1 program and think, what could be more tiresome than a Berlioz March? The Hollywood Bowl seats some 18,000 patrons, thus for everyone to see the action, it requires not only two large video screens that flank the stage, but also several more sets of screens higher up, for those in back. To me, the Berlioz seemed rather amplified and distant, and I had to remind myself to watch the real orchestra and not just stare at the T.V. screen. The Berlioz had not arrested anyone's attention, certainly not mine, when violinist Joshua Bell emerged on the stage to much applause but also still to much chair scraping, chattering, clanking of dinnerware and giggling.

That was until that first spellbinding utterance from Bell's Stradivarius, in Ernest Chausson's *Poéme*. Suddenly the audience quieted; the only extra noise came from the singing crickets on the hillside. If the performance had until this moment seemed like a distant concert on a screen, it now felt live, with Bell to focus it. What makes for a world-class soloist? It's this ability to grab people with your sound and hold them rapt.

The Chausson *Poéme* is a piece with an amorphous beginning in the orchestra, which slowly swirls around itself, until the solo violin takes over. It's a rather exposed beginning for the soloist, but I imagine that with the *Gibson ex Huberman* Stradivarius violin of 1713, one might not feel alone. Bell has Strad sound, and he's not afraid to use it in all its glorious range, from the laid-bare intimacy of the *Poéme*'s introduction, to a mounting series of double stops that flow into the all-out emotional wailing at the center of this piece.

You might say, 'Yeah, if I had a Strad, I could play like that.' But not so. It's the other way around. If you were driven your whole life to play like that, then you might recognize your voice in that Strad and bank your whole existence on buying it, like he did. He might be a violin superstar, but I'm still guessing that $4 million put a dent in his wallet.

The close-cropped TV images of Bell emphasized his considerable movement during performing; and they also allowed for a peek at technique, which I enjoyed especially during Saint-Saëns' *Introduction and Rondo Capriccioso*, a piece written in 1863 and dedicated to the technical wizard, Pablo de Sarasate. I noticed that Bell does indeed use a shoulder rest, but he by no means clenches with the neck; very often his head is far back and the fiddle is completely cradled by the left hand. His chinrest is right in the middle, over the tailpiece.

The day after this performance, I interviewed Joshua Bell at his publicist's home in Studio City. It was his last in what sounded like a marathon day of interviews. He wore white shirt and dark pants, his boyish mop of hair messy and tousled. He talked with patience and polish through most any subject. His face lit up a few times — when he spoke about writing cadenzas, and conducting. He said he also loves computers, science and gadgets.

We began with the topic of his new recording, of *The Four Seasons* by Vivaldi.

Laurie: What made you decide to record *The Four Seasons*? It's a very popular piece of music, and it's definitely been done before. Where were you coming from with this recording? What is there new to say?

Joshua: Well, you could say that about any piece of classical music. We're always retelling the stories, but they're stories that are relevant and very personal. You really won't find two interpretations alike of the Vivaldi, especially today. First, you have so many different ways of approaching Baroque music, from the hardcore early-instrument approach, to the people who dive into it wholeheartedly — the Romantic approach — which is, I think, equally valid. Also, the Vivaldi has so much room for ornamentation and improvisation. So I think there's always room for another version of *The Four Seasons*.

I've been playing it since I was very young, and I've probably performed it hundreds of times. I had been touring it with the Academy of St. Martin in the Fields, and I felt ready to put it down on disc. Basically, it's my version, at this point in my life. A year from now, I'd probably play it differently. But that's all you can really say about a recording, that it's a snapshot in time. Unfortunately, it lives forever, and people view it as being the way I play that piece.

I do the same thing, listening to the old Heifetz records. I think, "This is the way Heifetz did it." I have to remember that this is just a snapshot of the way he did it that particular day.

So it's a bit daunting, when you go in the studio thinking, "This is the way it's going to be down, for your legacy, for your grandchildren, as the way you did it." I'm careful before I record something, that I feel ready enough to do it. I felt ready for *The Four Seasons*.

Laurie: Where would you put your approach to this music, in terms of early-music approach and the Romantic approach?

Joshua: I've had a lot of different influences. My primary influence was Josef Gingold, and you might say, he comes from the old school. But within the old school, there were different approaches as well. Gingold was born in Russia, but yet he studied with Ysäye. His way of playing lent itself more to the French-Belgian school, rather than the traditional Russian school. But in his day and age, there was the common denominator among whatever schools there were, that there wasn't a lot of thought about, or worrying about, being authentic. In a way, I love that. I love the fact that the music was unabashedly expressive, not self-conscious about style. It was very honest. Of course, it wasn't the way Vivaldi would have heard it in his time. But there's an honesty to that way of playing which is really wonderful.

The early music approach has done wonderful things as well. It's raised our awareness as to what it might have sounded like at the time, and also done great things with tempo, that over the years had gotten heavier and slower in the approach to Baroque music.

It reenergized the approach to a lot of this music, even Beethoven's symphonies, when people like Roger Norrington and [John Eliot] Gardiner came along and took some of the weight and heaviness out of a lot of these pieces.

That's an important thing, too. I've performed with Roger Norrington, and I recorded a Beethoven and Mendelssohn (performance) with Norrington. I've performed with John Eliot Gardiner.

The musician I play the most with is Stephen Isserlis, a cellist who I think is one of my biggest influences. He has a very different approach to playing the cello, which is hard to categorize. It's not self-consciously Baroque, yet he's more leaning towards that camp than a lot of cellists today. So I've had a lot of influences. I'm a mishmash of all those things.

Certainly my approach to the use of vibrato is something that I feel I like to vary a lot, and not overuse. I think of vibrato as being an ornament, not a constant. I think that's the way that vibrato originally developed, as more of an ornament than as something that you just paint on every note.

My concern with Baroque music is that it doesn't sound too self-conscious. Often I find that the Baroque approach will sound so stylized, that the actual expression kind of gets lost. Also, *The Four Seasons* has a lot of humor and cheekiness and fun, and a peasant way of playing. It's not all refined. It shouldn't sound all perfectly refined and dainty.

Hopefully, some of that element came out in the recording. I think the harpsichord player (John Constable) did a lot of fun improvisation and irreverent improvisations that helped characterize a lot of the movements. I was happy with the collaboration.

Laurie: So you were riffing off the harpsichord player a little bit?

Joshua: Yeah. Sure. Definitely that happens a lot in concert. Every night was something different; he would spur me on to a different kind of ornamentation. A lot of the tone was set by him as well.

Laurie: So you didn't take out the manual and go, "I think in this case, I need to..." and plan out every ornament?

Joshua: No. Obviously, after doing lots of performances of it, varying it from night to night, I'd feel that certain things worked better than others, and I'd try to remember them. But I would experiment, even in the recording studio. When I was editing the record, I'd have to choose between which ones I thought sounded better. So I wasn't completely set on exactly what I was going to do.

Laurie: I noticed that you recorded *The Devil's Trill* on there too. Do you have any thoughts on practicing trills?

Joshua: Like vibrato, trills can vary so much, depending on the context. Sometimes I like a very slow trill. Like at the end of the Chausson *Poéme*, I like a trill that gets slower and slower, until it becomes one note.

Again, it's an ornament. One of the mistakes I feel that students make is that the trills all sound like you stuck your finger in an electric socket. (He laughs.) It may be impressive to do something like that. But it doesn't sound organic or musical at all, if it sounds like the way a synthesizer would do a perfect trill.

Laurie: The cell phone trill?

Joshua: A trill is not supposed to sound like that. So I play around with it, what feels right to me: sometimes fast, sometimes slow. There are tricks that I use sometimes. If it's a half-step trill, and it's very high up, sometimes I just actually do it like a fast vibrato and let it hit the note. But that creates a different kind of sound as well. Sometimes it sounds better to have a clean, independent motion with the finger. It all depends on what you think is appropriate for the situation.

The same with vibrato. Every note should have its own vibrato, depending on the color and the mood. When you're used to varying your vibrato, it happens naturally. You shouldn't even have to think about it; it becomes organic to your playing. But you can experiment in the practice room with vibrato. It's something very hard to teach. I think I developed my own sort of arm vibrato that works for me. It's sort of something very personal and distinct. When you listen to old recordings, Heifetz's vibrato was very distinct.

Laurie: That brings me to the idea of teaching. I know that you've developed a new affiliation with Indiana University. Are you moving in the direction of teaching?

Joshua: Well, although I live much of the time in New York; Bloomington, Indiana is still my home. My family lives there. I grew up around the university, so I've always felt very close to it. I wouldn't dream of taking on a teaching position anywhere else. They've been asking me for a while to teach at the university, so I've taken on a small commitment — two weeks a year, at the moment. It's just one week each semester. But eventually, hopefully, it will grow into something more. But I don't want to give up my concert schedule.

Laurie: It would be really hard to teach with a full concert schedule.

Joshua: And it's very, very time-consuming and exhausting to teach. But I've set aside two weeks each year, to start.

Laurie: Do you like teaching?

Joshua: I do. I enjoy teaching and trying to analyze something with the student. It makes me rethink things. It can be frustrating, when things that you feel are natural and obvious, are not to somebody else. Obviously it's nice to teach students that are talented. But I'm sure teaching students that are not so instinctual could be an interesting challenge as well. I haven't done that much. I haven't done a lot of teaching.

When I work with an orchestra — a youth orchestra, or I'm leading or directing an orchestra — I feel that I'm playing the role of teacher, explaining why I want to do something, and why it makes sense, and getting them to do it in a way that feels natural, and not just kind of imitating something I'm telling them to do.

Laurie: That sounds like conducting. Have you thought about that too?

Joshua: Well, I'm doing some, mostly from the violin. I've gotten a chance to do a lot of that in the last few years.

I had an appointment at the St. Paul Chamber Orchestra, where we got to do lots of Mozart, Beethoven's Seventh Symphony. We did it leading from the violin, but it was basically conducting. I'm gravitating towards doing more of that.

Laurie: People love the arrangements you used for your *Romance of the Violin, Gershwin Fantasy*; and *West Side Story* albums. Are you ever going to make them available? What is your take on possibly publishing violin and piano reductions on those?

Joshua: That's one of the things I really want to work on in the next couple of years, because I've worked with these arrangers and come up with, I think, some fun arrangements. I want to make a *Romance of the Violin* collection and *Voice of the Violin* collection. I get a lot of emails from people asking for arrangements that are just not available yet. I've just been so busy, that I need to take some time to figure that out. That is something that will come out soon.

I want to publish some of my cadenzas, as well. I've got to write them down! (He laughs.)

Laurie: How did you go about doing those cadenzas? You didn't write them down?

Joshua: No. I've had to write some of them down when I make the recordings of them, for the producer to have something to look at. But generally, I compose them with the violin. And by the time I've figured it out, it's so in my head, that I don't bother to write them down.

It's the most fun and creative thing I think I've done, to sit down to write a new cadenza. It started with the Brahms Concerto, when I was 20 years old.

Laurie: Were you scared at all? People have been using the same cadenzas for so long.

Joshua: Well, I was scared to play it. When I wrote it, I was doing it just for fun. Actually, the second it was done, I never went back to any other cadenza. Because I figured, "I've just written this, and it's different. And why not do it?"

The same thing happened with the Mendelssohn Concerto. I think I'm the only one that plays a different cadenza than Mendelssohn's.

Laurie: No barriolage or anything? Don't you have to get back to the orchestra with that —

Joshua: Well, I get into it in a different way.

Laurie: In a different way? (Laughter)

Joshua: That was one of the big challenges, is how to get back into it. And I had to come at it from a different angle, which was fun. But I did it for fun, for myself. The Mendelssohn Concerto is one of my top three violin concertos. It's the most sublime, perfect piece. But frankly, the cadenza was never my favorite part of the Mendelssohn. Except the end (of the cadenza). I don't know for sure, but I wonder how much Ferdinand David, for whom it was written, actually contributed to the cadenza. That's, at least, my excuse for saying that I should be allowed to do mine.

But the thing is, at the time, I was expecting more criticism about it. I haven't had too much — to my face, at least. I think in Mendelssohn's time, if someone were to say, "I'm going to play my own cadenza," it wouldn't even have been an issue.

Laurie: Right.

Joshua: I mean Mendelssohn himself wrote piano accompaniments to the Bach *Chaccone*. It shows how the view of music was very wide open. Here we had Bach's *Chaccone*, which is the most sacred and perfect piece — How could you ever improve on it? And Mendelssohn and Schumann and others, they added the piano accompaniment, just for the celebration of the music, in their own way. No one, at that time, would ever say, "Oh, you're defiling the piece." That's just what was done. Music was very much more free to experiment We're kind of obsessed a little bit too much with authentic playing of everything — authentically in the original form. That's why I enjoy being a little irreverent with the arrangements. I arranged, for the *Voice of the Violin*, the Mozart Piano Concerto, the famous slow movement. I always thought, "Actually, I think it sounds better on the violin."

The piano is not the most singing, melodic instrument. To me, those slow movements in Mozart can sing on the violin better. And it's also a throwback to my old heroes, like Heifetz and (Fritz) Kreisler, who did that all the time.

Laurie: Do you still play video games? How about Guitar Hero? (Laughter)

Joshua: My video game days are waning a bit. I've just built my house, my apartment in New York, and I did network the place for computers to play video games. I like playing over the Internet and playing with friends — mindless shoot-'em-up games, like Unreal or Quake. And I love computers. I'm always getting the latest. I just recently switched to Mac, so I'm giving that a try for a while. Of course, I have the new iPhone. But Guitar Hero, I've never played. I don't know. What's next? Violin Hero?

Laurie: What was the weirdest thing that happened while you were busking? (The 2007 busking experiment in a Washington train station, which led to the Pulitzer-prize winning article by Gene Weingarten in the *Washington Post* called *Pearls Before Breakfast.*)

Joshua: The weirdest thing about the busking thing is what's happened *afterwards*, like the fact that the article got spread everywhere. In almost every country I've been to, they ask me about it.

I was recently in Uruguay, on tour in South America. I had to perform, and I had an almost 103-degree fever. I was so sick, and I had to get up and play a recital, a two-hour recital with the *Kreutzer Sonata*, and F Minor Prokofiev, the *Devil's Trill*. I mean literally, I couldn't stand up the whole day.

That day, I called a doctor to come to the hotel room, because I was so sick. And he barely spoke a word of English. But he saw my violin and said, "Oh, you're the subway — the subway" In the middle of Uruguay, it was in the papers. I didn't expect to be talking about it a year and a half later.

Laurie: And the article won the Pulitzer Prize.

Joshua: Which only extended the discussions about it. It was fun to do. But I'm kind of ready to move on. I won't be doing it again.

Laurie: What is the worst, funniest, most interesting thing that's ever happened to you onstage?

Joshua: Probably the worst experience, that's funny now, would be early in my career, when I was playing in Alaska, and I had food poisoning. I was playing the Mendelssohn Concerto, and I was so nauseous and sick. I barely remember the slow movement, because I was trying to fight back throwing up. There's no break, even to run off stage.

Finally, I got to the end of the slow movement, and before the last movement, I just ran offstage. Actually, I ran offstage, and I couldn't find my dressing room! Finally, I made it, just in time, before I threw up. But that was in the middle of a concert. Then I went back on and played the last movement.

That was one of the most memorable. But it was not very nice.

In a way, another memorable experience was my debut with the Philadelphia Orchestra when I was 14. That was my first big concert. I was playing with a sponge and a rubber band as my shoulder rest, and the rubber band had sort of come off. I felt it slipping. So just before the cadenza of the Mozart Concerto , I had just a few moments to get it back. I was quickly trying to put the rubber band in the right place, and I accidentally let go of it. It flew all the way across and hit the principal violist in the head! (Laughter) So I played the cadenza without a shoulder rest, and then after the first movement, (the orchestra members) all passed it along up to the front, where I reattached it. That was my debut.

Laurie: That brings me to one of the most important things to Violinist.com members — shoulder rests. We have this huge controversy going with shoulder rests. It's insanity. It could start another world war, over the morality of using a shoulder rest. I've always just used one, and I don't think about it.

Joshua: Well, my teacher before Gingold was Mimi Zweig, whom I'm very close with still. And she has a great academy in Bloomington every summer. She professes that no one should use a shoulder rest.

So I'm going against her. (He smiles.) I think her advice is good. If you can do without it, it's good. But for me, I feel more comfortable with the shoulder rest. And in the end, relaxation is the key — and feeling that you're most efficiently using your muscles. So if you need to tense your shoulder to keep the violin in place, then playing without a shoulder rest is not doing you any good.

So I don't have a hard or fast rule. But you have to be comfortable and try relax the muscles that are not necessarily for playing the violin are not being used trying to hold your violin on your neck. So I use what Mimi calls a "Brooklyn Bridge."

Laurie: What about moving, while playing the violin, versus standing still?

Joshua: Actually, I think a lot about trying to minimize movements when I play, or trying to be more efficient in my playing. But if I try to be totally still, I feel inhibited, and I can't be as expressive as I want to be.

I'm sure certain people accuse me of moving around too much. And sometimes, they're absolutely right. I think there are times where you're actually making it more difficult, when you have a moving target.

But also, when you're playing with people, and especially when you're doing a lot more leading without a conductor — even with Mendelssohn and Beethoven concertos and Bruch concertos without a conductor — the movement can demonstrate. I use movement to show a lot, basically conducting and playing at the same time. If you're almost dancing with the instrument a little bit, it conveys a certain way that the orchestra can feel — almost like a conductor's movements.

If I were to stand totally still and just move my right or left arms, it may sound just as good. Heifetz hardly moved. But he's a rare person to be able to do that. It would be hard to convey that way, when you're playing with an orchestra. Even playing with a conductor, I think they get a lot of cues from the movement as well. In the end, they have to follow me as much as they follow the conductor.

Laurie: What is your advice for aspiring violin soloists? For example, is there anything that you can think of now, that you wish you'd known back then, just to make life manageable, to cope with being a soloist?

Joshua: You kind of learn on the job, your way of doing it. I think it's dangerous to even start extolling advice about what to do when you're a soloist. Because one of the biggest problems amongst students going into colleges and schools is that they think that's the only ultimate goal: to be a soloist.

It's not for everybody, and it's not the only way to have a career in music. The great example that I had in front of me was my teacher, Gingold, who was an incredible violinist. He always played so much better than his students, which is not always the case.

He had such a rich life teaching. He was in a quartet with Primrose. He played under Toscanini and George Szell and made recordings as a soloist. And he had a very full life of doing a lot of different things. I think that it's important that young people know that there's a lot of ways to be a musician, and it's not just about playing concertos as a soloist.

I play a lot of chamber music, myself. It's a big part of my life. I think one of the things I've learned, also, is that there's not just one path to success. You have to find your own way. When I was a kid, many people told me, "There's only one way."

They said, "You have to go to Juilliard. You've got to move to New York and study with this teacher." I won't say who.... "And then you'll get your connections there." And I did my own thing. I stayed with Gingold and found my own way. And I didn't go to competitions — international competitions. I managed to avoid it. But I found my own way, and there's not just one way to do it.

If I might begin a slight rant about one of the problems I find — even on websites like Violinist.com. It's a good thing that people talk about (the violin). But if you go on YouTube — especially among young people, they have this sort of competition-type attitude when they listen to violinists play.

They make comments like, "This person sucks." If one says someone plays something well — the idea that you need to trash someone else. Of course, you have your favorite. But I think it's really important for young people to open their minds to other ways of playing and other ways of appreciating music.

I find that it's sort of a novice mistake. I find it even more among complete amateurs, who are not even in music at all. They've grown up with their one recording of a piece. They'll complain to me, "Oh, I heard this opera sung by this person. And oh, it's terrible, because it should be this way." Because this is the way they view that piece.

They're not able to open up their minds and enjoy it on the terms that the person is presenting it — as a performance. I'm guilty as much as anybody. But if you can unblock yourself and try to get inside an interpretation of someone that may be eccentric, or listen to an old Mischa Elman, without saying, "Oh God, those gross slides. Listen to the tasteless stuff." If you can try to get beyond that, and really see the poetry that's underneath it — it's a different sound. There's room for a lot of ways of playing. That's what makes it so rich and interesting in the musical world.

Laurie: Who are some of your favorite violinists? Is there's a recording that you play for yourself, to remind you of why you love music?

Joshua: When it comes to the violin, (Jascha) Heifetz is always a big inspiration. Some people say that he's cold, which I don't agree with at all.

Laurie: Did you see him live, ever?

Joshua: I never saw him live. He stopped touring in the early seventies, I think, and I was five years old. There are things I don't agree with, times where I felt he rushes through things too quickly. But in a way, it's sort of an understatement. He didn't dwell in moment after moment. There was always this sense of the big picture in music. And also, of course, his incredible electricity.

I don't listen to a lot of violin playing anymore, just because I get so much of it. But sometimes when I feel I want inspiration, I'll watch or listen to a Heifetz record. He set the bar for the violin for the 20th century. He just raised it. And I always feel after I listen to it, I play better. I set the bar higher.

I love to listen to Arthur Grumiaux. I think he's one of the most singing violinists. I think of him as the equivalent of a great lieder singer. I love listening to great voices as well, like Dietrich Fischer-Dieskau.

Also, watching Carlos Kleiber on video conducting the Bavarian (State Orchestra). I love watching him conduct Beethoven's symphonies. Or even his Vienna New Year's Concert. He's conducting music that's not even my favorite music — Strauss waltzes and things. He elevates it to great music. And what I like about Kleiber is that it seems like every tempo that he picks is exactly right. He's not trying to make a statement. Sometimes you feel, with conductors or violinists, that they're always trying to make a statement or be provocative in some way, instead of just finding the exact tempo. It should just feel right. It should be about the music. And with Kleiber, there's no showboating. You feel like he is what the Beethoven Symphony is supposed to be.

Those are the kind of musicians I like. For example, with someone like (pianist) Radu Lupu, it's just exactly right. It's not extreme in any way, yet there's nothing unexciting about his playing. It's exciting when it's supposed to be. When he plays a Beethoven concerto, it just feels right. That's the kind of artist I like to listen to.

Music should be obvious, it should be like breathing. One of the great compliments is when someone comes back and says to me, "I know this piece very well. I've heard it so many times — and you played it exactly the way I always imagined it, the way I want it to be played."

Whether they conceived of it that way — who knows? They may not even be musicians. The fact is, when I played it, if they feel like — "Oh, that's the way I always imagined it," I'd take that as a compliment.

Anne-Sophie Mutter. Photo: Anja Frers

ANNE-SOPHIE MUTTER

Originally published on October 10, 2008

I spoke with the world-famous German violinist Anne-Sophie Mutter when she was in the midst of an American tour with Camerata Salzburg, in which she played works that she had recently recorded, including Concertos by Bach (A minor and E major).

It's easy to get a little intimidated by violinist Anne-Sophie Mutter, just looking at the record.

At age 45, she has a stunning discography: with 53 composers represented in more than 60 recordings over the last 30 years. When she was new on the scene, she was famously associated with the conductor Herbert von Karajan, who invited her to play with the Berlin Philharmonic when she was just 13. She has gone on to work with many, if not most, of the most important conductors and musicians of the late 20th and early 21st century.

She has championed new music, to say the least. Looking at her biographical timeline, one sees the breadth of her contributions: her world premieres include Witold Lutoslawski's *Chain 2* in 1986; Norbert Moret's *En reve* in 1988; Wolfgang Rihm's *Gesungene Zeit* in 1992; Sebastian Currier's *Aftersong* in 1994; Krzysztof Penderecki's *Metamorphosen* in 1995; Penderecki's *Second Violin Concerto* (dedicated to her) in 1998; Penderecki's *Violin Sonata* (commissioned by her) in 2000; Andre Previn's *Tango Song and Dance* and *Violin Concerto* (both written for her) and

Henri Dutilleux's S*ur le meme accord* (dedicated to her) in 2002; Previn's *Concerto for Violin and Double Bass* with bassist Roman Patkolo; and of course, the recording Mutter has released this week: Sofia Gubaidulina's *Violin Concerto In tempus praesens* (written for her).

This is not to mention Mutter's recordings of the more "standard" modern repertoire, for example Alban Berg's *Violin Concerto* and Bela Bartok's *Violin Concerto No. 2*, Igor Stravinsky's *Violin Concerto*...

Talking with Mutter this week about her new recording of Bach and Gubaidulina, I found her to be personally warm, and passionate about the new works she is bringing to the world. Like the rest of us, she is evolving: she spoke of her recent embrace of the Baroque bow for performances of Bach, and how this has opened her to a new kind of intimacy with these works. We spoke about her litany of shoulder rest experiments during her early development as a violinist (wasn't easy for her, either!), of new music and old, of motherhood, and even a little bit about beautiful, sleeveless designer gowns.

Laurie: Very few of us get to play a brand-new piece, a world premiere. I wondered how you approach a totally new piece of music — is it different from your approach to a piece of music that is standard repertoire?

Anne-Sophie: There is common ground, of course, like thoroughly studying all the details. But I feel that with a contemporary piece which has never been played before, you can be more innovative. You are less burdened by certain expectations. With pieces that have been studied and played for the last 250 years, much of what we inherit, in terms of cultural taste, has to do with our subconscious. It's something we just grow up with; it's almost the air we are breathing. Looking at a piece by Bach, for example, it is much more difficult to get away from habits, good and bad. If it's a violin concerto by Gubaidulana, your approach is fresher; it's probably also more objective. Although being subjective is ultimately what music needs in order to really bond with an audience. You don't just want to objectificate the notes. But you don't have the burden of history. It's a wonderful luxury, if that's the word, to set the path for future generations and their understanding of that contemporary piece you are bringing to the world.

Laurie: Sometimes, particularly as a violinist — I don't think guitarists have the same thing quite — there is such history. It can almost be a trap. I remember hearing a performance of yours, of the Beethoven Concerto, and you did something very different with the cadenza. I really enjoyed it, but then I wondered how many people would be...

Anne-Sophie: Appalled? (laughing)

Laurie: Appalled! Exactly, how do you deal with that?

Anne-Sophie: I mean, the only one who will hold you up for that is the composer. The composer is the only person you really have to serve, and whose intentions you always have to keep in mind. But as we know through history, composers have allowed themselves different viewpoints on different evenings and performances — especially the ones who were the conductors of their own pieces, or performers of their own concerti. There is not one formula.

I don't think history is a burden, but it makes us aware of the fact that we should not take interpretations for granted. Interpretations of great masters of the past — they are extremely valuable reference points. Yesterday when I was playing here, a young colleague came and we were discussing Bach solo sonatas. He was working on it and he wanted to know if I could think of a reference recording, and I mentioned the name of Nathan Milstein. He was probably 15 years old, and he had never heard of of him. I'm rather saddened and shocked to see that this goes across the border, it's no matter which country you are, there's a generation after me which is not aware of the grand masters of the last century; that's extremely disturbing. It's kind of a common disease of the young generation, who seems to think that whatever is out there as a new recording is the ultimate truth.

Laurie: Not by a long shot.

Anne-Sophie: Nope.

Laurie: There's been whole entire movement that has changed how we approach Bach. If you were to listen to an early 20th century interpretation of Bach, it would be very different than a recent recording.

Anne-Sophie: Interesting to see how different eras have brought a different focus on pieces which we've known for such a long time. The so-called original instrument movement has certainly brought enlightenment in some parts of the research, if it's only the fact that today we have scores which refer in every little detail of articulation and dynamics to what the composer wanted in the 18th and 19th century.

I remember when I started the Mozart concerti, when I was 10, 11, 12. There was no Barenreiter (urtext). You actually had to go to Salzburg, to the archive, in order to find the various different versions of the concerti. Sometimes notes even differ. It's not only a question of the trills, decorations and dynamics, but also articulation. So we really have all the tools at hand, but we shouldn't take that as an easy way out. With tools at hand, I also mean all these CDs out, to hear musicians make a conglomeration of what has worked. It's just exciting to find your own way of looking at a piece, still keeping in mind the stylistic period you have to serve.

In fact, one of the exciting things about playing a contemporary piece, to come back to that, is the fact that finally you have somebody to talk to, and ask questions and get feedback. It's probably the greatest moment, as a musician, is when the composer approves of your understanding of his work. It's such a relief.

Laurie: Now this is not the first time you have worked with a live composer...

Anne-Sophie: No, I've been giving world performances for 22 years, if I'm not mistaken. So half my life.

Laurie: What's sort of the common thread when you're working with a modern composer? I'm sure they're all different.

Anne-Sophie: I think that's the common thread! (laughing) I never disturb their work, I never ask for anything in particular. I'm just the receiver. And so far, I've been extremely lucky. I'm endlessly grateful for every single piece I was invited to premiere, because all of them have been extremely special. There is not one weak composition. That's very rare.

Laurie: That's very true, because you never know what you're going to get when you commission something.

Many people really don't understand 20th and 21st century music; they would just as soon listen to the Bach part of your CD and throw the rest away. So I would love to talk about what they are missing if they don't give it a chance.

Anne-Sophie: Of course, we cannot generalize, but you are not trying to do that. I just want to point out that I'm not a total and 100 percent fan of everything which has ever been written in modern times, and I don't like everything from the 18th and 19th century either. There are times in the life of a musician, and also of a listener and music lover, where certain periods or certain composers appeal to you more than others.

I needed long years to understand (Alban) Berg, for example. That always was a difficult composer for me. Eventually the moment was right (to record the Berg concerto), but it just didn't drop into the chair. I had to work for it. I was studying it thoroughly, but I just didn't fall in love with it. And I'm a musician who needs to have the emotional bond with music. Otherwise, if it only stays a cerebral exercise, I don't feel the need to bring it on stage — because I might not be able to play it in a way which would be good enough, convincing enough, exciting enough, for an audience to really grab it, enjoy it and be inspired by it.

So Gubaidulina is obviously a composer who has mastered the form. She has so much emotional depth and incredible, unbelievable intensity in her writing and in the way she orchestrates. The wonderful story she tells about conceiving the *In Tempus Praesens* concerto is that she hears this gigantic sound construction, which she tries to bring to paper, making it transparent, and kind of threading it out... As she's in the process of writing it down, it's fading. She is not able to act fast enough. And what is even more touching is the fact that she says often she hears sounds which there is no orchestra she could give it to. So what she brings to paper probably is only a fraction of what it could be. I tell you, the fraction she brings to paper is hair-raising. It's a life-changing experience, because she doesn't shy away from enormous intensity. Some contemporary composers do, because they feel the need for more of a total objectivity. That's not my cup of tea.

I'm a great admirer of Gubaidulina because, very much like Bach, she is able to be a masterful, skillful and extremely sophisticated writer. She has proportion in her mind: relation between the five sections of the violin concerto, for example. This is not a composition which is based on writing things down because they sound lush and gorgeous, no. This is a process of at least three different levels of work. First she paints the low and high registers in light and dark colors. This violin concerto is the story of Sophia, the goddess, the lonely soul against society. Sophia, of course, is represented by the high registers of the violin, which is the only violin in the orchestral score. Then you have the dark and haunting strings, which are the dark part of the score. After she lines out the balance between the light and the dark — the kind of philosophical approach — then she goes through the pain of putting everything in a formula, which has to do with tempo relations between the five segments. It is actually mathematical, so the relationship to Bach is very apparent.

But the genius of this piece is that you would never be disturbed by the architecture of it, but rather you would just be totally fascinated by the music. It's still expressivity, but it's music which is written in her language. It is nothing like anything else ever written. She comes from a tradition where she is obviously very much influenced by the music of the 18th and 19th century. But she makes it her own.

Laurie: It's not easy, is it?

Anne-Sophie: Whenever I talk to composers, I see how much – almost, pain is behind the piece. And specifically in this concerto, there is a lot of pain. Go to the 40 bars before the cadenza. She almost refers to that scene as a crucifixion of Sophia. It's a really intense moment, where the orchestra has this percussive motive, which is standing there like a stone: unmovable destiny — and the violin is trying to escape. After that there's an incredibly long pause, then the beginning of the cadenza. It's an incredible piece, and I was very moved to see that the audience in Switzerland, at the world premiere, really got it. I guess that there is a message in great art which we can relate to, even if it sounds alien to us.

Laurie: Since you've also paired this piece with Bach Concertos, and also you are playing a lot of Bach this month, I'd like to ask: will you ever record all the Bach Sonatas and Partitas?

Anne-Sophie: I don't have, and I never had, long-term recording projects. I just hate the feeling of having to do something for a recording in a three-year time frame. So I really don't have any answer to that, other than I don't think it's going to come soon. It is not something one can pull out of the hat. There are many other things one could pull out of the hat because they are in your daily repertoire, on stage. I really don't know. It's a little bit like the Berg Concerto: the moment has to be right. Of course, the longer that you wait, it's not going to get any easier.

Laurie: Tell me a little bit about your evolution with Baroque music. I'm about the same age as you, and this whole Baroque movement has taken place during our lifetime. The early mentors I had, at least, had a completely different approach to Bach than many people now would. I noticed you're using a Baroque bow for this recording, how long have you been using a Baroque bow?

Anne-Sophie: About two years. The Baroque bow works wonderfully for a recording. I just love the airiness, the transparency and the purity of the sound. But to play that subtle, doesn't really work well in a large hall. The articulation works in a large hall. It was very important for me to bring that quality of articulation and inner voicing to the recording. You can achieve those qualities more easily (with a Baroque bow). But on stage, it's a little lost. So there are some performance techniques which work in some environments, and some don't. You do have to adjust. On tour, we also play with Baroque bows. But I think on the recording, you hear even more subtle things than you will hear in a large hall.

Laurie: So you use a different technique in the concert hall than you do in the recording studio.

Anne-Sophie: Yes. But (using Baroque bows) has helped us for the articulation of the third movement of the Bach. The whole dance-like feeling, the whole spin, the joie de vivre — is totally gone if you use too moderate a tempo, and if you are not really taking seriously the articulation. The articulation — especially in the *A minor Concerto* — is really difficult to do, if at all possible to do, in an elegant way, with a modern bow.

I'm not a great believer in so-called authentic playing. We are all born in the 20th or 21st century, and we cannot shrug off what we expect, which is the diversity of colors we are able to achieve with a contemporary bow. But what you lose with a contemporary bow is transparency of sound and the ability to use Bach's phrasing, which is very important.

Laurie: What kind of bows do you have? Who made them?

Anne-Sophie: I have American bows, my concert bows are all bows by contemporary makers. One bowmaker is from Washington, D.C., (Donald) Cohen, and the other one is (Benoit) Rolland, who lives in Boston. I'm always switching between these makers. I don't know how many contemporary bows I have — a lot. My Baroque bow is done by a man in Munich, who specializes in 16th and 17th century, (Peter) Benedek.

Laurie: How else has your Baroque approach changed over the years?

Anne-Sophie: Tempis have changed, because of the Baroque bow, which gives it a totally different outlook. I would say, I'm crazy about inner voices. I'm not at all interested in the soloist's voice, in terms of musical structure. Every day, on this tour, there are little subtle things I'm telling the orchestra. I'm so excited about it because it's such complex music. I would compare it to the veins in a body. We shouldn't only look at the body, but be aware of the many arteries we have. These arteries in Bach's music are so vital, because they give the pulse of the music. That's where the blood is running, and that is what I am mostly concerned about.

So it's transparency, it's speed, it's inner voices, and it's a different sound aesthetic, a leaner sound aesthetic.

Laurie: I have a different question, one about being a woman with a successful career, and also being a mother. How have you handled motherhood, along with being a concert violinist and soloist? What kinds of adjustments did you have to make over the years, to make it work?

Anne-Sophie: For many years, when my daughter was born, (she's now 17), I cut down the amount of concerts, and I also started to shorten my trips abroad. For seven years after being a widow (which I've been now for 13 years) I stopped going to the Far East altogether, in order not to add that to my schedule.

Children come first, and being a single mom makes things a little more difficult in terms of organizing. But I guess everything in life is about passion. If you are passionate about your children and passionate about your profession, you'll find a way to make it work. I'm very unhappy every time I have to leave my children. But I probably am a more rounded person. I am a better person because I have had children; it drastically changed my personality. I suddenly started to see the world as a whole. And that also was when I started to do more extensive benefit projects. On the other hand, I know that without music, without the arts, without this connection to the audience and to great masterpieces, I wouldn't really be a fulfilled mom. I can't really think of being 365 days at home; that wouldn't have been it for me, either. So I guess it's just trying to meet with everybody's needs and not forget my own.

It's just wonderful, and I feel very privileged that somehow it seems to work for my children and it seems to work for me, too.

Laurie: Do they play instruments as well?

Anne-Sophie: Yes, my son plays the piano. Music is, of course, a natural part of our daily life. My son is very much into sports. And my daughter loves ballet, and has done that for over 11 years. She also does modern (dance), so she is the artsy part. She also plays the flute and is in choir. So yes, they do play instruments, but it's not really their great life dream, which is okay.

Laurie: My children didn't want to play the violin...

Anne-Sophie: I just remember my son, when he took up the violin. At first, when he was five or six, he wanted to study violin. After a few minutes — I mean they gave up so fast, it was incredible — he said, 'But Mama, why does it sound so much better when you play?' I tried to explain, 'Listen, I've been playing for 40 years!' But the prospect of having to play 40 years... (she laughs)

Laurie: Several of my readers wanted to know about your beautiful dresses...

Anne-Sophie: Oh holy cow!

Actually that's no big deal, I've gone the the same designer since I was 17 years old. Basically my dresses are all the same, just different colors, it's all the same style. It's comfortable, and it works. I don't have to think about it; I almost don't have to try them on. It's like a uniform. Sometimes I think it's like a plumber's uniform. (She laughs) I mean, it looks probably a little nicer. Once I get into them, I'm kind of in the mood. I know it really does help me, to look good.

Laurie: Who is your designer?

Anne-Sophie: It's John Galliano, at Dior in Paris.

Laurie: One more question: Do you use a shoulder rest?

Anne-Sophie: This is a very interesting and crucial moment in life, when you decide what shoulder rest you'll use, or if you'll use one at all. I remember, I went through a phase of almost seven or eight years. First of all, when I started, at age five and a half, I was still growing. Therefore, I frequently changed shoulder rests. I started with the Menuhin thing, and somehow it wasn't comfortable. A few years later, I started to use a little pillow, which felt way more comfortable — I didn't like the metal thing on the violin. But then when I was 11 or 12 and had nearly reached my final height, (the pillow) felt uncomfortable. So I changed from a relatively high pillow to a low rubber thing, which was extremely uncomfortable but the height was good. From that very uncomfortable but otherwise comfortable set-up, I went to a piece of deer leather, deerskin, because I needed something in between the clothing and the violin because the violin didn't feel secure. So the deerskin was kind of giving traction to the shoulder and violin. And then, when I started to play with Karajan, around that time, I discovered that playing without anything was actually the ideal solution. Then the next step was playing with sleeveless dresses — that gave the ideal traction. So it took me about seven or eight years to finally settle down and find the solution. But there is no real rule one can apply, because it all depends on the neck length and the position of your shoulder.

Most important is that you don't squeeze your shoulder up, and that you don't pressure your chin down, because you'll get terrible muscle pains in your neck area. Basically, the instrument has to just lie there, and you put your head on the chinrest and that's it. There's no force involved. According to the particular needs of the body, everyone has to play as relaxed as you can.

Laurie: When you're talking about this, you sound like a teacher. Do you teach?

Anne-Sophie: I taught at the Royal Academy of Music for a while when I was very young, and I'm teaching the scholars of my foundation, the Anne-Sophie Mutter Circle of Friends Foundation, now. I'm always grateful for intelligent, interesting string players applying for scholarship or just sending their tape. We have a number of artists we are working with. We have a double bass player, Roman Patkoló, I tell you, he's the Paganini, it's breathtaking. He has all these great composers writing for him. Andre Previn wrote him a double concerto which will be released on CD next year, and Penderecki's writing for him — this is exciting stuff. My foundation is giving commissions for this repertoire.

I think that's rather exciting, to do something for music history.

HILARY HAHN

Originally published on February 5, 2009

The yet-to-be-premiered Violin Concerto by Jennifer Higdon, which was sitting on Hilary's music stand as we spoke for this interview, went on to win the 2010 Pulitzer Prize in Music. Hilary released a recording of the work, paired with the Tchaikovsky Concerto, also in 2010. At the time of this interview, the Great Recession was in full swing, so some of our conversation focused on what that meant for performing artists and arts organizations.

The outside world may be in freefall, but inside Disney Hall, I feel no worries. Violinist Hilary Hahn just walked onstage, regal and steady, copper gown glittering in the stage light, still not a line in her young face. She's playing the Glazunov *Violin Concerto* with the Los Angeles Philharmonic, and from note one, she plays with unfaltering tone, solid and controlled.

Her effort is generous, without being labored. When the orchestra drops out for her cadenza, she holds her audience rapt, keeping the melody always at the forefront, embedded in perfectly in-tune double stops. During the last movement, the orchestra, with conductor Leonard Slatkin keeping the whole endeavor well in sync, is a wave, and she just rides her technique. It's a joy ride, too. For an encore she plays the *Sarabanda* from Bach's *D minor Partita*.

It's a busy week for Hilary Hahn; she is up for two Grammys this

Sunday, for her recording of the Schoenberg and Sibelius concertos that she did with Esa-Pekka Salonen and the Swedish Radio Symphony Orchestra. On Friday she will play the world premiere of Jennifer Higdon's *Violin Concerto*, a piece that was sitting on her music stand, backstage at Disney Hall, when I spoke with her after her performance of the Glazunov last Saturday. We talked about the Higdon premiere and new music, about violin cases and the economy.

Laurie: Tell me a little bit about this concerto that you'll be premiering; I understand that Jennifer Higdon wrote it for you. How did it come to be?

Hilary: I was her student at Curtis in her 20th century music history class — it was still 1990-something at the time. So Jennifer Higdon basically introduced me to my attitude towards the whole body of work from the 20th century — she got me familiar with everything in that whole group of pieces.

Every week she would focus on one or two composers. We had two classes a week, and in each class she would play the music all during class and write facts up on the board. We were never tested on the facts of the composers; we were tested more on how well we absorbed what we were listening to. The tests weren't nerve-wracking; she would ask us compose a theme in the style of one of the composers we'd been listening to, one that really resonated with us. Or, if we were studying percussion one month, she'd ask us to write a piece for percussion, no longer than three minutes, and perform it in class.

It was probably the lowest 'fact' class that I've taken, and the highest 'content,' because when we were listening, we could form our own opinions. We also talked about what we were listening to, as we heard it. If anyone had any questions, we could raise our hands. If there was a particular element, compositional style, or a particular unique aspect of a certain piece, she would point it out as it appeared in the music, as we were listening. Being exposed to this music by a composer was liberating and eye-opening at the same time.

So I had that history with her: that was the first time I was in her musical world for an extended period of time.

Then I did a piece by (Higdon) with some friends of mine at Curtis, called *Dark Wood*. It was for bassoon and piano trio. That was probably the first piece of new chamber music I'd played in which I knew the person who had written it.

Laurie: Did that give you a taste for doing new music?

Hilary: Well, I'd already done new music, but I hadn't done pieces where the composer was right there. That actually wound up being the premiere of that piece, because there was a group that was supposed to premiere it a couple weeks before but they canceled. So we inadvertently played the premiere; it was really neat.

Laurie: What is Higdon's new violin concerto like?

Hilary: I would say that this violin concerto pushes the instrument a fair amount, and it slightly pushes the concept of line and melody. The way the melodies are broken up is a little bit similar to Schoenberg. People won't hear it at all as sounding like Schoenberg, but it's a little bit similar in the sense that a lot melodies that would normally be on one melodic line are staggered. So you have two, maybe three, going at once. In Schoenberg, they call them tone rows. But to me, when I hear Schoenberg, I hear multiple voices, alternating with each other. That's the effect that I hear in her music, although you wouldn't call it a tone row.

Laurie: Did she consult with you at all for this piece? Was she writing it for your style?

Hilary: Well, she was writing it for me, and she asked me a couple things. Early on, I noticed she was asking me about what was do-able, whether this was possible or not, because she's not a violinist and she wanted something that really worked. Some people she'd worked with before had told her that things she was writing were not going to be so effective for that particular instrument. I think that's wrong, though, because all the things she was asking me to do, they were all very do-able. So I told her: Don't ask me, just do it. Do anything you want to do, and we'll worry later about whether it's playable on the violin or not.

She wasn't being tentative, she was just being very conscientious about it. I like it when composers write whatever is in their head, without worrying about that particular instrument, or about that particular musician. The composer may have that musician's sound in mind; then they should write what they're inspired to write, just total liberation. I wanted her to do that.

That's why I say that she pushes the instrument a little, because she did do that. She wound up writing things that are different from what existed before, that have a unique kind of language. Of course, her signature gift of rhythm goes all the way through the piece. In some pieces, there's a lot of rhythmic deviation, a lot of drive, and it's hard to put together. But this one, it falls right into place. The individual lines might seem like they wouldn't fit, but then you play it all together and it's really just lock-step, and not in a stiff way. It just all comes together really well. That bodes well for the future of the piece, for being able to get people to put it together effectively and quickly.

Laurie: Maybe that's the mark of a good composition, that it's crafted in a way that it just comes together.

Hilary: I think it should come together in the end interpretively, and that it should come together in the end ensemble-wise; but I think it's okay if the musicians have to work for that. I don't think a composer should write for ease of assembly, or ease of listening.

Laurie: That's something I wanted to ask you about. The Schoenberg concerto certainly isn't the easiest piece to listen to. Where do you see that line, between connecting with the listener, and doing something artistic?

Hilary: It's the performer's job to bring the music across. A lot of the pieces that we love, that are considered standard, that are considered absolutely gorgeous, were not heard openly in the beginning, because they were something new. I think when composers write for the purpose of being accessible, they lose a lot of their own purpose for existence in the whole line of musical development. If they write what's in their heads, and in their bodies, what's running through their blood, and it happens to be accessible, that's fine. But I don't think anyone should ever edit themselves as a composer or a creator of something — for an audience, or for a performer. I think that really minimizes their contribution. Often the things that are strangest to us are the things that are most defining in the history of music.

It's also the same in pop and rock music; the people who do really far-out-there things wind up being incredibly influential later on. It's the performer's job to take those things and bring them across to the audience. Why are we here as performers? If interpretation weren't part of it, then we wouldn't be necessary.

Laurie: I have not heard Schoenberg concerto live but I wish I could. Because I have a feeling that if I could hear it live...

Hilary: There's a whole sweep of it that happens, live, and people in the audience get caught up in it. The musicians on stage are into it, too.

The recording (2008 Deutsche Grammophon) is probably better than what you would hear in any live concert. Live, we put less time into it. We put a lot of time into the recording. Not just the sessions, but everyone in the orchestra was practicing backstage, and at every break that they had. We had a lot of dedication, and I think it turned out really well.

But to hear it live, to be with the other people in the hall, and to see people playing it, I think that could make a big difference for a listener.

Laurie: On another important topic, are you aware that your violin case has been Tweeting on your behalf? (@ViolinCase)

Hilary: I have heard rumors of this! I don't know what it's saying.

Laurie: Now, is this truly your violin case, or is it an impostor?

Hilary: You know, I gave it my Twitter password, and I think it went and set up an account. My violin case has insider info that no one else has.

Laurie: What kind of violin case do you have?

Hilary: The case is a Bobelock.

Laurie: It looks like it has sort of a wine-colored interior.

Hilary: Purple.

Laurie: And that's a beautiful silk bag...

Hilary: It's a Hermes scarf; I knew it would be high-quality silk. I had someone make it.

I got the new case because my other case was falling apart; I had it for 15 years. It's very difficult to find a case. People should be very careful when they buy cases to test every single aspect, especially if you're going to be taking it out of the house. When you're in the store, there are things you should check: You should put it down at waist level, put your hands on the top, and bounce with your body weight a little bit. That will tell you a lot. If it gives, no go. Then you take it and you open it, and you torque the two halves at a diagonal. If it bends too much, no go. When you close it, you push in on the sides, as hard as you can, and if they give, no go!

You want a material that's not going to melt, too. On my previous case, I have a little round dot of melted synthetic canvas, because in the overheard compartments on airplanes, sometimes the reading lights are right underneath the floor. So when you're putting your violin up top somewhere, feel the bottom of the compartment, where your violin is going to be resting, and make sure there aren't hot spots. Sometimes the heating units go through there, so make sure there aren't cold air conditioning fans blowing on it. This is true in a train as well. You can tell a lot just by patting where your violin is going to be. If there is a temperature deviation, put something down between, like a blanket or a coat, and put your violin on top of that.

Laurie: You wrote a blog about the state of the economy back in late November. What are your thoughts about the economy and the arts these days?

Hilary: I think everyone's facing the same thing. I have a friend who's a filmmaker who said a lot of his friends have no work at all.

There's always the debate with music organizations: Do you do fewer concerts? Do you do the same number of concerts for less? Do you ask the musicians to help out? If you ask musicians to do things for free, does it set up a precedent? Historically, with soloists, presenters will often negotiate a lower fee, and then say that will have no bearing on the next negotiation. But then when you come back, they quote the earlier fee and do a proportionate negotiation. So people want to help each other out, but they are wary of precedent. I think that goes with the orchestras as well. There's probably a lot of misunderstanding...Musicians want to blame the administration, they want to blame other people, but the administration keeps people going. They're trying to save the organization, and their jobs are on the line. They're taking pay cuts, too. So it's really hard for everyone. A lot of soloists are being asked to reduce fees, and a lot would gladly do it. I think some people may be canceling concerts.

But I haven't heard of a lot of people losing jobs; I think that's a good sign.

I think the arts have had to fight for survival so much that this is not coming out of the blue for us. We're used to seeing public funding in the States get cut. We've already developed ways we deal with that. In Europe, now, they're having problems because a lot of those organizations are still government-funded, and in some countries they don't have the experience of going to the private sector. They don't have a tradition of fund-raising, and right now is a bad time to start!

So I think we all appreciate the people who have been involved and who continue to be involved. If people just continue to help out if they can, even if they have less, we'll be all right. They don't have to contribute the same amount, they can contribute less, but it's just nice to see people continue to support and continue to care. That's the most important thing, because that means that when things start to look up, everything will be okay again.

I'm not so worried. It's a little bit hard to panic, when you've been in panic mode, or around panic mode, for 20 years. I've been hearing how bad things are since I started playing the violin. People have talked about the death of classical music, that classical music is fading, that there are only white-haired people in the audience, that if we're not careful we won't ever have funding again, that orchestras are shutting down right and left. And that was 15-20 years ago. That's when I came into awareness of classical music as a career. So, maybe for people who began in the "heyday" it's different, but me, I've just been around this all the time.

It's shocking to see it elsewhere (in the economy), that's what surprises me. There are a lot of fields, a lot of professions, where there was no concern at all (for the sustainability of the profession). I think we're going to see a reflection of what's going on in the greater society, but I don't think it's going to be worse for us than it is for anyone else, and I don't think that we're unprepared. I think we're very well-prepared.

James Ehnes. Photo: Benjamin Ealovega

JAMES EHNES

Originally published on March 4, 2009

James Ehnes' passionate search for the 'right instrument' illustrates how close this choice can be to a violinist's heart – and what a bumpy ride that journey can be. James still plays the Marsick Strad *of 1715. He has now won seven JUNO awards, and in 2010 he was made a Member of the Order of Canada. Since our interview, he has made nine more recordings, including Paganini's* 24 Caprices, *the Mendelssohn* Violin Concerto, *the Britten and Shostakovich violin concertos, and Prokofiev complete works for violin.*

You have to admit, this guy keeps good company: Stradivari, del Gesu, Guarneri, Bertolotti and Guadagnini...

I'm talking about Canadian violinist James Ehnes, whose latest project, a CD/DVD called *Homage*, involved performing on nine violins and three violas by the above makers, all from the collection of Seattle software magnate David L. Fulton. In fact, the project is more of an exploration, with Ehnes speaking about each individual instrument, then showcasing it with music he chose specifically to feature that instrument's special qualities.

Homage was just nominated for a JUNO award, of which Ehnes has already collected five. He won a 2008 Grammy for his recording of *Barber/Korngold/Walton: Violin Concertos* with Bramwell Tovey and the Vancouver Symphony Orchestra, and among his numerous recording projects are the Niccolo Paganini *24 Caprices For Solo Violin*, and a CD of all Mozart's works for solo violin and orchestra.

But somehow Ehnes has a special knack for finding what is special in a violin, for illustrating in both his words and his playing. This is no accident; Ehnes may have been destined to be a connoisseur of fine fiddles. He certainly started thinking about the instrument he played — and making important choices — at a young age.

Laurie: What was your very first violin like?

James: I received a violin for Christmas a month before my fifth birthday, and I think it was a half-size. It was too big, so I got a quarter-size a few weeks later. I had been wanting a violin for some time; there was always a lot of music in my house. My dad is a trumpet teacher, and my mom has a ballet school. To keep me out of trouble, they would prop me up on the radiator next to the stereo speaker, and I would listen to music.

So I wanted a violin, and I was so excited when I got it. I remember taking it out and having a momentary flush of insecurity because I didn't know which hand did which thing! I guessed right the first time, the violin goes in the left hand, the bow goes in the right hand. Still, I was so concerned that I would forget this, that for the first several weeks I always practiced in exactly the same spot in the house, where I knew I had my orientation correct.

Laurie: Tell me about your journey to procure a fine instrument.

James: When I was about 12, I was lucky to get a beautiful violin, a three-quarter-size. It wasn't terribly expensive, an old German violin. I've got such sentimental feelings toward it, I still have it. It was a really beautiful-sounding instrument, a beautiful antique. It was probably that violin that got me excited about violins. I became aware of how different they can be, and how special the right violin can feel.

Then I got very lucky: When I was ready to start playing a full-size violin, the Manitoba Arts Council, (I grew up in Brandon, Manitoba), was starting up an instrument bank. They had some money, and they organized a competition for young Manitobans to get grants to purchase the first instruments for the instrument bank. I played this competition, and I won. So they said, we've got $25,000, go find a violin. It was a pretty extraordinary thing. With my teacher's help, we looked at a lot of different instruments and settled on a Riccardo Antoniazzi. It's amazing that a Riccardo Antoniazzi was worth only $25,000, not that long ago. To this day, that's actually my violin. Later on the arts council unfortunately had to shut down this instrument program. They donated the instruments to various universities throughout the province, and we arranged it in such a way that they donated the Antoniazzi to Brandon University in my hometown, where my dad works. I was able to purchase the instrument from the university, and then the university took that money to buy some other instruments. So I have that violin to this very day.

Laurie: That sounds to me like unique opportunity, at a young age.

James: It really was. It was shortly after getting that violin that I went to Meadowmount for the first time. Of course, at Meadowmount there were 13-year-old kids playing on Gaglianos and Amatis — there was some serious money. But there were also some kids who were really struggling on not-so-great instruments, people from normal families like my own. I knew how lucky I was to have a nice violin. Then as I went through my teens, I would occasionally borrow different instruments, sometimes some really nice ones. I borrowed a Strad from a guy in Minneapolis a few times, and when I went to Juilliard, I borrowed a violin from them briefly.

My next major long-term instrument was a 1717 Strad (the *Windsor-Weinstein*) that belongs to the Canadian government. It was donated by an amateur from Toronto. I had to play a competition (to procure that instrument) and I received the loan (of the instrument) for three years. After that, I could do the competition again for another three-year loan, but that's the end of it. You can only apply twice. So I knew it was always going to be a temporary thing. It's a beautiful violin, but it's not really so much of a solo instrument. It doesn't have a particularly big sound; it was always a little bit of a struggle to project with that instrument.

I played on it for about five years, and it was during the period of playing on this violin when my career really started developing. Dave Fulton, whom I'd gotten to know during that period of time, was not particularly fond of that instrument. He thought that I needed something better, and it was during that period of time that I first saw the *Marsick* Strad, which I play on now. It was being sold in London.

When I would go to Seattle and see Dave, I would tell him about the instruments, but honestly, it never crossed my mind, that in a serious fashion, he would have an interest in buying the instrument. That wasn't the sort of thing he did, or the kind of relationship we had at that point. But he was becoming a friend, and so I would tell him about the violin. Basically I wanted his advice on how to deal with people who might be interested in buying it, how to deal with the sellers. My heart was really fixed on this one particular instrument.

Laurie: How did that come to be? Why this instrument?

James: It's actually kind of a random thing. It was being sold by Peter Biddulph, out of London, and there's a dealer in New York who works with Peter, and sometimes he brings violins back and forth, overseas. He's an old friend, I've known for years, I'd actually bought a bow from him, and he knew my playing really well. It was a very curious thing, he called me up one day and said, "You have to see this violin. This is the violin for you, you're going to love it." And of course, there are dealers who say that sort of thing every time you visit! But he knew for one thing, that there was no possible way that I could have afforded it, and I didn't know anyone who could have afforded it either, so it was not as if he was trying to make a sale, he just thought that this was something that I really needed to see. I've always really appreciated that, because I was basically the first person in America to see this instrument after it had been brought out of Russia and then gone through restoration. A 1715 Strad doesn't hit the market too often; I was just really fortunate to just know this guy and to have a chance to see it.

Then of course, having seen it, it was a several-year process to actually figure out a way to get my hands on it. There was a consortium of Canadians that was interested in buying it. That looked very promising for a while, then that unfortunately fell apart. There was a

Canadian auto parts company, of all things, that was thinking of buying it, and they'd gone as far as putting down a deposit, but then they pulled out of the deal.

Unfortunately, the bigger the stakes in the violin business, the more complicated and not-always-pleasant it can get. There were some pretty ugly sides of the business that I was exposed to in this period of time, and it took a pretty big emotional toll on me; I kept thinking I was going to get it, then I wasn't going to get it, and I had the violin in my possession and I had to give it back, and then it was sold to somebody else briefly, then their sale fell through...

Eventually, I think that Dave just got sick and tired of hearing me whine about it. The price was very fair for what the instrument was. He was of the opinion that someone should just step up to the plate and do this, and make it happen, because it's a good violin – it's a great violin, it was a fair price, and he felt that I should be able to use it. So he bought it. And that was that!

Laurie: And it's on permanent loan to you?

James: Well, he has no plans to take it back, I guess I'll say that. At some point, what Dave would really like is for me to buy it from him, so that I could really have it forever, which would be amazing. So we'll see.

Laurie: That must have been awful when it was sold to someone else, like the person you were planning to marry had married someone else!

James: It was kind of depressing. It was particularly depressing because some of my friends in the business, including this guy who had shown it to me in the first place, my friend Alex, he would try to get my mind off of it. He would say, 'Come over to the house, I've got this other great Strad passing through for a couple of days...' And I'd say, 'No, it's not the same,' and I'd mope about it.

Actually when I started searching on behalf of the Canadian auto parts company I'd mentioned before, the (*Marsick*) Strad, as far as I'd known, had sold, it was gone. So I was looking at different instruments, and I'd actually picked out a 1740 del Gesu. At that point, after I'd picked out that violin and I was pretty happy with it, I heard that this

Marsick Strad was coming back on the market, and so I was really excited to get the two in the same room. That was an extremely hard decision, deciding between those two instruments. I played for a lot of people, obviously, to get as many opinions as possible, and 50 percent of the people said one, and 50 percent said the other. In the end, it was just sort of a gut thing.

My roommate at the time, a cellist, had gone through all this with me. I'd bring back (instruments) to the apartment. He thought that I'd managed to pick out the most Strad-like Guarneri that I could find, and the most Guarneri-like Strad. So I was not dealing with extremes. I knew what I wanted, and it was sort of right down the center.

Laurie: You put yourself through a lot to get this instrument. Is there a way of describing what it is so compelling about a fine instrument, that would make you go through all this?

James: In terms of playing the violin and having a career on the violin, one is always dealing with...how much sacrifice are you willing to make? How hard are you really going to practice? How many weekends out with your friends are you really going to pass up, what is it worth to you? At the point when I was looking for a great violin, the concept of being the absolute best that I can be was paramount. That was the most important thing: reaching whatever full potential I had, because I was at that point where my career goals and dreams were either going to happen or not happen. There I am, getting into my early, mid-20s, and things had been going well for me, but I was by no means established. I could have disappeared pretty easily. I thought, anything I can do to get my playing better, anything I can do to improve myself as a player, as a musician...I have to do it, and I have to do it now. So trying to get a great violin was just a part of that. Looking back, there was a lot of time and effort and struggle that went into the process of getting an instrument, but in a way that was the easy part. I mean, the practicing was much harder!

Laurie: Does an instrument teach you something?

James: Absolutely. Different instruments can teach you different things, depending on what you want to learn.

For me, I think that the great Strads and del Gesus have a level of refinement in the sound that pushes the player constantly to be improving themselves. Sometimes it really kind of gets annoying, on a Strad, where in order for it to really ring correctly it has to be played with such precision that is just sometimes gets frustrating! (laughing) You think, is this really worth it? There are certain great del Gesus — you can afford to be a little sloppy with them, and they'll still sound great. But you start sounding bad on a Strad really quickly. That can get irritating, but I'm always so into the idea of self-improvement. I appreciate having a violin that is constantly pushing me to try to achieve greater and greater levels of tonal purity, accuracy and intonation. I always try to take the attitude that if I'm playing on a great violin that's worth millions of dollars, it's probably better than I am. I want to do my best to try to keep up with the greatness of the instrument itself.

Laurie: Did you happen to read *The Violin Maker* by John Marchese? One of the conclusions I got from that book was this idea that Strads and modern instruments sound essentially the same to an audience, if fiddle players could only get over some kind of obsession or mental hang-up with Strads. But it really isn't the same experience for the player, at least it seems to me. Maybe the end product seems to sound the same to an audience, but there's some kind of give-and-take going on, there's something the Strad is giving the player that is different than another instrument.

James: If an instrument can inspire you to be better, then that will make an enormous difference in terms of the actual experience.

I think that any sort of shoot-out — they're always interesting. But they're kind of foolish in a way.

Laurie: Comparing this and that, you mean?

James: In theory, it's a great idea. But if you've got two different instruments, first of all, different players are going to sound different ways on different violins.

For myself, I try out a lot of violins. I love it. I love trying out old instruments, new instruments, ones that are fresh out of a workshop...I've played on really, really nice violins. Do I think that I've found a modern instrument that is as great as my Strad? No. Absolutely not. And that's not a knock on some of these great violins, and it's not a knock on players who feel differently or who have chosen to play their modern copy over their old Italian. Everyone is looking for different things.

If someone can show me the violin that is as good as my Strad, sign me up, I'll write the check, I'll be done with all this headache. I'll buy two!

Laurie: I wanted to ask you about developing your technique. You have a technique that is superior to most, and yet, I can see you hold the violin differently than some of the conventional ways that teachers might ask for. At what point do you ignore what teachers are asking for, and just do your own thing that's working?

James: I was really lucky to have fantastic teachers who gave me a lot of freedom. I basically had two violin teachers, and they in fact were students together under (Ivan) Galamian. My teacher in Canada was a man named Francis Chaplin, at Brandon University. He died about 15 years ago. He was an amazing man, he's kind of legendary up in Canada. It's basically impossible to go to any major Canadian orchestra and not find lots of people who studied with him over the years. He was of the 'if it's not broken, don't fix it' kind of school. He could see what worked for me, and what didn't work for me. It wasn't like he just let me do my own thing and I was out on my own. I learned all my standard stuff from him. But I think that maybe some teachers get caught up in how it should be done, not taking into consideration that everybody's body is a little different.

I was with people who also made me aware of the importance of being aware of my body, and how things felt. If it hurt, then it was probably wrong. My dad was always a big believer in not wasting energy with needless tension. People sometimes say, "You're so relaxed when you play..." I'm not exactly relaxed; I'm pretty focused, but there's not needless energy being used where it doesn't need to be used. I take pride in — hopefully — the economy of effort that I use when I play.

And then Sally Thomas — she was such an amazing teacher for me.

Sometimes I look back on my years of studying with her, and it's almost like I was a wild horse or something...

Laurie: What do you mean?

James: Sometimes you'll see these horse races on T.V., and they're all going as hard as they can, and there are fences on either side of them, but the fence is pretty wide. So I could get going off in some direction on something, and until I started getting really off track, Ms. Thomas generally would let me do my thing. She had a lot of confidence that I would figure certain things out on my own, and that the process of figuring them out was more important than her saying, "Now do it this way." Every student is different, but I did have this independent streak that both of them indulged, and both of them were careful not to mess with things that were working. There were a lot of people that I would play for and they'd say, "Oh, your thumb's all wrong, your bow grip's all wrong, this is all wrong, that's all wrong." It's funny, about 10 years ago, a violinist who had seen me play many years before told me, "Your bow grip, it's gotten so much better, who taught you? What happened?" I said, "Well, I got a better bow." The bow grip that works on a $150,000 Tourte isn't necessarily going to work on a $3,000 Nürnberger.

Laurie: It's an interesting line that a teacher has to walk, between allowing someone to experiment and develop their technique in accordance with their own body, and then also, reining someone in. Do you teach?

James: Not really private teaching, but I do a fair number of masterclasses. I find it interesting. I realize that a lot of things have come easier to me than they do to some people, but on the other hand, I think that I'm pretty analytical. Even if it's something that I can do, there's a part of me that always wants to know why, and how. It's just the way I am about things in general. I used to take my car apart. I'm really into seeing how stuff works.

Laurie: How do you stay focused in performance? Do you have advice for people who get jitters before performing?

James: A major factor is just getting in the habit of doing it. People say to me, "You have such a weird life, you travel all over, and you play these concerts in front of all these people, it's so weird!" And I think, well, it's not weird to me, to me it's just totally normal. You have a weird life! You sit at a desk, and go to the same place every day...that so strange! The moral of the story: if it becomes normal to you, then it just feels more natural, for the mind and the body.

I think for some people, it's always more of a struggle than for others. It amazes me, certain great musicians out there, every concert is terrible for them. Obviously, these are bright people. If they had the answers they would fix it.

Giving oneself as much experience performing as possible is a good thing, and so is focused preparation.

Sometimes, when people learn a piece, they're very focused. They have to be, they're first getting it in the hands. Then when they are actually in the preparation-for-performance phase, they get into this sort of a trance-like run-through phase. They'll run it through, every day. I gotta run it through, gotta run it through...The mind starts to get a little bit on autopilot.

Then when you actually get to the performance, you think you're really prepared, but you're not prepared in that focused way. All of a sudden, you're at hypersensitivity in the mind at performance time. It's not that you start thinking too much, it's that you start thinking enough, but you haven't been doing enough thinking. And you start second-guessing yourself. I come across that a lot, people say, "I knew the piece so well, but when I got up on stage, I wasn't sure if it went here or if it went there, and I couldn't remember my fingerings or my bowings..." They're usually blaming it on their mind somehow blanking out, but I think that in a way they were blanking out on the preparation.

Laurie: It's the opposite from what everyone thinks.

James: Exactly, when you actually had to think about what you were doing, you hadn't really thought about it in so long, that it seemed very far away.

Laurie: How do you do that in a practice room? How do you make the focus happen?

James: I'm guessing we've all had this experience, where you're playing along, and you realize that you weren't really even listening.

Laurie: Definitely!

James: Just stop, start from where you last knew you had your focus, and really pay attention, really listen. People who practice well can get more done in an hour than people who practice poorly can get done in a lifetime. The focus during practice sessions is so important. Too many young people get caught up in "time," logging the hours.

If people can have a particular goal in mind, and if reaching that goal can take on more importance than just logging the hours, then I think real progress can start to happen. Of course, you want to make sure that the student is spending enough time to build up stamina, and build up that level of concentration. But when you are dealing with advanced students, if they're saying, "Now I'm 16, now I'm getting serious about getting into the conservatory so now I need to practice X number of hours a day..." Well, maybe you should think of it in terms of, "I want to learn this piece and the piece, by this time," that might be a more valuable way of looking at it.

Laurie: I did notice in all your bios that you are married, and I wanted to ask, how do you maintain a personal life, when being a soloist is so demanding?

James: That almost gets into the question, can you divorce an artist from his art? Maybe with some people you can, but for a lot of people you can't. I know that my music-making is best when I'm happy. As much a music has always meant to me, I've refused to ever let it take away from other things that were really important to me. Which meant that from a young age I really had to prioritize. There are certain things that are worth it in your life, that you don't want to miss out on. And there are a lot of other things that are just not that worth it. It's sort of like people who watch T.V. There might be a couple of shows that you really like and you don't want to miss. But a lot of people will watch hours and hours of stuff that they're not even really paying attention to. I think that's the way, unfortunately, that a lot of people go about living their lives.

JANINE JANSEN

Originally published on March 17, 2009

In this conversation with Dutch violinist Janine Jansen, we spoke about one of the most beloved pieces in violin literature, the Tchaikovsky Violin Concerto.

What intensity.

That's how I felt after watching a live recording of Janine Jansen playing the Tchaikovsky *Violin Concerto* — a fiery and physical ride that held me spellbound, in which she completely gives herself over to this concerto. Even the hair on her head comes unbound by the last movement, flying into her face, which also registers most every musical gesture and nuance.

Jansen said that she doesn't really notice how much she exerts in a performance, that she doesn't feel physically drained afterwards.

"I don't notice that, because it is the most natural thing for me to play like this," Jansen said, though she admitted she sometimes feels emotionally worn after a performance. "For example, with the Britten concerto, that takes so much emotionally out of you," she said. "For me, music is the strongest language, and it just goes through me."

Jansen's recording of the Tchaikovsky *Violin Concerto* and *Souvenir D'un Lieu Cher* is released in the United States today. Predictably, it is being released for digital download, as Jansen was long ago crowned "Queen of the Download" by the *The Independent* of London, for the successful

Internet marketing of her Vivaldi *Four Seasons* recording.

"When that was said, it was when my Vivaldi came out," said Janine, laughing. "It was one of the first classical recordings to be on iTunes, which has become a big part of today's world. I'm sure by now I'm no longer the queen!"

It wasn't her idea to go the digital download route. "Back then I hadn't even visited iTunes and didn't really know how to download music," she said. "I wasn't so much aware of it."

That success wasn't without its downside; the alluring cover art that appealed so widely may also have let to some of the condescending adjectives ascribed in the early days to her playing by people who had never heard her perform live. "Kittenish charm"? "Beguiling small tone"?

In what universe?

At 31, Jansen takes this in stride. "I really do enjoy the day with the photographer," Janine said. "It's also art in some way." For her more recent albums, "the last few photos are more grown up, I think."

"The most important thing, with album covers, or with anything else in life, is you just have to do what's right, and stand behind what you want, what you think is right, and not let yourself be pushed in another direction."

Janine learned the Tchaikovsky concerto — from scratch — in a matter of several months, a feat that I find astonishing due to a) my own 10-year battle with the piece and b) the fact that from the point of its very conception the concerto was labeled "unplayable" by its dedicatee. It's a hard piece to play.

Jansen was first asked to play the Tchaikovsky by conductor Vladimir Ashkenazy and the Philharmonia Orchestra.

"It was so intimidating to play it with these great conductors so early on," she said. But since then, she has played it frequently, even as a debut piece with important orchestras such as the New York Philharmonic and the Los Angeles Philharmonic. At this point, she has been playing it for nine years.

"You are never through learning it. But after all these years, I felt ready to share my view of it as it is now," said Jansen. For the recording, she said she loved working with the Mahler Chamber Orchestra. "Each and every player is so flexible," she said, "and Daniel Harding is an emotional musician."

Jansen recorded the album with her 1727 *Barrere* Stradivarius, which she has been playing since 2002, on extended loan from the Elise Mathilde Fund through intermediation of The Stradivari Society of Chicago.

She said that getting the Strad "was kind of like a fairy tale story." She had been playing on an Italian instrument, a Tomaso Balestrieri that had belonged to her former teacher, Philippe Hirshhorn. "His widow was loaning it to me," Janine said. "I tried to find a sponsor to buy it and loan it to me, but I was not able to do so, and so I was left with nothing." During the midst of this time of searching, a man approached her after one of her concerts and gave her a card, and that is what led her to The Stradivari Society of Chicago. Bein and Fushi brought her eight instruments to try.

"I tried all of them," Janine said. "All of the instruments were of the highest quality. But with this instrument, I felt immediately that it was right. You have an ideal kind of sound in your body — in your heart. For me, an instrument should have a richness and also be flexible. What I particularly like about his instrument is it has the ability to be soft and still really carry."

"I say that I knew it was the right instrument from the start, but that was only a start," she said. It takes years to get to know a instrument, she said, to unlock its strengths and to compensate for any of its weaknesses. "You learn so much from this kind of an instrument."

I was thrilled to see Tchaikovsky's *Souvenir D'un Lieu Cher* ("Souvenir of a Beloved Place") — on Jansen's new recording as well as the concerto. This is a group of three pieces that includes the moody and emotional *Meditation*, which begins like the richest dark chocolate — scarcely leaving the G string; then it winds up and calms down, loses its composure and gains it back, loses balance and finds equilibrium. In the end it expires at the other end of the spectrum, on a towering D that's too high for the ledger lines required to write it (would someone like to count?)

The *Meditation* also was written as the middle movement of the violin concerto — until Tchaikovsky thought better of the idea.

"The *Meditation* itself is a gorgeous piece. It's just very interesting to see the two of them together," said Jansen, comparing the *Meditation* with the *Canzonetta*, the more emotionally restrained movement that Tchaikovsky ultimately placed at the center of his violin concerto.

"The second movement (of the violin concerto) is the greatest, most beautiful piece of music, and it is exactly the right intimacy, the right character, everything is there," she said. "It's quite short in the concerto, but it is exactly right, and if this *Meditation* had been in the concerto, it would have been too much. Too much emotion, just too much."

Having played the *Meditation* with piano myself, and having listened to many versions of it with orchestra, I did a double-take upon hearing a solo cello making its elegant descent in the introduction — solo cello? And wait, what happened to the woodwinds, too?

Apparently Jansen wanted all strings, and she chose a version of the *Souvenir D'un Lieu Cher* that was arranged by Alexandru Lascae. Tchaikovsky originally wrote the piece for violin and piano, and the most commonly used arrangement is a full orchestration by Alexander Glazunov.

"I especially love the strings — the sound blends so well," Jansen said of the Lascae arrangement. "It's more of a chamber music way of playing it."

And it shouldn't be surprising that Jansen would love something that felt like chamber music — her affinity for this kind of music goes back to her very first teacher, Coosje Wijzenbeek, who is well-known in Holland for teaching young children.

"Every week there were lessons in chamber music," Jansen said of her lessons with Wijzenbeek. "For me, the essence of making music is this way of communicating with each other, this whole flexibility. Without each and every part, the music is not the same. You must be alert to each person."

Every year, during her winter holiday break (from a schedule that includes some 100 solo performances a year) Jansen holds a yearly chamber music festival in her hometown of Utrecht in The Netherlands.

"Most of the time I'm traveling alone, to new cities, and it's wonderful to meet new people," Janine said, "but it's also wonderful to come back, and to play chamber music."

Janine's festival culminates in a jam session of sorts, and "this year it lasted three days!" she laughed.

"It's a relaxed ending of the concert," she said. Everyone just kind of gets up, announces their piece, sometimes even talks about the piece a little bit. And the pieces come from a range of genres: This year, clarinetist Martin Fröst played klezmer music. Also, the Dutch jazz pianist, Michiel Borstlap brought music to play with Janine. "I never improvise, but he brought something for me, so that we could play together," she said. Even an audience member who worked as a TV presenter rose up to play. "The whole atmosphere is so relaxed."

I wondered if this was a bit like being in an orchestra, where all the familiar faces, togetherness and music-making makes people start feeling like family members.

"Sometimes people think, when we say that it's like a family, that it's just corny. But it's so true," Jansen said. "Those are the people I love playing with. It's so nice socially to be together, too. This whole communication, it's so wonderful to have."

Tasmin Little. Photo: Melanie Winning

TASMIN LITTLE

Originally published on April 14, 2009

Inspired by Joshua Bell's subway busking experiment, Tasmin Little did some busking herself in a London Underground tunnel. It made her re-think the whole problem: How do we get an audience for classical music?

British violinist Tasmin Little has faith in classical music — that the music itself needs no dressing up to appeal to people across a wide spectrum.

She's done her best to prove it, as well. In February 2008 she released an album of all solo violin works called *The Naked Violin*, in the form of a free download. Her idea was to bring violin music to an audience that might not otherwise find it accessible. To make it even more accessible, she created audio introductions to the pieces, and challenged people to download the music, get to know it well, and then write her if they still felt a barrier to enjoying classical music.

Her new album, *Partners in Time*, was conceived along the same lines, and though it is not free this time, Tasmin has created the same kinds of educational features on her website to lure the uninitiated — and also to offer insights for those of us who already love this music.

Tasmin, who is 43, has reached out in live performance as well. In addition to regular concertizing, she also has been performing monthly at schools, and even at prisons.

Tasmin, who plays a 1757 Guadagnini violin and also has the *Regent* Stradivarius of 1708 on loan from the Royal Academy of Music, talked with Violinist.com last month while she was in Seattle to play the Elgar *Violin Concerto.* She spoke about her early days at the Menuhin School, about her Josh Bell-like busking experiment in London several years back, and about her new mission to bring classical music to the widest possible audience.

Laurie: Let me start at the very beginning: what made you want to start playing the violin?

Tasmin: Actually my route into playing the violin was slightly unusual, though I grew up with a concept of performing because my father (George Little) is an actor. He didn't do a "normal" job either! So my sister and I were taken off to the theatre regularly as a part of our childhood. My parents also loved classical music, so they used to play a lot of records, in the days when there were black vinyl records. My father was in a lot of musicals, so there was a lot of music in the house, of all different types.

When I was six, nearly seven, I was cooped up in bed with chickenpox, and I was so incredibly bored. I knew some of my friends were learning recorder at school. so I asked my mom, would she be able to buy me a recorder and a book? Then I promised I wouldn't nag her any more to play games with me. So she bought me a recorder, and she bought me a book, and I actually taught myself to play the recorder and read music in a half an hour. I really loved it, and it was incredibly easy.

So I thought it would be lovely to play another instrument. At the same time, we had just met a young piano student who had just graduated, so my sister and I took piano lessons. By this time, I also was getting very interested in the violin. When at last I picked up the violin, I knew instantly that that was the instrument that I loved. I made very quick progress on 15 minutes a week, which was all that you were supposed to get at the school. But after three months I was playing in my first concert, and then about six months later my teacher said, "Look, you really need to go to a specialist music school." So I auditioned for the Yehudi Menuhin School and I got in. I'd been learning just over a year, and I went.

Laurie: How old were you, then, when you went to the Menuhin school?

Tasmin: I was just eight. It was quite young, bearing in mind that it's a boarding school. I effectively left home at age eight. But it was a very small school as well. At the time that I arrived, there were only 35 pupils, ranging from age eight to 18. I had only about three people who were actually my age in the whole school, which was a bit bizarre. It was a wonderful education, a fantastic atmosphere in the school. It was more like a family, really, but it was a big adjustment, having been in a large primary school in the heart of London. Suddenly I was right in the middle of nowhere, in this stunningly beautiful countryside, with lots and lots of fantastic, young players.

Laurie: Did you see much of the school's founder, the great Yehudi Menuhin, then?

Tasmin: He was amazing. He was very active, still performing at that point — this was 1973. He was playing, he was conducting, he was doing all sorts of things. Bearing in mind the fact that he probably spent only about 40 days in England in one year, he would spend three of them down at the school. He would come at least three times a year, and he would hear every one of us.

Laurie: I've always been curious about that school.

Tasmin: It's a wonderful school. There were so many not-very-nice rumors that used to go about, like what a hothouse it was, and how we were drilled like little machines, and how people were not really given proper academics education, and so what you got were these robots who just can play fantastically well... nothing could be further from the truth. The moment I arrived at the school, the two words that were sort of the mantra were "chamber music," and the first thing that happened was that you were put in a quartet and made to listen to everybody when you played. That was just the whole ethos of the school: the idea of being a listening musician.

I have to say, I meet quite a lot of musicians who don't listen!

Listening is the number one, most crucial element when you are making music with other people. How can you possibly make sense of anything if you're working in a vacuum? Then the performance is in fact nothing to do with the music, or even anything to do with anybody that's listening. It's your own little private world. That's very far from what I believe.

Laurie: It's obvious that's far from what you believe, because you're really reaching out. You've gone to great lengths, actually, putting out something like *The Naked Violin*, which not only was offered as a free download, but also had all kinds of educational audio introductions on the website. What brought you to this idea, of doing these downloads for free?

Tasmin: Various things. It wasn't that I just woke up one day and thought, "Ah, I'm going to do that;" it was an evolving process. For many years I have believed that anybody can enjoy classical music, despite the fact that at various points politicians have said, "Oh no, classical music is for a middle-class, white audience." Personally, I find that kind of statement insulting – insulting to everybody, actually. But also, it's just not true. So for years I've felt that I would like to do something to make music more widely available, to shake off something of the stuffy image – but not at the expense of the music.

I don't disagree with crossover; or quartets such as Bond, dressing up; or Vanessa-Mae doing her stuff — I'm not against that in any way. But I do feel that there is a very strong case to be made for reaching out to a diverse audience and playing classical music, unadulterated — not given a beat, and not dressed up in some other way to distract people from the music. Because when people do other things with the music, it's saying, "We don't think you're really going to enjoy the music as it is, so we'll do something else so that you don't really have to concentrate on the music." I don't want to do that myself.

A few things happened during 2007 that gradually led me to put out *The Naked Violin* download: You will remember when Josh Bell did the busking...*The Independent* newspaper in England said, "Ah, this was an interesting experiment, would you come and do the same thing? We're curious to see whether the same thing would happen." It was actually not any more successful than Josh's attempt, certainly from a monetary point of view! Which is fine, because that wasn't the aim of the game.

Laurie: Where did you do it?

Tasmin: I did it in the smelliest, most disgusting place! By Waterloo Station, in London. There were pigeons flying around, bird poo everywhere, it was really nasty and cold, and dingy. Most people just want to get out of that tunnel and back into the daylight. So it would take quite a lot to stop somebody, to make them want to stand there — and breathe the aromas! (laughs)

What happened was that I was absolutely surprised and shocked by the people that didn't want to listen, and the people that did want to listen. It was like a concert hall, turned on its head. Of all the people that would probably pay vast sums of money to go regularly to concerts — nobody even looked at me. They just walked straight on past. But the people that were so curious and interested were the young people. Also, there was some building going on nearby, I think at the Festival Hall, and a lot of the workmen stopped. British workmen are quite funny sometimes. They'd throw a line at me, in a very lighthearted fashion; it was great.

It was clear that out of the stuffy — or perceived-stuffy — environment of the classical concert hall, many people that you wouldn't associate with going to concerts will listen to classical music. I thought, okay, this has got something to do with the environment, that people don't feel comfortable going into a classical concert hall, never mind the expense.

So many young children listened — there were two ladies who walked past, and their young children wanted to watch, but they were being hurried away. I presumed that the mother didn't want to give any money, or maybe they had a train to catch, because we were by a train station. Anyway, they literally had to pick one of these children up and carry her away. She wanted to watch me. It was a fascinating experience, it just made me re-think this whole problem that people have often spoken about in classical music: How do we get these audiences? What is it that is preventing very young people from coming into the concert hall?

I was thinking quite a lot about that during the year. Then later on in the year, I was playing a fantastic program of solo violin works: the Bach *G minor sonata*, the Paul Patterson, the Bartok *Solo Sonata* and the Ysaye *Ballade*. The responses I was getting to this program were unbelievable. Music such as the Bartok *Solo Sonata* — which some people might consider very difficult listening — was generating this incredible response. Everybody just adored the program. Everywhere I went, this program really seemed to have an effect on people.

So I began to put the two ideas together: of wanting to reach people and wanting to play unadorned, wonderful violin music. I wanted to put out a range of very different violin music, instead of doing what is done most of the time on CDs, bracketing works of only one particular style, or just one composer.

So the idea was born: I thought, I will record this, and I will make it available as a download — and let's see whether anyone is interested in this kind of classical music, once it's taken away from the usual environment. And the response was quite phenomenal. I was amazed. I was getting 20,000 hits a day on my website. Within literally a couple of weeks I'd had 250,000 visitors from all over the world on my website, and right now we're currently marching toward half a million.

And the letters! These letters were so moving, some of them.

Laurie: I wondered what kinds of things people wrote to you, because I know that you had a three-step challenge, asking people to download and listen, then write to you about what they think and whether they still felt any barriers to wanting to go to classical music concerts or buy a CD...

Tasmin: People did write, they wrote from all over the world, quite often not in English. I speak some languages, so most of the time I could understand what people were writing — but sometimes I couldn't!

Two of the letters I loved the most came from the States. One was from a guy who introduced himself as a 50s-plus rock 'n' roller. He said, "I never thought I would ever listen to, or love, any other music than rock 'n' roll. I've never been interested in classical music, but your playing and your music makes me want to throw away my whole rock 'n' roll collection and replace it with classical CDs."

Laurie: Wow!

Tasmin: I was so thrilled, obviously, when I got that. And I got a really brilliant mash note from a five-year-old boy, here in the States, and he said, "I loved your download. I loved the Bach, but the Patterson is great, the Patterson is way gooder!"

I was so thrilled about that letter, first of all, because of the age of the boy; but also because of the fact that we are so boring and stuck in our ways when we make assumptions about what children will want to listen to. So often people think, Mozart's for children, and sure, Mozart is for children, but so is contemporary music. In a sense, children have got this amazing, open mind, and they don't feel that they have to provide a particular response, they just respond. So I love that letter.

Then another that moved me considerably came from a man in Nantong, China. He wrote to say, "You've got no idea of the value of the gift you have given. In China, we've got no credit cards, so we can't order anything off the Internet." Of course you and I, we wouldn't even think about that, it's so taken for granted, that you get on the Internet, you order something online, you give a credit card, and that's how transactions are done. So I was absolutely touched by his letter. He said that the opportunity to listen to world-class classical music was so limited for him, and therefore he deeply appreciated my download.

So that's just a small flavor of the hundreds of letters that I received. It was genuinely moving, and I still get letters.

Laurie: Tell me about your new CD, *Partners in Time*. I noticed that you provide extensive introductions to your album, and also to each piece, on your website.

Tasmin: People now are so interested in the Internet, and that was another reason why I wanted to provide, with my new recording, these facilities for people to explore classical music. I've spent a long time writing these introductions which are on the site, and I've also recorded them, so that people can listen to the introductions — for example, if somebody is visually impaired. You can read them and listen, or you can just listen, or you can just read. There are tons of musical examples as well.

Laurie: So your new CD, is not free, like *The Naked Violin* was, right?

Tasmin: This one is not free, but what I have done, in addition to making this listening facility available on my site; I recorded a bonus track for download, for people who do buy the CD. I know that it's a leap for people: one moment I'm saying okay, here, have a download, and now I'm saying you've got to pay for it. It's not sustainable to continue to put music out permanently for free. But it's an invitation.

I feel that it's so important that musicians continue to find ways of engaging people, of reaching out, of being imaginative in the works that they program and record, and then finding ways of capturing people's imaginations. I'm hoping that the little five-year-old boy is going to go and listen to this CD and say, "Wow, that's great as well," and that he'll find something he'll think is "way gooder" than Bach, or perhaps on this one the Bach will be "way gooder" than everything else...When you reach into different areas and you explore different ways, I think people really respond.

Philip Setzer. Photo: Lisa Marie Mazzucco

PHILIP SETZER

Originally published on May 22, 2009

At the time I spoke with Emerson String Quartet violinist Philip Setzer, the group had been together for 30 years. He had some of the best advice I've heard about working together long-term — and it could apply to any long-term collaboration, even a marriage! In May 2013, cellist David Finckel retired after 34 years with the group, with best wishes from his colleagues, and his position was filled by cellist Paul Watkins.

The Emerson String Quartet has played together for 30 years, as of this month. How do four people function together so well, for so long?

About a week before I spoke with Emerson String Quartet violinist Philip Setzer, I heard the quartet perform a recital, at the ACE Gallery in Beverly Hills. They couldn't have given me a better overview of their range, with a program that included Mozart's *String Quartet No. 22 in Bb Major* (K. 589); Beethoven *Quartet No. 11 in F minor*, Op. 95; Webern's *Bagatelles*, Op. 9; and Ravel's *String Quartet in F.*

Violinists Setzer and Eugene Drucker and violist Lawrence Dutton stood to play, while cellist David Finckel sat on a pedestal, as has been their standard practice since 2002. Somehow it seems right that time would raise these guys to their feet rather than making them sit back.

I enjoyed the well-oiled machine that is the Emerson. They made it look easy: all you need is perfectly well-calibrated pitch, time and volume control, and you'll have a fantastic quartet. As they played the buoyant third movement of the Mozart, I noticed what nice timing they had, "like a clock with a million motors, all going exactly right," I wrote. During the Beethoven I found myself wishing to have two such friendly-looking, attentive and competent partners in the lower strings, "The violist looks like he's having so much fun...I may kidnap him," I observed.

I turned my attention to Setzer and Drucker, who trade off playing first and second violin. Aw, come on, one of them has to be the hot dog here! I looked for signs of jealousy, dominance, dissatisfaction...I gave up. Each seemed perfectly happy sitting first or second. I let my eyes relax. Maybe they both secretly covet the second violin part. Hah! And maybe I'm having a second violinist's fantasy.

Back to the concert, the Webern was a modern collage of effects, a pizzicato here, glissando there, a tremolo sul ponticello; to me it sounded like mice scrambling around, knocking things off tables, disappearing into holes. Not completely my cup of tea, but Ravel, I love, as do many. As they played the Ravel I sensed in the audience a collective Beverly Hills kind of vibe: "Wow, this music would be awesome in my new documentary." As a musician, I was impressed with the way they could drive in five during the last movement — what a ride!

Setzer spoke to me in April, from his cell phone, as he drove to SUNY Stony Brook, where he teaches violin. We talked about the Emerson's new CD of works by Czech composers, and about what kinds of things help foster a long and fruitful professional relationship between four people.

Laurie: Tell me a little be about the Emerson's new CD, *Intimate Letters.* I understand the quartet has been championing these works by Janácek and Martinu for some time; how long have you been playing them?

Philip: We actually played the second (Janácek) quartet first, quite early in our career, so we've been playing that piece for at least 25 years. The first quartet, we learned a few years after that, so that's a newer piece for us — we've been playing it for 20 years! We don't play them every season, but I would say every other season we would probably program one of them.

Laurie: If you played these pieces so early on, you must have been drawn to them early on. What makes these quartets such interesting pieces?

Philip: His language is so unique; I don't know any other composer that you could really compare Janácek to. There are elements of Czech folk music, tunes that sound like something Dvorák or Smetana might have written. But his sense of color and sound, and the way that he uses music to express his passion...It's not that other composers don't do that, but they don't do it in the way that Janácek does. The other thing that's interesting about Janácek is that he was fascinated with speech, the spoken word – the rhythms of it, the pitch of it. I think he was especially curious about the way that the rhythm and pitch of speech changes when you add emotion: when you're speaking softly, or endearingly, or angrily, or passionately. He studied these things throughout his life and imitated that with his music.

When you turn the radio on, when you hear a few seconds, you can tell that it's Janácek; it's very distinctive.

Laurie: I read the liner notes, about *The Kreutzer Sonata* by Janácek, but when I was actually listening to the second quartet, my daughter, who is 11, was listening to it with me. She was making up a narrative to it that obviously had nothing to do with *The Kreutzer Sonata*. She was imagining a clown, who was dancing, but someone stepped on his toes, then he couldn't dance any more, then he was hyperventilating...it was funny to me.

Philip: It's so full of color, it does tease the imagination, for sure. I grew up in Cleveland, my parents played in the Cleveland Orchestra. (Conductor George) Szell didn't do a lot of 20th century music, but one of the pieces he really loved was the *Sinfonietta* of Janácek. I don't know if you've ever heard it live, but whatever recordings you've heard of it will never do it justice. It has something like nine trumpets in it, and a huge brass section. The prelude music and the way that it ends, sonically, is just overwhelming. It's very primitive, when you're thinking about the melody lines, they're very simple, but then he adds a lot of this color to it, and the way that it's orchestrated, it's extremely moving. It's very emotional music.

Laurie: I was thinking about the concert the Emerson just gave in Los Angeles — the Mozart was just so elegant, and then the Beethoven was stormy — it was almost as if you could characterize each composer in one word. I thought, what would be the one word for Janáček, if all of a sudden you switched gears and started playing Janáček? Maybe the word is something like "all over the place;" his music is very mercurial.

Philip: There's something kind of raw about it. You feel like the nerve endings are all exposed. That's what makes it so powerful, even if you don't know exactly what each line means. *The Kreutzer Sonata*, the first quartet, does follow the story of *The Kreutzer Sonata* (short story by Tolstoy) pretty accurately. The music toward the end, where it just gets faster and faster and wilder and wilder, is related: he's chasing her, and then he kills her. It's a murder scene. You have songs without words, but these are operas without words.

Laurie: To be honest, I liked the Martinu *Three Madrigals* for violin and viola, the other piece on the new CD, an awful lot. I hadn't heard those before.

Philip: It's fun, isn't it? My wife, who is a big music fan, is not a huge fan of Janáček, but she really likes the Martinu pieces. They're beautiful, too, the slow movements are beautiful. You don't hear violin-viola duos all that often, but I think the *Madrigals* are some of Martinu's strongest, his most consistently excellent pieces, from beginning to end.

Laurie: I especially liked the middle movement, where the violin and viola just circle around each other. This piece was written for Lillian and Joseph Fuchs, wasn't it?

Philip: Yes, (ESQ violist Lawrence Dutton) studied with Lillian Fuchs at one point, and (siblings Joseph and Lillian Fuchs) premiered the piece... A little side story: I remember when I was at Aspen, as a student when I was young, I was supposed to meet someone at the music tent, I think we were going to have a rehearsal. I didn't see them, and I sort of walked around. As I was walking past one of the openings in the tent on the side,

I heard this yelling going on inside. I thought, what's going on? So I peeked in, and on the stage there were Joe and Lillian Fuchs — I think they were actually performing the *Madrigals* that night on a concert, and they were rehearsing. They were standing, facing each other, nose to nose, and both of them were screaming! (He laughs). They were both about five feet tall, they were like these two little snarly dogs, yelling at each other, it was very funny. I'd be willing to bet you that she ended up winning the argument, too! She was a tough lady.

I can tell you that the *Madrigals* are very difficult, but Larry and I actually never yelled at each other while we rehearsed.

Laurie: You two play very much in sync in the Martinu piece; do you actually trill exactly together? Is that something you practice?

Philip: For the most part, yes. You're really playing the same rhythms together a lot of the time; you have to follow the same direction or the same way, or it just doesn't match.

Laurie: I get the feeling you've been together so long, you can match the oscillation of your vibratos, the speed of your trills.

Philip: Some of that does happen naturally after enough years. You don't sit there and say, "Okay now we're going to vibrate together, ready, set, go..." I think it's something you just hear, and you're used to adjusting. It's tricky sometimes. If you are playing down in the lower range of the viola, you would tend to make the vibrato a little bit wider, and a little slower. Many times in Martinu, and more modern kinds of music, where you will play together, the violin will be way up high and the viola, or cello, will be low. You can have a very wide range between the instruments. If you want to be matching vibrato, you have to be careful, as the violinist, that you're not vibrating too fast, and the cello or viola is not vibrating too slow or too wide. There is adjustment that has to be made.

Then there are other places where it sounds fine not to match; in fact, it sounds more interesting sometimes if the person not playing the tune is more relaxed with the vibrato, and then you add the color with the other instruments. Sometimes we do different takes different ways, and then we decide later which sounds better.

Laurie: Aren't there a number of places in the Ravel (*String Quartet in F*) where the voices were two octaves away, in unison?

Philip: That's a good example. The second theme in the first movement of the Ravel is between viola and violin, and they have to be able to shimmer together so you have to want to match vibrato there.

Laurie: Something I didn't realize until I went to your concert in April, was that you all stand to play, and that (cellist David Finckel) sits on a pedestal. What brought you to the decision to perform this way?

Philip: We've been doing it for seven years now, so it feels quite natural for us. What I wonder now is why we didn't do it before! All those years of battling uncomfortable chairs...We're all pretty tall, and there were never enough piano benches to go around. I used to carry a heavy pillow, a thick, dense pillow that I would put on chairs because I was always uncomfortable unless I was at the back of the chair, which you can't do, it's not good to play sitting back like that. Then if the chair was too low, the bow would hit my knee, so I'd put my leg back and under the chair – there were a lot of reasons why it wasn't good to do that.

So for our 25th anniversary, we were playing six Haydn quartets, and we decided to try standing up for that. It's so much easier for the first violin part.

The other thing that happened around that time, around 2000, was that we collaborated on a theatre piece called *The Noise of Time*, about Shostakovich. In that, we moved around. We played standing up and we played by memory the 15th Shostakovich quartet. Our movements were kind of choreographed. That was so liberating — very challenging, but very liberating.

When we got back together after that, we played in Wigmore Hall in London. After we had done this theatre piece in New York, it felt so strange to be sitting there, in this clump in the middle of the stage. It felt very unnatural.

So we tried this Haydn program, and not only was it more natural and more comfortable, but we found that it really sounded better! When you're standing, you're not getting so much of the early deflection of the sound off the floor. It was much clearer; you could really hear everybody's sound. There was more color in the sound, and there were more overtones. It was less confusing, and the basic sound of the group was just more vibrant.

It's just natural for us to do it that way, and so after a few minutes it becomes natural for the observer as well.

Laurie: I enjoyed the way everybody interacted — there is more range of motion when you're standing, at least there can be.

Philip: I think the audience can see better, and they can see your body language better. If you watched a play for two hours, and the actors all just sat there in the same spot, it would be a little boring after a while. Even if what they were doing with their voice was wonderful, you'd want them to get up and move around a little bit!

Laurie: You and Eugene Drucker, the violinists in the Emerson, switch between playing the first and second violin parts. I think every quartet debates what to do about that — or they don't, and then there are lingering feelings about it. Was this the way you structured it from the beginning? And what is your perspective on it now, after doing it for years this way?

Philip: For us, it was a very natural thing to do, even though it had never been done before and a lot of eyebrows were raised. Gene and I started out playing in quartet in 1970, when we were students in our second year at Juilliard. We've been playing together almost 40 years, if you go back to our student days. A lot of student groups switch. It's not even a question of who is better on first; you want to learn to do both. It's part of learning to play in a string quartet.

That's the way we were all the way through Juilliard, and we decided to go with it professionally. Basically, he and I just couldn't make a decision. We both wanted to play first, but also we both liked playing second. Both of our fathers had played second violin in string quartets. Gene's dad was in the Busch Quartet for a while, right after the war, and then he went to the Metropolitan Opera Orchestra where he worked for many years; and both my parents were in the Cleveland Orchestra and my dad also played in a string quartet called the Sinfonia Quartet, which was made up of members of the Cleveland Orchestra; he was the second violinist in that quartet. So we had grown up with an appreciation — a genetic appreciation – of the second violin's part. If we had made the decision one way or the other, I think it might not have worked.

I think for some groups, it's natural to switch, and for some groups it's not. It's like with actors, some actors are just better at doing the supporting roles and some are better at doing the lead. Playing second violin, you have to be really smart, you have to be able to change gears and go from being an inner-voice accompaniment to suddenly having a solo, usually not in a very good range, usually in the lower range of the violin, often on the D string. You have to figure out a way to project through the texture a little bit.

Viola has its own sound, cello has its own sound, but the "other violin" has to find a way to make its personality known, so it's a very challenging role, and often underrated. Yet the old saying goes, "A string quartet is only as good as its second violinist." I think it's very true. Sometimes you don't get noticed as much there, but for some people, that's fine. If I had to pick, if somebody said to me, "Unfortunately, there's a new law that's just been passed, and you're not allowed to switch in string quartets, you have to choose now, which part would you like to play?" there's no question that I would pick the second part. I enjoy playing first violin, but if I had to give up one, I'd give that up and just really enjoy playing the second part.

Laurie: Well, this is very heartening to hear. I've certainly played a lot of second violin in my life.

Philip: I mean it, too. I'm not being falsely modest about it. There are so many great second violinists in quartets, who've made it an art unto itself.

Laurie: Every part is important.

Philip: Especially when there's only four!

Laurie: What is your schedule like, as a member of a quartet?

Philip: I'm a full professor at Stony Brook. Everybody has other things that they do. David and his wife are the music directors of the Chamber Music Society at Lincoln Center, and they have their summer festival out in California, Music@Menlo, they play a lot of duo concerts together. I'm joining them, playing Schubert trios over the next couple of years, we recorded that, so there are extra performances of that. The quartet plays about 90 concerts a year, plus recordings, plus meetings..it's not an easy life, to do all these things. Gene Drucker wrote a novel, *The Savior,* which has been published by Simon and Shuster; Larry plays in a string trio and also has three kids, and he teaches at Manhattan and Stony Brook. The quartet is in residence at Stony Brook, so we do chamber coachings.

You have to be organized about your time; if you're successful, you're busy. I feel very fortunate to be working, and these days, I have friends who are out of work. I'm lucky to be busy. Sometimes, it's difficult to juggle with your personal life. My wife would, I'm sure, like me to be not as busy as I am, but that's sort of the way it is.

Laurie: For those just starting on this path of playing chamber music, what are some of the important habits to form, things to develop, as you are gelling as a quartet?

Philip: Every group is different, every person is different; I can tell you what I did, what we did.

In the beginning, we listened to a lot of recordings, went to a lot of performances, copied a lot of things we liked and avoided a lot of things that we thought were not-so-good. Eventually you stop looking at other people and you start listening to yourself. We had the good fortune of being able to listen to ourselves a lot.

In the beginning of our career we did not have a recording contract for a long time, but we did a lot of performances on the radio. It was when public radio first started and was broadcasting a lot of concerts from around the world. Usually we didn't get paid anything extra to have a concert broadcast. It was extra pressure and all that, but it was our way of getting our name out there without having recordings, and we thought that that was important. We would have to listen to these concerts and approve them. So we ended up listening to a lot of performances of ourselves, and I think that's something that groups don't do enough of. It's tough, it's very tough. It's like looking at yourself in the mirror and — augh! You look at yourself play, and you really listen carefully. It's painful; you hear a lot of stuff you don't like. But you also learn very quickly what sounds good and what doesn't. As a group, it's helpful. It takes the subjective out of it a little bit, if you are able to step back and listen to a performance.

Laurie: Did you listen to yourselves together?

Philip: Sometimes, but usually not. Usually we just passed things around, but sometimes we listened together, especially when we were preparing for a recording later. In fact, we're going to do that tomorrow; we just did a performance of Dvořák Op. 106, the G Major quartet in Houston last night, and it was taped and we were handed a CD of it after the concert for approval. We're going to be recording that Monday, Tuesday and Wednesday. We have a rehearsal tomorrow, and I'm sure that we will sit down and listen to it together, with our scores. It will save time, having done that, rather than coming in there and hearing it for the first time. That way, the process will have started already.

The other thing that has helped us a lot has been using machines: each of us individually practicing with tuning machines, agreeing that we're going to tune to A=441, or whatever you agree to. I practice a lot with a drone, so that I'm used to adjusting to another sound. I'll change the tone, depending on the passage or the key of the piece. I practice scales that way, I practice arpeggios that way, I practice double stops, always with a drone on. It drives people crazy, but for me, I'm used to it. And the other guys do that, maybe not as much as I do, but they do it to some extent.

Also, using metronomes helps: agreeing on basic metronome markings for a particular movement. If everybody practices at that tempo, with a metronome, it's not that you're going to play metronomically, but it at least you're starting off somewhere in the same ball park. It helps you avoid situations where you play something, and somebody says, "It was too slow," and "Really? I thought it was too fast," or "It's out of tune, you're sharp," and "No, you're flat..." That kind of thing happens, but the more work you can do individually, the less it happens.

Sometimes we actually rehearse certain passages together with the metronome, and even with the drone. It takes away that subjective, "I know what's wrong with this, and you don't." Which most quartets go through.

Laurie: It makes sense to take that away, because that can cause a lot of contention.

Philip: The less self-righteousness that occurs in a string quartet, the better.

Laurie: Even just the way you say, "That sounds a little bit sharp," can be a deal-breaker.

Philip: I've seen it in my own group. A lot of groups fall apart. A lot of people come and talk to me, and they say, "We just can't seem to work together." A lot of it is that it becomes too personal, and not about the music.

Here's another very good piece of advice: in the amount of time that you argue over how you want to do a particular phrase, or even the end of a particular phrase, in, say, five minutes of arguing about that, you could have tried it 10 different ways. You could have done each way, talked about it a little bit and tried it several times. Maybe you would have come up with a different solution, or maybe no solution at all. But the process of working that way — playing different ways, trying it different ways — encourages a certain flexibility. The inability to be flexible can be a problem with groups.

It's not always a question of people not wanting to be flexible, it's that they don't know how to. It almost becomes a kind of technical thing, even though what you're talking about has to do with emotion. If you don't have the technique to be flexible, how do you expect to be flexible? It has to be developed, and you have to experience it, to feel what that's like to bend a phrase in a way that you don't feel. You still have to do it — and make it convincing. That's technique, to some extent.

Laurie: I think you're speaking to what I was going to ask next, which is, how on Earth has the Emerson String Quartet stayed together 30 years?

Philip: It's sort of a standard response, but it's very true: you have to keep a sense of humor. If you lose that, if you get too serious for too long, forget it. I don't care how good you are; if you don't have a sense of humor, and you can't tease each other and take some ribbing from the other people, you're just not going to make it.

Laurie: Just watching the quartet perform, everybody seemed happy.

Philip: This year, this month, it's 30 years since David joined. That's 30 years with the same people. We have our tensions, but on the whole, we get along very well. We have a good time, we laugh a lot. We take ourselves seriously, but not past a certain point. We don't allow each other to take ourselves too seriously. Whereas, the music is always taken seriously. The greater the music, the more serious we take it. That's the key: where your priorities are, and how you spend your energy, both negative and positive, how you channel that.

Philippe Quint. Photo: Lisa Marie Mazzucco

PHILIPPE QUINT

Originally published on July 1, 2009

Since this interview, Philippe changed violins; he now plays the 1708 Ruby Stradivari, *on loan from the Stradivari Society. He also released a number of new recordings, including John Corigliano's* Red Violin Caprices, *Ned Rorem's* Concerto, *Miklos Rozsa's* Complete Works for Violin and Piano *with William Wolfram, Bernstein's* Serenade, *and a compilation of works by Paganini arranged by Fritz Kreisler. He also acted in a movie called* Downtown Express.

Apparently it is not possible for Philippe Quint to play the *Violin Concerto* by Erich Wolfgang Korngold enough.

"If I could play it three times during the concert — I would!" Philippe said, laughing. "It's one of those works that gives you an incredible amount of positive energy." He spoke to me on the phone from New York in early June, about his new recording of the Korngold, about the great Juilliard violin professor Dorothy DeLay's uncanny ways, and about the day the Strad he plays went flying away in a taxi — without him.

"I instantly had something that's called 'love at first sight' with the Korngold concerto," Philippe said. "I heard Jascha Heifetz's recordings, and I heard Perlman's performance and I instantly knew; I literally ran right into the library and got the score and started learning it, right away."

"I started the piece with Dorothy DeLay," Philippe said. "Right after the first lesson, Miss DeLay said, 'Philippe, this is your piece!' Strangely enough, the (Juilliard) concerto competition that year was the Korngold concerto, and the winner was to play with Kurt Masur at Avery Fisher Hall. I won, and I also got to play the piece for Isaac Stern beforehand."

That was back in 1997.

This week Philippe releases his recording of the Korngold, on Naxos with conductor Carlos Miguel Prieto and the Orquesta Sinfonica de Mineria, and also including orchestra works by Korngold (*Overture to a Drama*, Op. 4 and *Much Ado About Nothing Concert Suite*, Op. 11). This is not his first recording; Philippe also was nominated for two Grammys for his 2001 recording of the William Schuman *Violin Concerto* and has recorded works by Rorem, Bernstein and Rozsa.

Korngold was a prolific composer of film scores, and he never lived that down.

"It's strange, the Korngold is still underestimated repertoire," Philippe said. "It's being performed more frequently these days, but it still has the whole Hollywood connotation, which is exactly what Korngold suffered from during his lifetime; he could never quite cross back from Hollywood to classical.

"What is interesting is that it's really not Hollywood that made Korngold, it's Korngold that made Hollywood," Philippe said of the film music that Korngold produced. "If you look at the harmonic structures and if you go into the analysis of his works, deep analysis, you will see that it's very Wagnerian."

"Of course, each movement (of the violin concerto) is derived from a film score," he said. "But if you take away the knowledge that Korngold was a film composer, then what you will see is that he followed the great tradition of Wagner, and Strauss, continuing with the idea of music drama, where the violin, or voice, plays the main part. In a way, it's like a mini-opera. Even in his own words, Korngold described his concerto as a cross between Enrico Caruso and Niccolo Paganini. In fact, he said it was very nice to have both Caruso and Paganini in one person, after Jascha Heifetz premiered it."

I wondered, not having ever played the piece, is it hard to play?

"It actually is quite difficult," Philippe said. "It's awkward; it's not violinistic at all. To be honest with you, this is the kind of challenge that I absolutely love. I love composers that did not write for violin particularly. Works by Paganini, Wieniawski and Sarasate seem to be very difficult technically, but at the same time, you know that those works were written by violinists. Essentially, once you figure out what is the little tricky technique behind it, then you can actually get it pretty well because it's still under your fingers. Like if you take the Wieniawski Concerto, it's all under your fingers, just a matter of practicing over and over."

"But if you take concertos like Brahms, Tchaikovsky, Stravinsky, Beethoven," he said, "those were mostly pianist composers, and they didn't really have much concern about the violinist's difficulties, or making things comfortable for us. Naturally that presents a little bit of a challenge — you have to figure out the bowings and fingerings that make sense in terms of phrasing."

Philippe was born in the Soviet Union, and he came to New York in 1991 to study with Dorothy DeLay.

"It was, of course, a major change, not to mention that I did not actually speak English at the time," Philippe said. "What happened was that somebody brought my cassette to Miss DeLay, from some concert in Russia, and she listened to it and she said she would be happy to give me an audition. I came, and I played for her, and she invited me to the Aspen Music Festival right away."

"It had been my dream for many, many years to come study at Juilliard, and with Dorothy DeLay," Philippe said. "It was like a myth. In Russia — at that time it was the Soviet Union — nobody really knew what was going on, but we were told that if you get into Juilliard, you're going to get a stipend, and they will pay for your apartment, you will study with Dorothy DeLay, you will have a recording contract the next day," (he laughs) "and you're the next Jascha Heifetz!" (He laughs again.)

"So sitting in my little apartment in Moscow, I had all those dreams; I was envisioning life in America," he said. "And of course, when Perlman came to Russia in 1991, I saw in his biography that he was also a student of Dorothy DeLay."

Philippe said that DeLay was a master of getting her point across without insulting students. Many of her former students mention the same story, when she would say to a student, "Sugar Plum, what is your concept of F#?"

"It's quite a brilliant way of saying, 'Your F# is out of tune,'" Philippe said. "In Russia, if you're not prepared, or if you're playing out of tune, the teacher would take your music, take you, and just throw you out of the class with a few unpleasant words. So suddenly, I come to Juilliard, and somebody's asking me, how do I feel about this work? Or what is my concept of this piece? Or what is your concept of F#?" (He laughs.)

"At the same time, she would always make sure that the point gets across," he said. "It was just as embarrassing if somebody is screaming at you that you are playing out of tune as somebody saying, 'What is your concept of F#?' I mean, you don't even know what an F# is supposed to sound like? It was a very interesting approach."

He described another incident in which DeLay gave him a strong message, but in her unique way of communicating.

"I was working on the Wieniawski second violin concerto — I loved the work, and I particularly loved Perlman's recording of the piece," Philippe said. "I was playing for Miss DeLay for the lesson, and when I got to the last movement, in the cadenza, right before the fast part, I did this glissando somewhere there. Suddenly, I hear, from Miss DeLay's corner, 'Yuck!'"

"I stopped, and I looked at her, and I said, 'You didn't like it?' And she said, 'That was absolutely disgusting, where did you come up with this?' I said, 'Well, Miss DeLay, your student, Mr. Perlman, does exactly the same thing in the recording.'"

"And she said, 'Come here, Sugar Plum. I'm going to tell you a little story.'"

"So I came to her table. She looked down, and she was silent for a few moments. And then she said, 'Philippe, did you know that I had an older sister?' And I said, 'Ah, no, Miss DeLay, I didn't know.'"

"'Well, in any case,' she said, 'I had an older sister, and I really loved the clothes that my sister used to wear.'"

"And I said, 'Ok....'"

"Then she said, 'But particularly, I loved her red shoes. She had this beautiful pair of red shoes. When my sister wasn't around, I would wear them, all the time. There was just one problem. They were a size larger than my foot. They didn't actually fit me.' And then she looked at me."

"Basically, the point was, when you become Perlman, you can do anything you want," Philippe said. "But the way she showed it to me was utterly brilliant. She could have said, 'Stop imitating or copying great artists.' Or she could have said, 'You're not Perlman, when you get to that level, that's when you can do it.' But she actually told me a story that was just incredible, to indicate her thinking."

Philippe plays on the 1723 *ex-Kiesewetter* Stradivari violin, an instrument that took a little solo adventure in a Newark taxicab during the wee hours of the morning one day in April 2008, leaving Philippe to a frantic search. The incident generated much press but did end in a happy reunion — as well as a gratitude concert for the cab drivers.

Philippe can talk about it now with a sense of humor, but it was an ordeal, he said.

"First of all, I would like to thank Violinist.com for a wonderful poll that took place when it was happening," he said. "I was giving an interview to the *New York Times* about the whole incident, and that was probably about an hour after I got the poll from Violinist.com! So I told the guy that, by the way, there's this site, you should check it out, it's called Violinist.com..." The poll showed that 37 percent of respondents had left their violin somewhere, and people also shared their harrowing stories about forgetting their fiddles in various places.

"Honestly, I thought this would never ever happen to me," Philippe said. "When I read about Yo-Yo Ma, or Lynn Harrell, Kramer or recently, Glenn Dicterow — I thought, that is impossible. It must be a publicity stunt. But now I realize how quickly this can happen, how your mind, for one second, is not there. Like when (Gidon) Kremer left his violin on the train, he was studying scores, and that was what was in his head. I think Yo-Yo Ma was coming from some performance, as well. We do get tired, we get fatigued, we think of many things."

"This incident certainly was not an accomplishment of any sort. It was a great misfortune that was slightly turned around when I gave a concert for the drivers," he said. "The whole story was largely twisted by the media, because when it happened, I actually refused any interviews. I was completely scared. I was getting calls from NBC, ABC, and everyone was calling my cell phone! How do they have access to my cell phone? It was actually quite nerve-wracking and scary experience, and the twist of the story was I did not actually forget the instrument. It was two o'clock in the morning and I was a little bit not-alert-as-I-usually-am, and I was putting the bags off the road and closed the trunk. The violin was still in the backseat, I was perfectly aware of that, and the guy took off. Everything happened in a split second; the guy just rushed off and I saw the cab in the distance."

"A lot of papers and channels said the violin was in the trunk, and I kept saying no, it's not in the trunk! Did you forget it? No I did not forget it! Did the driver return it to you? No he did not return it to me, I found him! Some article said the driver was looking for Quint, no, nobody was looking for me. I was looking for him, he was sleeping! He was actually happy because I was his last customer. He was rushing home because he was done with his job, forever. He was perfectly fine, sleeping at home. I think people were trying to reach him, but he had his phone off. And then he must have turned it on, around noon. By that time, I was in Newark, on my feet, from 7 a.m., running around, talking to people. I was barely walking. The problem was that the more people I was talking to, the less it seemed possible to retrieve the instrument. Nobody could help me at the time, they didn't know where the violin was, they couldn't figure out who the driver was. I didn't have a receipt, and I tried to recognize the driver from the pictures at the taxi authority there and I pointed out the completely wrong guy!"

He said there were probably hundreds of pictures of taxi drivers in the book he leafed through, and "believe me, it wasn't the greatest book that I've ever read," he said.

When the violin was finally found, Philippe actually missed the call. Then he listened to it: "Mr. Quint, we have located your item."

Mr. Quint's "item" — the 1723 *ex-Kiesewetter* Stradivari — is an instrument he has been playing, on loan through the Stradivari Society, for about three years.

"It's a great, great instrument," Philippe said. "It's been a wonderful get-to-know process between me and the instrument. I always feel that the relationship between an instrument and a player is a very particular one, in a way, like marriage. Having played on in for a few years, to my ears it sounds like a completely different instrument. I know it so much better; it's extremely responsive. I feel that it mainly adds to my personality. There's a lot of talk, are you a del Gesu player? Or are you a Strad player? For me, there is no question: I love the Strad. I'm a little bit on the hyper side of a person, very passionate...the Strad, in way, is the opposite of me because it's warm and soft and serene and calming, so I feel that we have this beautiful rapport."

Philippe has been a U.S. citizen for 12 years. I asked him, what made him decide to stay in the U.S.?

"The biggest reason was to study at Juilliard," he said. "In the late 80s, early 90s, it was very difficult to live in the Soviet Union any more, particularly for musicians, there were just no opportunities, so everyone was leaving. Also, personally, it had to do with the death of my teacher, whom I absolutely adored, Andrei Korsakov, who was a well-known concert violinist in Europe and Russia – and some sort of a distant relative of Rimsky-Korsakov. He died at a very young age, and that was just another push to start thinking about a different direction in my life. My family left, though my mother stayed because she's actually a well-known pop composer. She's still there, and she's working for film and musicals, she has many projects. We meet about once a year, which is not enough, but now with Skype and all the technology, it's a little bit easier to communicate on a regular basis."

Philippe also has explored an interest in acting.

"There were some possible projects; they never took off," he said. "But I got to meet very interesting people like Robert DeNiro and Matt Damon and a few others. But then I didn't have the time to pursue this any further because I was concertizing so much in the last few years, that whole acting thing died out."

"But it was a fantastic learning experience," he said. He took acting lessons on and off for three years from Sondra Lee, whose credits include Fellini's *La Dolce Vita* and a supporting role in the original movie, *Peter Pan.*

While studying acting, "I discovered a lot of things that benefited my playing" Philippe said. "Any acting coach will tell you the most important thing about acting is listening, and I think that for a great musician, the most important part is also listening. The second thing is being in the moment. As an actor, you have to be in the moment, you have to understand the character. And as musicians, we also really need to be in the moment, and understand the character of the work that we're doing. If you study a work, you have to subdivide it, you have to dig into the history; if you study a play, you also have to subdivide it and understand the history, and the style. It's so similar; it's not even funny."

"You can't fool an audience," Philippe said. "You don't have to have this profound knowledge of what you're watching, but one thing you do know, does a performance touch you, or not? Are you involved by the performer? Do you come out with something after this performance? People know that, they feel that, they talk about it. Would they come back to see this performer again, yes or no? Without the actual knowledge, people will tell you, yes, this was exciting. Something magnetic was going on, and it's irrelevant whether you have the knowledge or not."

Gil Shaham and Adele Anthony. Photo: Mark Gardener

GIL SHAHAM AND ADELE ANTHONY

Originally published on September 30, 2009

It has to be said: Israeli-American violinist Gil Shaham is one of the nicest and most humble people one could meet. And boy, can he play the violin! Here, I spoke with both Gil and his wife, violinist Adele Anthony about the legacy of the great 19th century violinist, Pablo de Sarasate, and also about how a family of four functions, when both parents are touring soloists.

Ponder this for a moment: playing more than an hour and a half of music brimming with harmonics, octave runs, left-hand pizzicato, high-speed arpeggios, up-bow staccato — all the fanciest licks and tricks you can imagine on the violin — with a Spanish flair.

That's the music of Pablo de Sarasate.

The married violinists Gil Shaham and Adele Anthony admitted: they had to practice like crazy to prepare for the creation of *Sarasate: Virtuoso Violin Works*, the recording they released today on their own record label, Canary Classics.

"I don't remember ever preparing this hard, working this hard," said Gil a few weeks ago, when I spoke with both him and Adele over the phone. "There were times when we were playing late at night, here, squeaking up in the high register...We're lucky to have tolerant neighbors."

The recording was made in Valladolid, Spain in 2008, at *¡Sarasateada!*, a festival celebrating the centenary of the great violinist Pablo de Sarasate (1844-1908).

"It was just several months of one or the other of us playing really high, fast music. It really took a lot of practice to get it all ready," Adele said. "The more you listened to it, the more exciting it became. It was nice to hear Gil practicing his pieces that I wasn't playing, to get to know them vicariously."

When they performed at *¡Sarasateada!*, "it was really kind of fun to play in front of a Spanish audience, with a Spanish orchestra," Adele said. "The audience was so familiar with Sarasate. They enjoyed the pieces they knew well, and they knew a lot of background for the dances. They had posters up everywhere, with big pictures of Sarasate on them...It was a lot of fun. It's always nice to record things, but there's nothing like performing them in front of people, getting some reception. Some of it we recorded live, and some we just recorded, but it was all done in Valladolid."

Gil and Adele not only recorded the pieces we violinists know, love and often struggle with, like *Zigeunerweisen*, *Introduction and Tarantella*, *Zapateado*, *Habanera* and *Carmen Fantasy*, but they also unearthed a few lesser-known works.

"Discovering more about Sarasate was amazing. We are really lucky to have this legacy," Gil said. "Maybe my favorite track on the disc, and definitely one of my favorite pieces, is the *Song of the Nightingale* that Adele recorded, which is so beautiful. It's true, Sarasate likes all these difficult techniques, but it really is always in service of a musical message, which kind of magically appears. A lot of his other published works are arrangements of operas and works that are 'in the style of' Scottish airs, or Gypsy airs, or Spanish airs, or Spanish dances. This one is really a Sarasate-original composition. I think the same is true of *Romanza Andaluza*. He very humbly calls it an Andalusian romance, but it really is a very beautiful original composition. I find that the writing has incredible perfection to it. It's very concise, it's meticulously clean, full of melodies and full of imagination."

"It was kind of an eye-opener," Adele said. "I've grown up with Sarasate, my whole violinistic life, but to discover all the repertoire he wrote — the rest of his compositions are really quite amazing. When you're younger, you just learn the famous pieces that everybody plays. When we were choosing repertoire, looking at all the things he wrote, it was hard to choose! They were all interesting in their own way. I lucked out with the *Song of the Nightingale* – that's a very interesting piece, and it's unlike any of his other compositions. It really describes the nightingale, perfectly, with a Spanish flair, and with all the violinistic fluency that comes with Sarasate. He always manages to get some left-hand pizzicato in there! It's a very beautiful piece and I really enjoyed playing it."

That's not to say they didn't enjoy doing the old favorites.

"I also love *Introduction and Tarantella* – I've been playing that piece since I was young, so it's something that feels very at home to me," Adele said. "And we also always enjoy playing *Navarra for Two Violins* because it's just kind of a crazy, fun piece. It's hard to take it really seriously! When we play it it's always so much fun."

I wondered what the biggest challenge was, playing so much Sarasate.

"(*The Nightingale*) has a lot of harmonics, and the challenge is to make it sound fluid, singing and melodic," Adele said. "In Sarasate, (the challenge is) always trying to make things sound effortless, so it doesn't impede the musical flow. But he was also a violinist, so he wrote very well for the violin — everything is possible, if you work at it hard enough."

Both Gil and Adele found inspiration from the rare recordings that Sarasate himself made in 1904.

"The legacy of his recording is so staggering," Gil said. "He's in his 60s, it's 1904, and since it's 1904, you know (the recording is) all done in one take. He's playing his own compositions. I think there are only eight works that he recorded. These are works that were recorded by all the greatest violinists of the 20th century. Sarasate's technique is so clean, and his sound is so beautiful, and his style is so perfect."

"A lot of people say that those older violinists weren't clean – but he was just amazing," Adele said. "He was just a great, great violinist."

I wondered what life is like for this married couple, both touring violinists, who have two children, Elijah, 6, and Ella Mei, 3.

First of all, not every married couple can also work together. How are they able to do this kind of intense project together, without wringing one another's necks?

"We don't play together very often, but when we do, we really have similar musical tastes, luckily," Adele said. "The nature of our relationship is not competitive, so we really enjoy playing together, we have a lot of fun. It's nice to play with someone you know so well, and you don't have to work on the more fundamentals. We always enjoy it."

As for the kids, "we try to make it work as best as we can," Gil said. "We were very lucky, I started working very young, and so when our son was born, I was very lucky to be able to cut back. So both of us play a lot less. We try to play as much as we can around New York, keep it close to home. Nowadays I try to play about 50 dates a year, and Adele does about 30. It's so complicated! Now we have four schedules around the house. We try to work it so that when Adele is working, I'm free, and when I'm working, Adele is free."

And if they are playing together? Sometimes they just take the kids on the road, Adele said.

"Your priorities completely change, the kids are the number one priority," Adele said. "We both really enjoy playing. We have limited time to practice and prepare things, and sometimes it's a real escape, to get away with your violin for a little while...maybe I enjoy it more now! We juggle our schedules, we've cut back on a lot of things so we can be home more with the kids. You don't want to miss out on the important things. I feel like we're very lucky, because we have flexible schedules to some degree, that we can spend a lot of time with our family and still have our careers at the same time."

As for projects this fall, Gil will be touring, playing many works from the 1930s.

"When I was thinking back to violin concertos, I noticed that many of my personal favorites were all written in a very short period of time, between 1931 and 1939," Gil said. "The list is staggering, and it kind of reads like a Music 101 course: Stravinsky, Berg, Bartok, Schoenberg, Prokofiev, Samuel Barber, William Walton, Benjamin Britten, Hindemith and Milhaud — they all wrote violin concertos at the same time! I love all those pieces. They're so different, too. Roger Sessions wrote a beautiful concerto, and Szymanowski, and Ernst Bloch. What an amazing time. It was kind of a coincidental confluence of violin concertos by great composers."

Gil said he is not the only person to have noticed this.

"When I played Stravinsky Concerto, earlier this season in Cleveland, I was speaking to a gentleman on the radio broadcast, and he said to me, 'What is it about 1930s, everybody was writing violin concertos, was it something in the air?' " Gil said. "And when we played it in Washington, one of the patrons came after the concert and spoke very eloquently. He said that the 1930s were a time of great turbulence and trepidation, and the feeling among the population was as if they were standing on top of a volcano, ready to erupt. Then he asked, 'How is this reflected in the music of the time, and how does that relate to our times, and to the music of our time?' Great question — and one that I'm not equipped to answer. It's very interesting to think about, it's very thought-provoking."

Augustin Hadelich. Photo courtesy Augustin Hadelich

AUGUSTIN HADELICH

Originally published on December 10, 2009

In 2010, the critic Alex Ross called Augustin Hadelich "a young artist with no evident limitations." That is because he overcame considerable adversity, with grace and dedication to his art, as this interview attests. Since the time of this interview, Augustin Hadelich's career has grown steadily, and he has released two more recordings: Echoes of Paris *(2011) and* Histoire du Tango *(2013). He now plays the 1723 ex-Kiesewetter Stradivari — yes, the same one that "drove away" from Philippe Quint.*

In the three years since winning the 2006 International Violin Competition of Indianapolis, Augustin Hadelich's career has taken flight. Hadelich's new album, called *Flying Solo*, features all works for 'solo' violin, by Bartok, Ysaye, Paganini and Bernd Zimmermann. But the name of the album could also come from the fact that Augustin spends a lot of time on airplanes these days, flying to debuts from Cleveland to Carnegie Hall, Los Angeles to Tokyo, winning the 2009 Avery Fisher Career Grant and playing with orchestras the world over.

The new recording is his third. His first, from 2008, featured three Haydn concertos for violin, for which he wrote his own cadenzas; and the second featured Telemann *Twelve Fantasies for Solo Violin*, released in early 2009.

Born in Italy to German parents, Hadelich spent much of his early years taking lessons from various violinists who were on holiday in Tuscany, where he grew up on a farm. When he was 15, his life's activities came to a sudden halt when he suffered severe burns to his upper body in a fire at his family's farm — an accident that required two years of painful recovery.

I spoke to Augustin over the phone a few weeks ago, after meeting him at a recital he gave in Los Angeles. We talked about life on constant tour, about competitions and about the 1683 *ex-Gingold* Stradivari violin he was granted for use until he hands it over to the next Indianapolis competition winner next September. We also talked about how his desire to continue playing the violin helped him during his recovery from the accident.

Laurie: How do you cope with your schedule as a soloist, when you are in Santa Barbara one day, Berlin the next week, then back to New York, across the country to Los Angeles, then on an overnight plane to Indianapolis for a recital the next day, and all of this is in the course of a month. Then you are playing different music at all these concerts. What kinds of strategies have you figured out to handle it all?

Augustin: There are certain little tricks that you learn. First of all — anything, if you do it very often, becomes easier. A lot of what stresses you out about flying is how you yourself feel about it. So I don't get very stressed any more at airports; I'm more used to it than I was a few years ago. If you are flying during the day, it's important to be productive on the plane. If it's overnight, you need to sleep.

Laurie: So one thing you have to cope with is the travel. How about having the repertoire ready?

Augustin: I don't have a specific method, but a lot of these pieces I've played many times before. It doesn't take as much preparation, but it does take intense preparation to get a piece at the highest level again. For some pieces, I can do that in the couple of days before a concert. I just work very intensely on it.

In certain pieces, it's always the same places that are an issue. The same goes for rehearsals with orchestras; regardless of what orchestra, where in the world, there are certain places that always need rehearsing. After a while, you just know where those places are, and you can make the rehearsals more efficient because of that.

A few years ago, when I first started to play this much, I sometimes made the mistake of practicing too many pieces at once. I was practicing ahead — I was practicing what I had to play in a few weeks. Of course one needs to do that, but only up to a point. When I practiced too many pieces, then I didn't immerse myself in the piece I was playing that weekend. One needs to focus on (the upcoming weekend's performance pieces) with enough intensity, to be completely comfortable and at home in that style again, and in that work.

There are always at least a few pieces I'm learning that are new. For those, I make a plan for a few months or a half a year before the performance, so that I am working on it on and off, really trying to get to know it and internalize it.

Laurie: How did you get started with the violin?

Augustin: I started playing when I was five years old. My two older brothers were already playing instruments; they were playing cello and piano. I heard them practicing, and I wanted to play something, too. My parents had this vague idea of forming a piano trio...

Laurie: Did it ever happen?

Augustin: No, no. (He laughs) It never happened. It can be difficult for siblings to play together, and I think maybe it's just as well that we never did that.

But even before that, I grew up hearing music. I still have a great love for the cello repertoire because of I heard it so much at such a young age.

Laurie: Do your brothers still play, did they become musicians?

Augustin: They're not musicians, but they still play as a hobby.

So, I didn't know what I'd signed up for, because I was five. My father was not a professional musician, but his mother was a violin teacher, and he started teaching me the basics. He was my teacher for the first three years, essentially. It was tricky to find good teachers in that area of Italy where grew up (Tuscany), so I did some traveling to Germany, and to other places in Europe.

Laurie: Was it readily apparent that you were really serious about it, or that you really liked it?

Augustin: I did always enjoy it, but I didn't always enjoy practicing!

It was when I started to take lessons with other people that I became really inspired. Some of (my teachers) were musicians who were in Tuscany on holiday, like Christoph Poppen, who at the time had a string quartet that went to Tuscany to rehearse.

Also, when I was eight, my father took me to Siena, where Uto Ughi was giving masterclasses. It was the first time that I saw someone who was really, really great at the violin up close, and it was a huge inspiration. I went back the following three years and took lessons with him. I was so impressed because he had such a beautiful, singing tone; his sense of lyricism was beautiful. I also was impressed by the fact all these people would play in a masterclass, and he would just pick up his violin and start playing out all of these concerti. He could play any piece, and he really liked to play in his own masterclass, he liked to demonstrate. It was fascinating to watch him, and it made a big impression on me back then, to see everything he was doing up close.

Laurie: I don't want to dwell on your accident, but I know that it happened while you were growing up, and I wonder if the violin helped you recover.

Augustin: I think it did. At that time, the violin had become a huge part of my life. I was playing more and more concerts, and spending a lot of time with it. When the accident interrupted everything, it was a huge crisis. I didn't know if I would be able to play again. But then as I recovered, eventually I started again. I tried playing, and I realized that it was possible.

It's very helpful, I think, if people can go back to their job, or to their work. It gave me a lot of hope when I realized that I could play again. Of course, it was a long road. I started playing again, but I had to get better physically and psychologically. Also, suddenly I was an adult; I was no longer a prodigy child. So there was less of an interest in my playing — I was being compared to adult violinists, as opposed to just being compared to prodigies my age.

And I had lost a few years in my musical development, my technical and violinistic development.

Laurie: I would think that it would not be just losing a few years on the violin, but then also having to completely recover physically.

Augustin: Well, to some extent, when I started playing again, I was technically at the level I had been before. But of course it takes time to get the physical strength back again.

Then when I was much better, I had the opportunity to play some concerts again. Through one of those concerts, which was at Chautauqua Festival in upstate New York, I found management in New York, with Michal Schmidt of Schmidt Artists. They convinced me to get out in the world a little more. So I went to summer festivals and I started to realize everything that was out there there. Eventually I decided to go to Juilliard.

Laurie: How old were you when you went to Juilliard?

Augustin: I went to Juilliard when I was 20 years old; I went into a graduate program. I did have a diploma that I had received at an Italian conservatory. So for a few years I was doing all the requirements for that as I was recovering. Then I also spent one year in Berlin before I decided to go to New York.

In hindsight, it was a great decision (to go to New York) because the city provided a fresh start. And the school was a really inspiring environment — the people that I met, the students and faculty, it was really stimulating. I also had a very, very good teacher — Joel Smirnoff — who helped me develop my technique more. Because of the odd way I had been taught — by so many different people but not so regularly — there were a few issues I had that he helped me to fix.

Laurie: Tell me about the Indianapolis competition — how did that change your life, and what are your thoughts on competitions, after it's all said and done?

Augustin: Well, I never had fun doing competitions. I'm happy that it's behind me. But they have their purpose, and in some ways they are a great thing because they provide these opportunities. Suddenly my career took off.

When it comes to that particular competition, the community in Indianapolis gets very involved and very excited about it. It feels like a big violin festival. They get to hear all this violin repertoire, all these violinists and great players. It might not be fun to compete in it, but one does have a very supportive and enthusiastic audience.

Laurie: Tell me about the *Gingold* Strad, has that changed your playing at all? Have you had any insights as a result of playing that instrument?

Augustin: It's a very unique violin, it took me a while to get to know it, to figure out how the sound production on it worked. It's very different from the instrument I had before.

Laurie: What did you have before?

Augustin: I played on a Guarneri filius Andreae — it was a beautiful instrument, but it had some issues with the size of the sound. It's not del Gesù, it was made by del Gesù's father. It had a great sound, the sound was fantastic, but it was a smaller tone. I really enjoyed my time on it, but sometimes there were those days when it was really tricky to produce the sound. Luckily it had a good day for that competition!

The *(Gingold)* Strad can also be moody sometimes, with temperatures and humidity changes, but most of all, the sound production works very differently. For some reason, one can't put too much pressure onto the string, it has to happen with bow speed. Over the course of about a year I slowly got to know how it reacted. You can't just do anything to it, it has to be played a certain way. Not all Strads are like that. But if you approach it in a specific way, then there is a lot of sound that can come out, and the sound is just really, really beautiful. It's been a great three years, playing it, especially from the time when I really started to know how to handle the violin, and how it works. It's fantastic.

So this competition has done a lot. It was definitely very stressful while it went on. Although, they do their best. There's something nice about the Indianapolis Competition — they really try to make the process as easy as it can be, for something that's so competitive.

Laurie: How do they do that?

Augustin: It's the little things. When you are under that much pressure, the little details can make a big difference. For example, at Indianapolis, you can go off stage in between pieces and take a drink of water. Some competitions won't allow that. Also, the host families for the competitors are very nice, and the whole competition is run extremely well and efficiently. These are things that sometimes can create additional stress, in addition to the stress of being in a competition. And that's the kind of stress that then can be too much — you finally do go insane! (He laughs) It makes sense; this way it's easier for everyone to play their best, which is what everybody wants.

In some ways I felt that the first round was the hardest; you feel like nobody knows you, and starting the repertoire is so hard. In a way, it gets easier afterwards, but the level of tension keeps rising. It's very nerve-wracking, when you suddenly realize you might win, and what would happen if you did? It's really bad to think about that, but you can't stop yourself.

Laurie: You have to be very psychologically strong, don't you?

Augustin: Somehow it's possible to get through it, but it can take a lot out of you. I think it's very helpful that the hall is always full, with all these people, so it feels a little bit more like a performance.

Laurie: Do you like a performance better?

Augustin: Yes. Definitely. This may not be the same for all musicians, I think it depends on what you've done more. But for me, since I was small, I've played for relatively large groups of people, and it's the sort of setting where I'm reasonably comfortable. When it's small room, just a few people, and it's more like an audition setting — it's a lot more nerve-wracking for me. Most competitions are kind of a hybrid: you have a judge panel that you can see out there, and but then you have all the other people. So you try to pretend that you are playing for all the other people, that you are trying to give them a good performance, and if the judges like it, great. That's how you try to approach it. But of course, the thought keeps creeping in: What do the judges think? What is going to happen? I have to say, when it was all over, I was incredibly relieved. Part of the relief came from the fact that I didn't have to go through it again.

Laurie: What are some of the more important technical exercises you need to do on a regular basis to build and maintain a high level of technique?

Augustin: I don't know if I do anything very unusual… I try to find the balance between the quantity and quality of practicing. I'm very interested in very efficient practicing. I don't want to put more stress on my body and on my shoulders than necessary. When it's about the interpretation and musical decisions, a lot of work can be done away from the instrument. Oftentimes when I do that work, suddenly I realize I actually don't agree with what I'm doing when I'm playing.

Laurie: Do you listen to recordings of yourself playing, or do you look at the music and sort of run it in your head?

Augustin: One can imagine the music, one can sing the music. Even though I can't sing at all, when I start singing, the phrasing happens much more naturally. Suddenly everything happens the way it should, and then when I'm playing it, all these things that get in the way — because of the technique, or because of whether I start up-bow or down-bow — you somehow overcome that. It can be helpful to to realize, "Oh, that this is actually how I would want it to sound."

Analysis, in all cases, is really useful. We're not necessarily trained to do that in a conservatory. They teach us some harmonic analysis, but there's no class where they say, this is what you really should do with a violin concerto score, this is how you should approach it, these are the steps. Whereas conductors will often learn that, how to study a score, how to approach a score like that.

If you study the score in itself, you may suddenly realize something that you never would have realized if you just had been playing it. For example, maybe you have a sonata, and as you study it, you realize there is a pianissimo, and that is the only pianissimo that the composer employs in the entire piece. Maybe when you were playing it, you weren't doing that place that much softer than the others, and you certainly weren't thinking about the importance, or why this composer chose this dynamic in this place. When you play it on your violin, you are distracted by the technical challenges. So when you study the score, you notice things that you wouldn't, just playing your part. At the same time, of course, it is really important to also learn a piece in a physical way, to feel it physically. Both things have to happen and come together.

But there's no magic formula. It's just a lot of work. Work efficiently, and work on all the different aspects of it: not just the technical problem-solving but also on the analysis and emotional component of the piece.

Laurie: How do you keep yourself enthusiastic about it after all this work? Once all that's done, how do you go into a performance and really put your heart in it?

Augustin: With some pieces it can be tricky. But there are pieces you can play your whole life, and think about your whole life, and it doesn't get boring. Violinists have quite a bit of music like that. After all this work, at a certain point you have to stop obsessing and worrying. You have to just perform and enjoy the music, to try to get the character and interact with the audience. It can be a danger — sometimes I'm onstage and I'm still worrying about something, or I'm thinking about a fingering — that's completely the wrong place to do that!

Laurie: What do you think is the best piece, for still being interesting after you've played it a hundred times. Just in your opinion.

Augustin: I wouldn't say I have a single piece like that. I feel that way, for example, about the Beethoven *Violin Concerto*. I can't even remember how long I've played it, or how many times. But I still do have fun, and I've never been bored onstage with that piece. Any time I walk off stage after playing the Beethoven concerto, or the next day, I find myself thinking about everything that I need to do completely differently next time. It's an indication it will never get boring – there is always room to improve.

Sarah Chang. Photo: Cliff Watts

SARAH CHANG

Originally published on December 18, 2009

What is it like to be a child prodigy, how do you keep your playing strong, and what do you wear for all of it? Talking with Sarah Chang was delightful.

Violinist Sarah Chang has recorded everything, hasn't she?

Well, okay, she hasn't. But she is one of the few 28-year-olds on the planet who can record the Brahms and Bruch concertos for the first time, and do so with more than 20 years' experience playing them at concert halls around the world.

I spoke with Sarah when she was in Los Angeles to play Vivaldi's *Four Seasons* with the American Youth Symphony, and we talked about a wide range of subjects — from her perspective on life as a prodigy to how she picks out those gorgeous concert gowns.

Laurie: What was the first thing you ever played on the violin?

Sarah: I started on the Suzuki method, so probably one of those songs; I didn't do it for very long, only about 4-5 months. My dad is a violinist, so after that I studied with him. I went to Juilliard when I was six, and Dorothy DeLay was my teacher from that point onwards. So the first thing was most likely Twinkle Twinkle, or one of those Suzuki songs.

Laurie: How was Dorothy DeLay with a six-year-old?

Sarah: She was possibly the best teacher that I could have asked for. Very grandmother-like, very encouraging, very gentle. But she never told you to fix anything — this was something I found frustrating a little later on, but I realized it was just her way of working: She always got you thinking. Sometimes you'd go in for a lesson and she'd ask, "What do you think you can do to make this better?" or, "What is it you're unhappy with?" instead of telling you, fix X-Y-Z. She'd go inside your head and get you to think.

Laurie: That sounds pretty sophisticated for a six-year-old...

Sarah: In the very beginning, she was really hands-on. Then I started traveling and concertizing more — and not really being there. I would play, and then I'd go away for a month on tour. Then I'd come back for one or two lessons and go out again. So it was extremely irregular, and I think she realized that I needed to start listening to myself. She once said to me, in the very early years, that I was probably going to spend a vast majority of my life working by myself in hotel rooms or backstage in dressing rooms, and I couldn't always rely on her being there. She told me, you know, you really have to learn to open up your ears and listen to yourself.

Laurie: It was wise of her to tell you that. I don't know that everyone knows what to expect from the soloist's life.

Sarah: She had so much experience at that point, (having taught) so many people.

Laurie: It is a little bit of a unique life. Not many people have the experience of being a child prodigy. I wonder, looking back on it, what would you advise somebody who showed great talent early on, who was looking at that kind of situation? What would you advise their parents?

Sarah: I'd tell them to wait. Juggling school, homework, assignments, exams, career and constant recordings — was no fun. I'm not going to kid you, that was no fun. Not only that, when the ball starts rolling, and you get caught up in the moment and everything is so new and exciting and you want to put yourself out there and play as many concerts as you possibly can — you forget that the early years are when you should be learning the most amount of repertoire.

I think my parents were really good about that. They controlled my schedule so that I did the important concerts: I did the New York Phil, the Berlin Phil, the Vienna Phil. I did all the debuts, I did all the big dates that I needed to do. But then they would stick me back in school. They put a really tight grip on the schedule. I had – still do have — a variety of managers. But it was very much my parents who would end up just saying, "No," to everything. They said that I needed to go to school, and I needed time to learn repertoire. I'm glad they did that — because now the schedule is insane.

Laurie: So the ability to say, "No," is important.

Sarah: And they did. It's really good, especially at the beginning, so you don't get too caught up in everything. If I try to learn new pieces now, with a full-time schedule, it really is a day here, and a day two weeks later. It's not the ideal way to learn new pieces, but unfortunately that's the only time to do it now. So I'm really glad I got the majority of the violin rep under my belt when I was a student.

Laurie: What about becoming famous at a young age, and coping with that? Or is it so much a part of your life that you don't think about it?

Sarah: You really don't think about it after a while. I started so young that the focus was heavily on the whole child prodigy thing. Any sort of label they could have stuck on me, they did: "prodigy," "wunderkind," anything that has to do with kids. So to grow up with that and then to go through a transition stage where you're not exactly a kid any more but they don't really know quite where to categorize you...I've been the the business for over 20 years now, and I'm still reading articles about me that call me the ex-prodigy. That label just follows you around. There's not much you can do about that.

But I'm very grateful that I'm in the classical music world. I think people in the classical music world are extremely sophisticated, they know what they're listening to, they're musically educated, so they know what they want. They also know good music when they listen to it. I think it's one of the last remaining really honest forms of music-making. We don't lip sync, we don't have light shows, we don't have special effects, we don't have anything to distract or add fluff. We go out and we play, and we either play well or we don't play well. It's really clean, you either deliver or you don't. I like that sort of pureness to the industry.

I also like the fact that I started out at a time where everything – the classical music world, the recording industry — was in full swing. It's different now. But I started out when child prodigies were still accepted, and I was cranking out recordings like you wouldn't believe. It's a different sort of world now. You can't just slam out a record for the sake of slamming out a record. I'm still recording with EMI, and I'm very grateful that I'm working with the same company that I started out with, I know that's very unusual. Now every project that we do — there has to be a reason for it. You can't just go into a studio and make a record like you used to. First and foremost, there has to be a good musical reason for it, then there has to be a marketing reason for it, and there has to be an audience for it as well. Everything you put your name on now has a lot more thought behind it.

Laurie: Tell me a little bit about the thought behind your new Brahms and Bruch recording. You know, I didn't play the Bruch concerto until I was in college, so I was 18, or something like that. And I remember that the first thing my teacher said was, "I played the Bruch when I was seven!" Which of course made me crumble. (Sarah laughs)

But I thought about it, and I wonder how a seven-year-old views the Bruch, versus how a 20-year-old views it, versus how an almost-30-year-old looks at it?

Sarah: No disrespect to your teacher, but I think the whole age thing — I learned that when I was six, I learned that when I was seven — means nothing.

Laurie: Really? What do you mean by that?

Sarah: I learned the Bruch when I was five. It means I played the notes, and I had enough emotion in me then to play it well – at least well enough to get into Juilliard; it was my audition piece. Mozart 3 and the

Bruch were my two audition pieces for Juilliard. And then I put it away, I didn't touch it. I didn't touch it for another 10 years, and then I started performing it in public when I was 17 or so. Same thing with the Brahms; I learned it when I was eight, at Juilliard with Miss DeLay — learned it meaning learned the notes, scratched the surface. It got to the point where I thought I knew the piece, but obviously that was nothing. I wouldn't have dared go on stage with it at that point. So again, I put it away for about 10 years. I was probably 18 or 19 before I even went on stage with the Brahms. From that point on, with every concert, that's when the learning actually begins. That's when you realize how very little you do actually know about the piece! (She laughs)

There are certain pieces that I'm really grateful that I waited (to play). Because if you learn something when you're so young and it gets embedded in your head...Memory's a really funny thing, especially when you learn something when you're so extremely young – you can't shake it off. You really can't shake it off! With some pieces, I learned the piece when I was five or six, and I learned it in a specific way. Then 10 years later I try to pick it up and it's still stuck in my head — you try so desperately to shake it off because there are certain habits that you really don't want to continue on with.

Laurie: What are some of the pieces you're really grateful that you did late?

Sarah: Shostakovich. I waited until I was 20-something before I even attempted to learn that. That's a huge monster of a piece.

Laurie: It's huge emotionally.

Sarah: Just draining.

Beethoven, as well. I'm glad I waited. I was probably in my late teens. Brahms, I learned when I was younger and put it away.

There are some pieces you have too much respect for — just because you can play the notes doesn't mean you necessarily should be on stage playing the piece.

And yet, I think there's also a lot to be said for being on stage and getting the piece under your skin and fingers — living with it a bit. I started that process with the Brahms when I was about 18 or 19 and did countless concerts with it before I even attempted to bring it up with EMI, saying that I really want to record this.

Same thing with the Vivaldi. It's so popular; everybody knows the piece, every violinist in the world has either played or recorded the piece. There's really no reason for another record of the *Four Seasons* to come out, unless you really feel that you have a special version and you're convinced about it. The Vivaldi was on EMI's wish list for me for about a decade. I kept saying no – just because I knew that everybody had recorded it. I wanted to be in a place where I not only understood the piece but was comfortable enough to say, okay, even if there are 6,000 recordings of it out there, this is my version, and I feel really good about my version. It takes time before you can actually feel good about that.

Laurie: Where do you currently live, then?

Sarah: Philadelphia. That's where I was born; my family's still there. My brother goes to Princeton, everybody's around the area.

Laurie: How many siblings do you have?

Sarah: Just him. He's younger. He played the cello — he played really well, so talented. But he wants to do something else. He's seen me grow up and he's seen the insanity that is my life and he wants something a little bit more normal.

Laurie: You mentioned that your father's a violinist, does he still play?

Sarah: Not so much, he lives in Korea, and he teaches a bit.

Laurie: So it's possible to live in Philadelphia and go to Juilliard.

Sarah: Philly's close enough that I never really felt the need to live in New York. I was never there for any blocked out kind of time, I was always traveling.

Laurie: But you went to grade school?

Sarah: I did that in Philly. And then I went to Juilliard, when I was in the pre-college division, only on Saturdays. Then later on I would go up more.

But it was a really great school. They were very supportive. They're ultimately nurturing performers, so at the end of the day, if you say, "I've got nine weeks of back-to-back-to-back concerts, I'll be out for nine weeks, but I need all my assignments before I go," they were understanding. But at the same time, they needed the stuff done. I finished school only because I was able to fax stuff. Email was just starting up at that point.

Everybody there was so incredibly talented.

Laurie: What are some of the things you have to do to keep a high level of technique and to keep it in your fingers?

Sarah: Basics, every day. There's no other secret, really. I wish there were! (She laughs) Scales, arpeggios, thirds, octaves — the regular stuff you would hate as a student, you need to do it every day. When you have a schedule like this... some days when you can manage to squeeze in 4-5 hours, that's great. There are other days when you've just gotten off a 15-hour flight and you're so exhausted you can't even see straight, then I do my scales, all the basics. Even if it means I'll just touch the violin 30 minutes before collapsing in bed, I'll still do the basics. Even if you have three concertos and four sonatas that you need to look at, I'll start with the basics.

Laurie: You never get to a point where you can graduate from the scales.

Sarah: I wish! I do the Galamian and the Flesch, I certainly use both.

Laurie: Etudes?

Sarah: There are some I do to get the fingers warmed up in the morning. The normal stuff: the Kreutzer, the Sevcik, the Dont, the Gavinies, Ysaye — all that stuff. All the stuff you hated as a child. (She laughs)

Laurie: I actually love scales, I find it kind of therapeutical to start out with those Galamian acceleration scales. But I can't say that my students have taken to them! (Laughing)

Have you ever taken a sabbatical? Do you see life changing as you approach that big 3-0? Do you want to keep doing the whole solo thing?

Sarah: I'll be 30 in two years, and I've already set aside that day. This year I've got a concert on the day, I don't mind, I really don't. But I just thought, for 30 I want a big party, and I want my friends there and I don't want to have a concert that day.

It's very comforting for me to have the schedule and the concerts. It's a big part of my life, that's where I actually feel the most comfortable.

Laurie: So what you still enjoy most is soloing.

Sarah: It is. The majority of what I do is concertos, what I love the most. I adore chamber music, I love doing recitals. I don't get to do them as much as I get to do concertos. I would say about 95 percent of what I do are concertos. I love working with orchestras, I love working with conductors.

Laurie: Sometimes people find themselves going in other directions — composing, conducting or teaching.

Sarah: I see a lot of my colleagues, a lot of the violinists out there, branching out and going into conducting. And a lot of them settle down and have families, start having kids — you have to sort of scale back on concerts when you do that. But I still feel that there's a lot that I need to do musically, to make myself happy.

Laurie: Like what?

Sarah: There are a lot of pieces I want to learn, a lot of rep. Conducting, I don't think is in the cards for me. I think you get to that when you feel that you've done everything in the instrument's repertoire and you want something new — I'm not at that stage yet, I still feel that there's so much violin music out there that I want to learn, that I want to commission...

Laurie: Commission!

Sarah: I've only worked with three living composers until now: Donald Sur, Richard Danielpour and Christopher Theofanidis — he wrote a concerto for me last year. I had so much fun with that! It was a huge responsibility, and not something that I do all the time. But it piqued my interest enough that I definitely know that I want to do more of that.

And there's so much that I want to do before I even think about branching out and going into conducting, composing….

Also, just trying to squeeze in what little life that you can.

Laurie: And clothes shopping, you have to squeeze that in.

Sarah: I love shopping!

Laurie: I do, too. It's important.

Sarah: You know what? It really is.

Laurie: It makes you feel so much better.

Sarah: I love clothes; I love shoes. I'm a big shoe freak. It's my one weakness in life: shoes.

Laurie: What is the best kind of shoe?

Sarah: (She laughs) Anything that makes you walk taller. Dior has great shoes. Louboutins are, on occasion, great — some of them are quite painful — I mean these are Louboutins (she points to her high black boots) and I don't wear them on stage. But I love shoes.

Laurie: What makes a good concert dress? What factors does it have to have?

Sarah: For me? Personally?

Laurie: Yes.

Sarah: Everyone's going to give a slightly different answer, but I love color.

Laurie: What do you mean by that?

Sarah: First of all, I love black. When I'm not on stage, you'll most likely see me in black because I never get to wear black on stage. But on stage, I've only worn black a handful of times.

I love color, — color meaning something that's bright and happy and makes your coloring look good, and for everyone, that's a different color.

Cut, how it fits. How it fits is more important than anything else. As long as it's altered to your body and fits well, it doesn't matter if it's a $1,000 dress or a $10,000 dress or a $20,000 dress, I really believe how it fits and how it hangs on you is the most important thing.

I also think that beyond all of that, the most important thing for a musician is that is should be repertoire-appropriate.

Laurie: Oh really?

Sarah: For me, that is a major factor. Some people, when I say that, they don't quite get it, they say, 'What do you mean, it has to be repertoire-appropriate?' But if you have a red, hot, sexy number for Carmen, I'm not going to be wearing that for a Beethoven concert. I'm not going to be wearing that for a Brahms concert. And vice-versa.

You know how, sometimes when you put on a really hot slinky red dress it just makes you feel different? It makes you walk differently and feel differently? If it's not the mindset I want to be in for Brahms...It's really weird, but I think that for a woman, it affects the way that you walk and you feel; even subconsciously, it will overflow into the way you're playing that evening.

Laurie: What is a Brahms dress?

Sarah: I try to go more elegant and more classical when it comes to stuff like Brahms or Beethoven.

Laurie: Mozart.

Sarah: Mozart, I think, fresh, young, simple.

Laurie: Shostakovich.

Sarah: Whatever the heck you want! (Laughter) It's so complex, and obviously it's very modern, so sometimes I try to go modern. But really, across the board. You can do whatever you want with that one, I think.

Another important thing is, can I move in this dress? Can my arms move freely in this? I've had enough wardrobe mishaps on stage that I know that the last think I want to worry about is: Is this going to fall off? Are the straps going to fall? The worst thing you can do for yourself, as a woman on stage, is play a 40-minute concerto and worry the entire time about your dress. There's nothing more unsettling. You do not want the dress to become a distraction when you're on stage.

For example, when you have a beaded dress — I always ask the designers to not bead the last inch of the dress, because you always end up crunching on them on stage. Little things like that. Straps, if they fall, no way. You're focusing on that.

When I had my debut at the Sydney Opera House — I was wearing this new, sky-blue Dior dress which I absolutely loved. It was my first grown-up dress, my first dress where I didn't have to go to the teens section. My mother let me go to Dior and get an actual formal gown, and I was so in love with this dress. It had a row of about 20 buttons that you actually had to do yourself, and I thought, I'm never going to have the patience, so I asked the seamstress to make them into snap buttons, which at the time, seemed like a really good idea.

Laurie: I think I know where this is going...

Sarah: So I did the whole test — stand, play — it was fine.

Then I went on stage, took my first bow, and the whole thing just ripped. It just came undone. (she laughs)

Laurie: What did you do!?

Sarah: I wanted to cry. I literally wanted to cry. And the conductor just didn't see, he just started the orchestra. It was a short introduction, so I had the violin and bow in one hand, and the other hand was trying to get the snap buttons, as many as I could – and that's not really what you want to be thinking about before you have to play! For the entire concert, you're thinking, please stay on, please stay on...

I didn't wear that dress again.

Laurie: Oh that's sad, your first lovely dress!

Sarah: But I think, at the end of the day, a concert is an event. With operas, you have costumes and lighting, and you're telling a story, in a character. At a concert, you can basically wear whatever you want. But at the same time, you are, in a way, loosely representing the composer, and I think you should keep that in mind.

I love, when I look out into the audience — in a gorgeous hall, so beautiful with the chandeliers and the lighting. You look out into the audience, and you know that the audience has also made an effort. The women look beautiful; the orchestra, they're in tails. I just think that it's appropriate for the soloist to make an effort as well.

I remember, there was an orchestra, several years ago, that was thinking of new ways to bring in young audiences. They asked if I would support this new idea of Friday afternoon casual concerts, where everybody would show up in jeans, including the performers. They asked if I could just wear jeans and a T-shirt or a top or whatever. I thought, this is a concert! I seriously doubt that wearing jeans is going to bring in more people.

Zachary DePue. Photo courtesy Zachary DePue

ZACHARY DEPUE

Originally published on January 30, 2010

Zach DePue is an example of someone who lives comfortably in the classical world as well as the world of popular music. He is the Curtis-educated concertmaster of the Indianapolis Symphony, but also a member of a band, Time for Three, *which promotes itself as "the world's first classically-trained garage band." Since this interview, the group signed a recording deal with Universal Music Classics.*

What exactly is *Time for Three?*

I'd call it a group of serious musicians, geeking out on everything that finds favor with their ears. The three of them – violinist Zach DePue, violinist Nick Kendall (grandson of Suzuki pioneer John Kendall) and bassist Ranaan Meyer — met as students at the Curtis Institute, but it's pretty difficult to pin down their "genre." Amazon gets close, calling it "a fusion of classical and fierce folk fun."

When I spoke to Zach last week over the phone, he didn't have a tidy answer, either.

"I'm not really one who is able to say what its place is on the shelf in music," Zach said of the group's new album, *Three Fervent Travelers.* "I think we're just doing what we like to do."

At 30, Zach also serves as concertmaster of the Indianapolis Symphony. Add that to 22 weeks of touring for Time for Three, and Zach's one busy fiddler.

"I grew up learning a very distinct style of Appalachian fiddle tunes, for the purpose of playing with my family," Zach said. "Appalachian-style is not as swung as, say, a Texas-style fiddling; it's a northern fiddle style, and there are endless, countless tunes to learn."

"I learned all those by ear from my brothers," Zach said. "They literally sat down with me when I was nine, and I learned by trial and error: I play it for you, you play it back, and then go back and forth until you have the tune. I remember Wallace teaching me *Wake Up Susan* for two hours down in the basement."

That kind of early experience has allowed the members of *Time for Three* to arrive at their tunes through a combination of both live experimentation and written arranging.

"We compose with the instruments in our hands," said Zach. For their new album, the group brought in another Curtis friend, Steve Hackman, a conductor, pianist and singer-songwriter. "He's been delving into the pop world a little bit, but he still brings that classical attitude to everything." He helped them with their arrangements and also created an arrangement of Imogen Heap's *Hide and Seek*. As with all their arrangements, the final edit happened when they went through the song bit by bit, taking this out and adding that.

"We like to say we have a garage-band mentality," Zach said. "That really is our process, though, through trial and error, with the instruments in our hands."

Having both the classical and garage-band mentality, they also like to break the rules in both realms.

"We don't like those rules, as a group," Zach said. "I find that we like to be more about expression and by any means necessary."

What does that mean? Well, for example:

"If Ranaan brings a straight-ahead jazz tune, for instance, or a melody that maybe Ranaan intended for jazz, we'll play through it. As we play through it, Nick will say, 'Man, it works well with this beat,' and he'll start chuckin' a beat, and I'll do it again. 'That feels a lot more up my alley,' and then I'll join him on that, and Ranaan will say, 'Wow, I didn't figure this piece like this, but this is cool,' and he goes with it," Zach said. "This is opposed to, 'We're going to play the head and the deck, you're going to take the solo, and then if you and Nick can trade off two-bar phrases, and then I'll take a bass extension solo and we'll play the ahead again in unison, with a trash-can ending.'"

In other words, even garage bands have their standard vocabulary, and *Time for Three* likes to stand all of it on its head.

"We try to re-invent the structure," Zach said. "We never say, 'You'll play through it once,' it's more like, 'It feels like you should play that through half, and take it into this cool thing we just jammed out on,' so it never follows a structure. It ends up being more thought-out and more through-composed, rather than saying, 'This session will be completely open to you improv-ing; we'll be laying down harmonies for you.'"

"We've also found that free-styling has been successful," Zach said. "Rather than stopping and talking to an audience, we literally will free-style our way into the next tune, based on what's going on in the room. There is no structure to that, whatsoever. But there is an art form to it and the audience has to be open to it, as well. They have to come expecting it."

"We've been experimenting with this with outreaches with high schools," Zach said. "The high school kids — when we ask, 'Is there another question?'...about the third question they'll say, 'Yeah, can you guys just keep playing?' So we just we stop talking and go back to playing."

Much of *Three Fervent Travelers* was recorded live – remarkable for the energy this creates and for the fact that these guys joyously perform their stunt-filled high-wire act with no safety net. Listen carefully, and *The Simpsons* theme floats out of the *Orange Blossom Special*; a thread from Dvorak's *American Quartet* peeps out of a tune about Pittsburgh called *Of Time and Three Rivers.*

"We pull from a lot of things, and we all listen to a lot of different music," Zach said. "Right now, for example, I'm big on Muse. They're basically U2's opening act right now. Their music is very orchestral, and it's very clear to me that they are classically trained, in one way or another. They have a pianist, and they totally lift classical pieces. I've heard Rachmaninov in their music; I've heard Chopin in their albums, not even re-done; the Tchaikovsky piano concerto....They can be like

Bruckner, in terms of the epic quality of a lot of their tunes."

"It's funny, because for years, Ranaan and I didn't listen to a lot of music because we didn't want any influences on what we were creating," Zach said. "We wanted it to be purely organic, from us. But it's been hard. Once I hear something that really catches my ear, I have to go discover it. It's just one of those things."

One of the songs they discover on *Three Fervent Travelers* is Imogen Heap's pop hit *Hide and Seek*. To me, the original version is a song with a mechanized, monochrome aesthetic — but it becomes a poignant exploration of sound and harmony in this trio's hands.

"We spent quite a bit of time getting that right — or getting it where it is," Zach said of the *Hide and Seek* arrangement. "I shouldn't say 'right'; it feels good."

"We bring a chamber music attitude to it," Zach said of their work on this piece. "If we handed the piece off now to a student group, there would be a lot for them to learn about playing together, creating homogenous sound together, just like you would in a Beethoven quartet. We're kind of proud of that. We hope, in the future, groups will play this stuff."

It's not available yet, though.

"We're working on that," Zach said. "We need to work on that, because it's fun to hear other groups play what we do."

Speaking of students, how does one work toward being a successful fusion musician?

"I think that for any instrument, the best starting point is training classically, for better or for worse, because it's so refined," Zach said. "Hands down, it's the hardest to play well and sound good. If anybody ever argued that, I would be strong-pressed for them to prove that, by studying jazz, you could then cover, on a violin, all styles of music. I feel like if you start from classical, you have the capability, the tools, that can allow you then feel jazz, to feel bluegrass, to understand it. Certainly the guys that pushed the envelope for the violin — Bach, Paganini, Ysaye, Bartok — those are classical composers. Classical been very successful in pressing the technical aspects of the violin forward."

"My family is almost a study in what happens when you start from classical but you're open to all styles," Zach said. Zach has three brothers: Jason, who is in the Philadelphia Orchestra, Alex, a rock fiddle player who plays with electric guitarist Steve Vai, and Wallace Jr., who is also a violinist.

"We all come out of classical music," Zach said. Nothing is better than classical training, from purely technical perspective, to give you capability on the instrument, he said. As for cultivating that creative side and learning to play in different genres: listen, and imitate.

"Listen to Stephane Grappelli, listen to Ricky Skaggs," Zach said. "Listen to different artists and mimic what they do. Then also listen to other instruments and try to somehow recreate that on your instrument. Obviously, there are some limitations, but I think just learning by ear, trying to capture styles, is one of the first steps."

This March, *Time for Three* will be premiering a new concerto by Chris Brubeck, son of great jazz icon Dave Brubeck, with the Youngstown Symphony, then playing it again in June with the Boston Pops.

"It covers a lot of different styles of jazz, in the jazz idiom," Zach said of the concerto. "We've been getting our mind wrapped around that type of world and living in it, so it's going to be fun to recreate that piece. Of course, in that idiom, Chris always says, 'Man, if something doesn't fit well on the fiddle, just change it...' He's very cool, but I always like the challenge of doing what he wrote, first and foremost."

Simon Fischer, with student. Photo: Laurie Niles

SIMON FISCHER

Originally published on March 4, 2010

Simon Fischer changed the world of violin technique with his book, Basics, *which was first published in 1997. He has continued to write books on violin playing and pedagogy, including* Practice, Scales, *and* The Violin Lesson; *as well as producing the DVD* The Secrets of Tone Production.

Violin playing is a basic matter of proportion and balance.

Hah!

With all the bowings, fingerings, pitch, tone, rhythm, phrasing and sheer agony that goes into it, just how does one boil violin playing down to that basic matter?

This is the brilliance of London-based violinist Simon Fischer's contribution to violinkind: In his books, magazine columns and teachings, he cuts a path straight to the issue at hand, whether it's wobbly vibrato or out-of-tune scales. Sometimes he even makes the solution seem so simple as to be self-evident — such is the genius of good pedagogy.

I first met Simon at the Starling-DeLay Symposium on Violin Studies in New York in 2007, when he was giving a lecture on tone production. By then he'd already written the two books that many consider essential to any violinist's library: *Basics* and *Practice*.

Most recently I spoke to him on the phone about his latest projects: books called *The Scale Book* and *The Violin Lesson*, and an epic DVD on tone production. He also has been working on a number of transcriptions, including the Purcell *Chaconne*, and he recently released a recording of the Brahms *Violin Sonatas* that he made with his father, pianist Raymond Fischer.

Simon has taught at the Guildhall School since 1982, and at the Yehudi Menuhin School since 1997. He also writes a monthly column for *The Strad* magazine. In addition, he plays all over London, from the studios to the concert stage.

Laurie: How did you get started with the violin?

Simon: My late brother Mark, who was six years older than me, took up the violin when he was nine, so I was three at the time. We lived in Sydney, Australia, and I remember walking with him to his violin class. Pretty soon, he gave up the violin, but I wanted to learn. However, my father wanted me to wait.

Laurie: Why?

Simon: He's a professional musician, a pianist, and because of the difficulties of the profession, he was wary of parents who push their children too soon. He wanted to be absolutely sure. What he wasn't taking into account was that earning a living as a pianist is a very different matter than earning a living as a string player. When you play the piano, you tend to spend an awful lot of time on your own. The violin is a completely different world — he shouldn't have worried.

I kept on pestering my parents until I was seven and a half, and finally I was allowed to start violin lessons.

Laurie: How did you end up in England?

Simon: He and my mother both wanted to come to London, so in 1961 the whole family uprooted to here, and here we've been ever since. My father had to start again from scratch in a foreign country at the age of 32 — very, very difficult, especially for a pianist. When I was growing up, he was forever telling me that I was going to enjoy an advantage that he had not had in this country, in that I was growing up here, with my generation, and all of those contacts.

Laurie: So then was he Australian?

Simon: He was born in Australia, my mother was born in England.

Laurie: Tell me about your schooling.

Simon: I was briefly at the Junior Guildhall at age 11, where I studied with Christopher Polyblank and Clive Lander. But then at age 13, I left and studied privately first with Homi Kanger, then with Eli Goren, then Perry Hart, then Sydney Fixman. It was only when I met Yfrah Neaman, at Guildhall, that for the first time I stayed for many years with one teacher.

I stayed five years at Guildhall. In those days it was a three-year course, and some students just left and started free-lancing. I was offered a full scholarship to do a fourth year, and I thought, why go out to work if I can be paid, in effect, to stay at home and practice and have lessons? That seemed an obvious thing to do. Then I was offered another scholarship to stay a fifth year, and so the same applied. By then, I was teaching myself, really, by watching the fantastic players that Yfrah Neaman had in his class.

Laurie: It sounds like you were soaking it up like a sponge.

Simon: Well, I got terrible shock when I went to Guildhall. When I went to Guildhall, I thought I was the best. And the reason I thought I was the best was because as far as I knew, I was! We're talking pre-Internet days. Today is the day of information, but it certainly wasn't in the 1960s. I didn't even play in the National Youth Orchestra. I won the prizes in the local little competitions in Wimbledon, and I didn't really know anybody who could play the violin at all. I could play anything that was put on the music stand, but people didn't put Paganini Caprices on the music stand, they didn't even put the Bruch Concerto on the music stand! I very easily got my place at Guildhall, nevertheless. Then in my first week at the Guildhall, Mincho Mincheff, the fabulous Bulgarian violinist who had just won the Carl Flesch Competition, was standing there, about five or six feet away from me, playing the Brahms Concerto — on Szigeti's Guadagnini, which had been left to him. I thought, my God, I can't do that, I'd better learn how to!

By my fifth year at Guildhall, I won the top competitive scholarship auditions to go to America, playing the Paganini Concerto No. 1. Also at that time I won the Noel Millidge Concerto Prize at the Guildhall, playing the Bruch G minor with the Symphony Orchestra. I have a recording of that performance that I am very proud of. Two weeks before that competition, I went from London to Aspen to audition for Miss [Dorothy] DeLay, and it was the Bruch that I played to her there.

Then, after I came back from studying with Miss DeLay for two years, over the next few years I had between one and about four lessons with several teachers, including Zakhar Bron, Hermann Krebbers, Igor Ozim, Frederick Grinke, Sandor Vegh, Emanuel Hurwitz and Eric Gruenberg. At that time I was playing some international competitions, though I didn't win any of them — though I did get to the semifinal of the Carl Flesch — doing them partly simply to try to power or force my playing up to new levels. After I was past the age-limit to play competitions, I carried on studying by myself and ended up doing all kinds of nice things, from playing recitals on the BBC, to leading lots of the orchestras here, to playing the Mendelssohn and Tchaikovsky concertos with the Philharmonia at Kenwood (London's equivalent of the Hollywood Bowl) in front of audiences of 10,000. I often say to my teenage students who can already play Paganini Caprices in tune and easily, that if I could do what I have done, starting from where I was at the age of 18, they can do anything!

Laurie: Do you remember your first student?

Simon: I remember my first student very well — two students. I left school when I was 15. Because I was too young to go to Guildhall, I went to what was then called a Polytechnic. I took Music "A" level, kind of the highest exam you take in high school before you go to college. That was a two-year course, and it was a fantastic time. In the second year, somebody phoned to ask if there was somebody who could give two children violin lessons. I was 17, and I was the violinist there, so I was asked. I taught a little boy and girl, 9 and 7, both from Ireland, and I taught them for about two terms, every week, and took them through the associated board exams, Grade 5 and 3. Each took an exam, then the family moved back to Ireland, and I left Chiswick and went to Guildhall. But I used to skip down the road after those lessons. I just loved teaching those kids, it was just the best.

Then, I went to the Guildhall. Seeing Yfrah — with his master classes there — the way he was enjoying this whole violin world and this repertoire and all these students, it was this feeling of camaraderie amongst his class. I just looked at him doing that and thought, that's what I want to do. It was as simple as that.

Laurie: You've managed to teach quite a lot, and to continue playing. How do you keep the balance between the two?

Simon: What I've always found is that the teaching improves my playing, and of course my playing improves the teaching. Then I've found that writing about playing improves my playing as well. It has to do with mental rehearsal and mental visualization: When you are practicing something, then you decide to play it in a different way, you are changing your mental picture. Galamian was talking about it in the 1950s and 1960s; he said that all practicing is a matter of training the mind — nothing to do with training the muscles. When you make a change in your practice, you change your mental picture. This is why mental practice is so fantastic. You don't need a violin; you can go sit on a bench in the park and do fantastic work on whatever piece you are playing, There is a catch, though: you have to know what are the images you're meant to be forming in your mind. And there's a limit to it; you can't learn repertoire like that.

Laurie: Was there ever a time when you came across a student who just could not get something?

Simon: You mean have I ever found myself unable to cope with a particular student, can't sort them out? I've occasionally come up against a brick wall with a student, but very rarely. It's almost impossible that that happens.

Laurie: How do you avoid it?

Simon: I'm passionate about proportions, and this is something I got from Dorothy DeLay. I've put this in the *Practice* book, and in the *Violin Lesson* book, there's a big new section on this.

The story DeLay told me is simply this: Leonardo da Vinci was asked to go along and inspect an ancient statue that had just been unearthed. When he turned up, the statue was surrounded by a group of people, all talking about it in what today we would call 'artsy-fartsy' language. He stood there in silence. Then he got out one of his famous notebooks, and he got out his measuring tools. He measured every angle, every width, every diameter, everything. He wrote it all down and went home.

As a man, he could see the beauty of the statue: the light and the line, the radiance and the expression. But as an artist, he knew that everything he was looking at was the result of certain proportions, and that was the key. Everything is a question of proportions: if you're a painter, if you're an architect, if you're a cook, if you're a designer of anything whatsoever, what you're dealing with is proportions. When you're making yourself a cup of coffee, you're dealing with proportions.

To me, this is the be-all and end-all, it's the answer to everything: Proportions.

Occasionally, you get a student come to you for a first lesson, and they say that their teacher just didn't know how to fix their problems, so they had to move on. Then you look at the student play, and all the proportions are completely wrong: the bow isn't straight to the bridge, the hand isn't round and nice on the bow...you don't know where to start. You think about the previous teacher not knowing where to start, and you wonder, how is that possible?

If you think in terms of proportions, as a teacher, you never reach that stage where you simply don't know what the next step to take with a student is. And as a player, you never reach that stage – you always know what to do next and improve next. If you can improve and refine the proportions, it's just endless.

Laurie: What exactly does this mean, when you are in a room, looking at a student?

Simon: What it means is, that everything technically can be described in terms of proportions. For example, tone production, every sound that comes out of the violin is the result of certain proportions of speed to pressure to distance from the bridge. Spiccato — every sound in spiccato is the result of certain proportions of length of bow to height of bow, with the added ingredient of how much hair you're using. And intonation, in the major scale, it starts whole-tone whole-tone half-step. You don't want a narrow whole-tone for the first two notes and then a wide whole-tone for the second two, they've got to be equi-distant, and that's a matter of proportions. You play an arpeggio, and if you go A C# E, A C# E, A, all the C#s have to be exactly the same, that means the proportion of two to one. It's all numbers, in the end. Vibrato is a question of mixing different proportions of speed and width, and another extra ingredient, how much finger pressure. Every single aspect of playing the physical violin is describable, and in few words, and the language of the describing is proportion.

You can also use proportion to describe music. To describe an accelerando, each note must be proportionately sooner than the previous one. If you make a crescendo, each note must be proportionately louder, and you can gauge and grade these things accordingly. Of course, lots of people think they make a crescendo when they don't, because they don't listen — actually every note is the same volume. But if they would listen — it's just proportions, everything is.

Laurie: How did you come up with your ideas for your most popular book *Basics*?

Simon: Thinking in terms of proportions, or practicing with this in mind, you get flooded with ideas for new combinations of actions that lead to fantastic exercises which are entirely original, and yet based on completely sound principles and elements of violin playing. Many of the exercises in *Basics* are entirely original, as a result of this. All the great violinists have played in these ways — but not necessarily knowing what they are doing or being able to explain it to somebody else.

The *Basics* book and the *Practice* books are simply the record of all the things I had to learn, in trying to learn how to play the violin. The *Basics* book started because, after a year or two of teaching in the early 1980s at Wells Cathedral School and continually writing out the same exercises for students in their notebooks, I finally woke up one day and thought, why don't I write it all down just once, photocopy it and hand it to them? Thus the very first *Basics* book was born, and it was 20 pages, typed, on a typewriter. Then I kept revising it and producing better copies of it. A few years later, I bought my first word processor and decided to make a better version of the *Basics* book. I thought it would take only a week, but it took three months. It went from 20 pages to 50 double-sided pages because I added all the things I'd been doing in lessons and in my practice in the meantime. A few years later, I got my first proper PC, and that was when I thought I'd make the real super-duper *Basics* book, which then eventually led to it being published.

Basics and *Practice* books are just glorified lesson notebooks. If you had five years' worth of lessons and if you went to the trouble of writing down everything at the end of each lesson, you'd end up with a pile of hand-written notes. And if after five years you collated them and put them into order and gave them nice bold headings, what you'd end up with would be these books.

Laurie: What are some of the top exercises in the books?

Simon: Many people ask me that, and it is difficult to answer because I always want my pupils to do them all. But the intonation exercise in *Basics* (number 255) is perhaps one to mention. It is simple to prove how good it is: play, say, a three octave scale in A major; then practice number 255 for 10 minutes in A major; then play the scale again. The scale will be very much easier and more in tune. The question is: If you had practiced the scale itself for 10 minutes, could you have improved it that much? Normally the answer is: No way. I always like to say that if there is a violin heaven-world, then Dounis, Flesch, Sevcik and all the rest are up there either shaking their fist at me in annoyance — because they did not think of it themselves — or else (hopefully) they are nodding encouragingly.

Then there are the tone exercises. I call these "million-dollar tone exercises," because they are worth a million dollars each. They will be in my *Tone Production* DVD, which is set to come out in about six weeks. Three or four of these were taught to me by Dorothy DeLay and Masau

Kawasaki, the rest are my own combinations out of the basic exercises. But just 10 minutes a day doing these exercises in the first few weeks, then 10 minutes three times a week for a while, then once a week after that (or used briefly as a daily warm-up), is all it takes to utterly transform your tone.

Laurie: Tell me about the recording of the Brahms sonatas that you did with your father, Raymond Fischer. What is it like to collaborate with a family member?

Simon: We played the complete Brahms in Wigmore Hall in 1988 or '89. Prior to that we played them in at least six or seven music club performances around the U.K. Something about those sonatas remind me of my childhood, of my mother. I just love playing them to death, and to play them with my father. We played them in a big concert in Australia in 2004, and that was my first visit back to Australia since I'd left as a child. My mother passed away a long time ago, and so she never lived to see my career unfold in the way that it has. So it's very significant to be playing those pieces in Sydney with my father, as an adult.

As for Brahms, Benjamin Britten said that, once a year he would listen to a piece of Brahms just to remind himself how awful music can be. In the Brahms vs. Berlioz clash at the time, the composer Hugo Wolf, as a young man, wrote as a music critic to make some money on the side, and he wrote that in one cymbal crash from Berlioz you had more music than in the then-three symphonies (he hadn't written the fourth yet) of Brahms put together. This is what he wrote! All I can say is that if these people do not understand Brahms, then what can you say to explain it to them? I just can't be bothered.

Laurie: I actually love Brahms. He's one of my favorite composers.

Simon: Mine, too. The second piano concerto, the piano quintet, the clarinet quintet, the fourth symphony, the second symphony....

Laurie: ...and the first and third as well!

Simon: The first and third! And the fiddle concerto! I have to say I'm not the greatest Benjamin Britten fan...I would exchange the entire works of Benjamin Britten for one of the violin sonatas, any day, without thinking twice about it!

Laurie: Now one last question, I hope you'll indulge me. I know that you've played a lot of studio gigs, and also that you played with Sting. I'm a pretty big Sting fan — what was it like to work with him?

Simon: Yes I did play with Sting. The recording for *Ten Summoners Tales* took place at his house in Wiltshire — it's a 16th-century mansion that you have to see to believe. I don't remember this, but someone reminded me recently that at one point in the day I met Sting in one the hallways. "Nice place you've got here," I said. (Don't ask me why I said that, but I did.) He looked around thoughtfully, and said, "Yes, and I got it for a song. Well, two songs, actually!"

Clara-Jumi Kang. Photo: Denis Ryan Kelly Jr.

CLARA-JUMI KANG

Originally published on September 29, 2010

We all know that winning an international violin competition is grueling business; this interview with Clara-Jumi Kang puts a personal face on the whole process, from the tears of frustration to the tears of joy. Upon winning the International Violin Competition of Indianapolis, she took possession of the 1683 ex-Gingold Stradivari, the same instrument that Augustin Hadelich had been playing.

Gold medal laureate Clara-Jumi Kang appeared to be in tears Friday night, after her performance of the Beethoven *Violin Concerto* at the 2010 International Violin Competition of Indianapolis finals.

Actually, the real tears came the day before.

"I cried for 40 minutes the day before I played the Beethoven," she said. For the competition, Clara-Jumi played on a 1774 Guadagnini from Turin, on loan from the Kumho Foundation in Korea. The fiddle was not always an easy partner, especially for the Beethoven *Violin Concerto*.

The Guad has a very bright sound, and "sometimes it has a personality I can't control." By contrast, her normal violin has a darker sound. "I was used to that phrasing" that comes out of a darker violin, and "somehow nothing seemed to work."

Clara-Jumi, 23, has perfect pitch, and she was accustomed to a 443-hertz "A" in Korea, or a 444 in Europe. The Indianapolis Symphony used a 440 "A" — much lower. "I was used to the higher sound," she said.

Putting all those things together, everything felt out of her control.

But then she came to a profound realization: "I found myself thinking that Beethoven is much too great for me to control it," Clara-Jumi said. "It's from above this earth, and I should just play it, just worship it as something from above. That is what I focused on all evening."

"I was so into the music," she said of her performance of the Beethoven at the Finals. "I am blessed to have played the Beethoven with orchestra eight times — nobody wants to play the Beethoven with you when you are 23."

"(On Friday) I was playing it like I was worshipping it – that's why, after the performance, I had tears running," she said. They came from her deep emotion for the Beethoven and from her sadness at the piece coming to an end, the competition coming to an end. "It wasn't because I was upset or because I didn't like my playing."

"I love Beethoven too much," Clara-Jumi said. "If this concerto didn't exist, maybe I wouldn't love the violin as much."

Clara-Jumi started playing the violin when she was three years old. Her parents — both opera singers — had planned for her to play the piano. "I said, 'No,' I wanted something with a longer sound."

The Beethoven was always her favorite violin concerto, and she had more CDs of it, with more violinists, than she can count. She used to fall asleep listening to the Beethoven. "The timpani would make my heart beat," she said. "I guess it just grew into me."

"With Beethoven, every time you play it, it's so different – the feeling you have, the phrasing," Clara-Jumi said. "I get surprised with what feeling I come to."

She said she has eight or nine scores of the Beethoven and tries to use a different score each time she studies the piece, without writing in many fingerings or bowings.

"I try not to touch Beethoven's dynamics — Beethoven has a strong dynamic," she said.

Performing Beethoven, "sometimes you feel like you are getting all your weaknesses pulled out of you in public," Clara-Jumi said, "but sometimes it touches people's hearts."

I spoke to Clara-Jumi Kang on Sunday, right after she rehearsed Waxman's *Carmen Fantasy* at the Scottish Rite Cathedral in downtown Indianapolis for her final appearance at the IVCI awards ceremony. It would be her first performance as the competition's gold medal recipient.

Clara-Jumi was admitted at age four to the Mannheim Musikhochschule, and at age seven to The Juilliard School. Her teachers have included Zakhar Bron, Dorothy DeLay and Nam Yun Kim.

The IVCI was by no means Clara-Jumi's first international competition — she won first prize in the 2010 Sendai International Violin Competition, second prize at the 2009 Hannover International Violin Competition; and first prize at the 2009 Seoul International Violin Competition. I wondered if the Indianapolis competition was different in any way from these other competitions.

"It has an incredible host family system," she said of the Indianapolis. She had worried about whether or not she would be able to perform her best, under the circumstances of living with a host family, but she found that it worked very well. Her host family gave her an attic bedroom with its own bathroom, and "I could be upstairs alone for two hours and not feel bad about it," she said. "They made me feel like, 'You play a concert, and then rest.'" They also showed her around town and fed her well, she said.

She also felt happy with the audiences in Indianapolis. "The feeling I had onstage was that the audience seemed happy to hear the music. I can feel it when I play, if someone is into me, listening to me," Clara-Jumi said. "Something about America is attractive; the audiences don't hold back their feelings." For example, they don't hesitate to give a standing ovation. "Sometimes you play in other countries and they tend to show feelings in a different way."

She said that she used to have a bad attitude toward audiences when it was clear that people were not listening. Over time, she came around to a different feeling about it. "Now I want to play for everyone. My love for music was bigger than other people's negative thoughts in the audience."

"I think it helps if you are on stage more often," Clara-Jumi said of finding the right mentality for approaching performance. "Having a stage presence is important, even in competitions."

For her, the competition went in four stages, coinciding with the four rounds.

"The first round really felt like a competition," she said. That was the round in which competitors had to play movements from Bach unaccompanied Sonatas and Partitas; two Paganini Caprices; a Mozart violin-piano sonata and an encore piece. She played the *Adagio* and *Fuga* from Bach *Sonata in G*; Paganini *Caprices* 7 and 11; *Sonata in G*, K. 301, by Mozart; and *Beau Soir*, arranged by Heifetz.

The second round felt completely different, playing a Beethoven violin-piano sonata; a non-Beethoven violin-piano sonata and a showpiece. She played Beethoven *Sonata No. 3 in E flat*, Op. 12; the Ravel *Violin Sonata*; Joan Tower's *String Force*; and Waxman's *Carmen Fantasy*.

"It should have felt like a competition, but the Ravel and the Beethoven made me enjoy playing," she said.

The Classical finals were made even more interesting for her by the selection of a new Mozart for her — or at least one that had been in storage for a while.

"I had played Mozart No. 4 for eight years and recently won the Sendai Competition playing that," Clara-Jumi said. "I changed in July to Mozart No. 5 — I have not played it since I was eight years old."

"I wanted a fresh start for Mozart," Clara-Jumi said. "I felt like I was playing Mozart Four out of habit. And I like the Turkish (section in the last movement of the fifth concerto) very much, "though that last movement proved hard to memorize, the way it keeps repeating with different decorations.

"I was very nervous for this competition. I ate this many blueberries," she laughed, indicating a large bowl with her hands. "I think a nervous feeling is always a good thing, as long as it doesn't interfere with your playing.

When she was about to go on stage for one of the final concerts, conductor Samuel Wong asked, "How do you feel?"

"Nervous!" she said.

"That's good!" he said.

"And somehow his comment really helped," Clara-Jumi said. She was grateful for his support and for that of the the orchestra. "Samuel Wong made me feel like I didn't have to give him too many cues," she said. "I could close my eyes and just play."

Clara-Jumi tends to think in terms of a singing line — her parents are opera singers, and her father sings things such as Wagner.

"When I was in my mom's stomach, she was singing at La Scala," Clara-Jumi said. Her mother stopped singing publicly when Clara-Jumi was born, but her father has continued. Though she looks up to violinists such as Anne-Sophie Mutter, David Oistrakh, Jascha Heifetz and Ivry Gitlis, her father counts high among the people she admires.

"The reason my father is one of my idols as a musician is not just because he is my father," she said. "My father has always been true and honest to music." He has tried to ignore the politics of music.

"He said, 'Try to win with your music, never try to concentrate on how you affect people. Think of your language as a musician and be true to yourself as a musician.' I think I'm about to follow his path," she said.

She said she would like to bring music to places where people may have never heard a violin, in poorer countries.

"I would like to heal people with music," she said. "There are so few thing that can heal people's hearts — music is one of them."

Lara St. John. Photo: Rachel Dellinger

LARA ST. JOHN

Originally published on October 21, 2010

Lara St. John is a fantastic violinist with a great sense of humor. Since this interview, she has made several more albums, including Bach Sonatas *with French harpist Marie-Pierre Langlamet, whom she mentioned the story below, in 2012; and another Polkastra album called* I Do: The Wedding Album, *in 2013.*

Lara St. John doesn't really go for the idea that Mozart is "really hard to play" and that a great deal of worry, fret and fear should go into it.

After all, she's been playing Mozart's *Sinfonia Concertante* with her brother, Scott, ever since they were little kids.

Lara St. John is well-known for her solo and recital appearances around the globe, and for her recordings of Bach's *Sonatas and Partitas* and Gypsy music, not to mention her *Polkastra*, a polka orchestra she put together for musical fun. (The album is called *Apolkalypse Now.*) Scott St. John won the Avery Fisher Career Grant in 2003, is one of the violinists in the St. Lawrence String Quartet, ensemble-in-residence at Stanford University, and teaches in the Bay Area.

After some 20 years of playing Mozart together, the sibling pair decided to make a recording of Mozart works, which includes the *Sinfonia Concertante* – for which Scott plays scordatura viola ("scordatura" being tuned differently) — as well as Mozart Violin *Concerto No. 1 in Bb Major, K.*

207, played by Scott, and Mozart Violin *Concerto No. 3 in G Major, K. 216*, played by Lara. They are joined by The Knights orchestra of New York City.

Lara spoke with me over the phone last week about what it's like to work with your brother, about why Mozart would ask to tune the viola a half-step higher for the *Sinfonia Concertante*, and about why she loves Mozart *Concerto No. 3* so much.

Laurie: I've been listening to some Mozart, thanks to you, and your brother. When did you start playing together?

Lara: We did our first concerto when I was four and he was six — we did the *Bach Double*. So it's been a long time! We've been playing together all our lives.

He's not a violinist who plays viola, he's a violist. He started playing the viola at eight years old, very early. At first, he was pretty little, so he played a re-strung violin. As he got big enough, it was a real viola. Even as a kid, he was so into chamber music. And of course, when you're kids, the one thing that's always lacking in the string quartet is the viola. Everyone plays violin or cello! He's so quick; he taught himself the clef and everything. Then he was in incredible demand, chamber-musically, and that has continued to this day.

Laurie: When you say he was so into chamber music, how did that manifest when he was eight?

Lara: He wanted to play more chamber music, and I think that's a good part of why he took up the viola. Also, our first chamber music coach, Ralph Aldrich, was a violist.

I thought of learning to play the viola as well, and he was like, no way, man! (She laughs)

I can't sight-read to save my life. You do sort of need to be able to read at least one clef before you start another; it's probably a good thing I never took it up! Once, when I was teaching I had to play viola because they didn't have enough violas. I had to finger every note, do it by ear. Then I sounded like a trumpet!

You really have to do it from a young age. I can tell when it's a violinist, playing viola. The vibrato's a bit chainsaw, and it's just not the same thing.

Laurie: How long have you been playing the *Sinfonia Concertante* together?

Lara: We toured Europe with the *Sinfonia* when I was 11 and he was 13. I remember going to Portugal, Spain, Hungary, France... We've done it with a lot of orchestras since, I'd say an average of once a year. That actually means in a specific year we'll do it four times, and then not for four years.

I've got my own label, Ancalagon, and I've been thinking for a while that this is definitely something we needed to record. So for the last few years I've been casting about for the right orchestra, and when The Knights came around, I knew, that's it!

Laurie: Did you ever have any sibling rivalry?

Lara: Funny enough, not really.

For example, all over Canada, they have these little Kiwanis competitions, so even at the age of six, it was a way to perform the pieces that you learned. We were always doing these, and other competitions. Sometimes we'd end up in the same class, because we're pretty close in age, and if he would win, I would think that was about the same as me winning, because it was my family. If I would win, then he would think that way as well. We've been really supportive of each other — never against each other.

I also have the distinct advantage that my brother is one of those people who just has no enemies. He's one of the nicest, most genuine guys in the world. I'd really have to be a nasty piece of work to pick a fight with him.

We're really different players and individuals. Obviously when you're doing a little contest when you're a teenager, then I guess the objective is to win first prize. But later on in life, we didn't really have the same objectives all the time, or the same interests. We didn't even play the same repertoire quite a lot of the time. That's one reason why, for example, I learned the Mendelssohn Concerto in my mid-20s. Growing up, that was his. It made sense that I didn't learn it; I never needed it for one reason or another. So little funny things like that come from the sibling-ness, but there's not anything wrong with that.

Laurie: Do you find it different to work with him than to work with other collaborators?

Lara: Of course, because I know exactly what he's going to do, and vice-versa. We don't really rehearse, exactly. We just play through things. If he does something that I think is stupid, I'll stop and say, "I think that's stupid." And there will be this little fight and then of course he'll say, "Well all right, I won't do that," and vice-versa. But in general, on stage, even if somebody does something completely different than has been rehearsed, somehow we know. It's a connection.

People always ask, are you guys close? I guess we're close, but... I know some siblings who talk every day. We talk every couple weeks, maybe. And he calls me up when he needs a place in New York. (She laughs)

Laurie: I didn't really know there was a scordatura in the Mozart Sinfonia Concertante, that Mozart asks that the viola be tuned in a different way than usual. What's up with that?

Lara: We knew about it, but since nobody really does it except for maybe a few period recordings, we always had that impression that it's just for period instruments, if you're going to do an historically-correct performance. Then we started thinking about it, and... I think Mozart did (the scordatura) in order to make (the instruments) more equal. Mozart's not an idiot; he knows what he's doing.

Scott had always done it in E flat, on a normal viola. About a month before the recording, I said to him, "Why don't you just try it?" To me it's just unfathomable, but he said he thought he'd probably be able to do it. He said that, actually, even though he had played it for decades in E flat, the scordatura makes it so much easier, clearer, brighter — even though he had to re-learn every note. It makes perfect sense to play it in D major.

Laurie: How is the viola tuned for the scordatura?

Lara: The viola is tuned exactly a half-step higher. Instead of C-G-D-A, it's D-flat-A-flat-E-flat-B-flat. Here you are playing in E-flat major, and all of a sudden you have two open strings that you didn't have before. Not only that, but the whole thing is just a little bit brighter. It makes it just about equal, if not completely equal, to the brightness of the violin.

Laurie: And he could do that.

Lara: It took him a week or so, to really get it down. He sight-reads so well; the guy never misses a note. He's Mr. Perfect. But every once in a while, when we were recording, he came in like a ton of bricks, a semi-tone off. I think it happened twice. Somehow I was so happy! (She laughs) Made a mistake, ha-ha! It was funny.

In the last movement, that's got to be one of the most awkward A-flat major solos in the world. It's very difficult to do on both the violin and the viola. But if you have a violist play scordatura, you've never seen a happier guy! It just comes in open A-flat, open E-flat. Just watching him play it, the string crossings are in different places.

Even playing the octave passages that are together with him were slightly different because I had a different open string. We did have to go through it, so I could get used to this new timbre. It feels a little different, even for the violinist.

Laurie: The violin is not scordatura.

Lara: Exactly, so we no longer have any open strings that correspond. There's quite a lot of octave work here and there, in the cadenzas, and it does change things a little bit. But once again, Mozart knew what he was doing, and I think it works absolutely fabulously; it's great.

Laurie: I didn't even know about this.

Lara: For years and years, people used another edition. But now there is a Barenreiter, and that has two parts, one in D and one in E-flat. I think for a while, the tradition was to not think about how he wrote it. The original manuscript is written in D. It's probably no problem to do the scordatura, if you don't have perfect pitch. But if do you have perfect pitch, like my brother, I think it would be quite difficult.

The Barenreiter is one of those great editions that are really expensive. They have the normal, viola scordatura arranged for normal tuning. And then, they have the original notation. I guess the editors transposed the manuscript, so that you could play it in E-flat, so you could play it not in D major. Mozart apparently only wrote the one, he wrote it in D major.

The whole thing is really fascinating.

It's hilarious whenever we play it the oboe has to give him a B-flat. At first we wondered, how do we tune to each other? We had to figure out these weird major sixths, okay I think we're kind of about right...

Laurie: Have you done it live like this?

Lara: We will — I think there are a couple next year.

Laurie: But it was the recording that made you try the scordatura.

Lara: Yeah, it's always possible to experiment.

Laurie: It's kind of cool to be able to do something new with Mozart.

Lara: Well, actually, old!

Laurie: Exactly! You have also recorded the first and third Mozart violin concerti — with Scott doing the first. The first concerto is not one I'm terribly familiar with; like a lot of people, I know the third, fourth and fifth.

Lara: I don't know it that well, either, I've never performed it. For some reason, my brother's done it quite a bit.

The point of this recording was the *Sinfonia*. Then I thought, I'll make an album of it. I told him, I'll take number Three, and you can have your choice of the other four.

To me, One is this little genius going "Hey look, I can write a violin concerto!" There all these flashy runs. To me it sounds almost on that cusp between the Baroque and the classical. The Third -- not at all any more, but the First and the Second, you can hear the Vivaldi and the Bach. You can't really hear that in the last three Mozart concerti and in the Sinfonia. I think it's a lovely piece.

Laurie: What made you pick Three, since you got first choice?

Lara: I love Three. The first time I ever read number Three was with harpist Marie-Pierre Langlamet, in a practice room in Curtis. We were sight-reading the last movement, and she was playing the piano part on the harp. She's now principal harp in Berlin, and before that was principal harp at the Met. But this was back when we were kids and students. Even though I was a pretty bad sight-reader, I could usually pull off Mozart, which was usually familiar.

We got to the little Andante (m. 252) — this beautiful moment, just so gorgeous and so heartbreaking, in the midst of all this laughter. The first time I ever played it was with harp. Of course the orchestra has pizzicato strings there, I found out much later. I thought maybe it was the most beautiful moment I'd ever experienced, up until that point. My most beautiful Mozart moment! It was just one of those moments that you always remember. So because of that, the Third has always kind of held a soft spot for me. Like most people, I've only done the last three, really: Three, Four and Five.

The second movement of the Third is so gorgeous, just one of those perfect arias he wrote for violin. And it's so joyful!

Laurie: At least for me, in the early days that I studied Mozart, people had a very Romantic take on it, the bowings were even kind of Romantic, and then lately people seem to be going back to the urtext, streamlining a little more. I wondered what your approach was. Did you change things? Have you changed things over the years? Or maybe playing it exactly the same for 20 years?

Lara: I got pretty tired, early on, of people saying, "Mozart is so difficult." I don't agree with it. Yes, there is a certain delicacy, and it's usually very exposed. Maybe if you miss one note in Mozart, it means a lot more than if you miss one note in the Shostakovich Concerto. But if you think that way, it makes people play Mozart butt-clenchingly. The whole genius of Mozart is how, with such simplicity, he was able to get so much emotion and so many ideas across. It's not good to over-think or over-analyze. Of any composer, this is the one where it's all laid out, right there! You just have to enjoy yourself and love it. If you're having a lot of fun, that comes across to an audience. And if you're super, super worried, that come across, too.

ANNE-SOPHIE MUTTER

Originally published on November 29, 2010

In this interview, Anne-Sophie Mutter says something that for me is one of the most profound statements about the compelling quality of a live performance: "Psychologically, there is a huge difference between an empty, silent room, and a room silent, with attentive, listening people."

When I caught up with Anne-Sophie Mutter earlier this month in Orange County, California, she was in the midst of so many projects that I had to write them on a piece of paper to keep track: a series of Beethoven trio concerts with Lynn Harrell and Yuri Bashmet; the release of the complete Brahms Sonatas on CD and on DVD with Lambert Orkis; and a New York Philharmonic residency in which she is playing premieres of works by contemporary composers this fall and next spring.

We spoke about her more-than-20-year collaboration with pianist Lambert Orkis, the Anne-Sophie Mutter Circle of Friends Foundation for young soloists, and more.

Anne-Sophie and Orkis started their collaboration in Carnegie Hall in December of 1988. "We've covered an enormous amount of repertoire together — not all of it is recorded," she said.

"We have totally different backgrounds," Anne-Sophie said. "Lambert Orkis comes very much from the background of contemporary music and of historic practice of performing, which is not at all my upbringing — though it has rubbed off quite a bit on my understanding of Beethoven and Mozart, for example, and Bach, of course. So we are not naturally one mind! But we have great respect for each other, obviously."

"We are both passionate rehearsers, and on the other hand, passionately un-doing things during the concert. We try to push each other to the edge. Not every evening, but there are moments when we drive it to the wall, just because the music is intensely speaking at that particular moment and the dialogue is always fresh," Anne-Sophie said. "It's like if you talk to your husband: you pretty much know where his thinking is going. But still, you would hope that a dialogue is always something which also is surprising and enriching. That's what we have achieved over the years."

"We have a musical life apart from each other, which is very helpful," Anne-Sophie said. "We bring our experiences with contemporary music, with world premieres, with his trio, and with his recording of Beethoven Sonatas, for example, on historic instruments. We bring that together, and shake and bake, and let it fly."

The moment felt right to re-record the Brahms. "I have played the Brahms Sonatas a lot over the years, sometimes as a cycle, sometimes as single pieces in a mixed recital, and we felt that we had reached a new understanding, a very personal viewpoint, different from my very first recording with (pianist) Alexis Weissenberg from the early '80s. It was ready, it was ripe to be harvested."

Though they are being released at the same time, the CD and DVD were recorded separately.

"The DVD is pretty different from the CD," Anne-Sophie said. "They were all produced in the same time frame. The CD is not a studio performance, but a performance without audience. On a rainy morning, we ran through the G major and nailed it. There was a wonderful atmosphere that morning for that particularly dark and very private piece. I think that the G major sonata that is captured on the CD could never have been that private, that personal, that whispering — with an audience present. I particularly like the recording of the G major — and I don't easily say that.

"The performance with audience (for the DVD) is simply different," she said. "We all like to play for an audience more than playing for the microphone. Standing in front of the microphone, you just have to forget the purpose of you being there, because it's going to hinder you very much."

Communication works differently in the presence of an audience, she said.

"Psychologically, there is a huge difference between an empty, silent room, and a room silent, with attentive, listening people," Anne-Sophie said. "It's a totally different atmosphere, and in that atmosphere wonderful things can happen.

Does she have a favorite of the three sonatas?

"The G major," she said. "There's such a wonderful history between Clara and Johannes, and the piece itself is really a jewel. It's wonderfully constructed, and so thoughtful, and personal."

The G major sonata, though it does not officially bear a dedication to Clara Schumann, was written following the death of one of Clara's children. Brahms uses one of her favorite tunes, from *Regenlied*, (rain song) which serves as a theme through three movements.

"There are letters going back and forth, where Clara is very much moved by the thought that Brahms would even pick one of her favorite songs as a theme," Anne-Sophie said.

In the spring, Anne-Sophie will perform with New York Philharmonic for the New York premiere of Sofia Gubaidulina's *In Tempus Praesens, Concerto for Violin and Orchestra*, which was written several years ago for Anne-Sophie.

A piece that remains in the works for a world premiere in the spring in New York is Wolfgang Rihm's *Elf and the Bear*, a piece commissioned by Anne-Sophie's foundation, for her and for bassist Roman Patkoló. Who is the elf and who is the bear? "That's the question!" Anne-Sophie said. Patkoló is a current recipient of one of the Mutter foundation scholarships, and "I'm in total awe of his talent," Anne-Sophie said. "He's not just a great technician but also a thorough, grounded, very knowledgeable musician."

And speaking of her foundation, "I'm always looking for greatly talented students for my foundation," Anne-Sophie said. Young artists between the ages of 16 and 22 are eligible to apply to be scholars.

Anne-Sophie began the foundation in Munich, Germany, in 1997, to help young soloists find the proper instruction, instruments, performance opportunities, and more.

"I wanted to have the perfect foundation, the perfect tool for young string players," Anne-Sophie said. Because the foundation is run by a musician, "the understanding of what a young string player needs is very high, out of my own experience. We also give commissions, not only for double bass but also for chamber ensemble, and we buy instruments, pay for tutoring. (Some of the scholars) are traveling with me. They are auditioning for conductors, playing for producers of CDs...there's basically nothing the foundation isn't providing. Depending on what every single person needs, from a driver's license to lectures in German or English, literature, scores, you name it. Rowing, mountain climbing, getting to know painters, I mean it's very varied, and most of the time it's really great fun."

Anne-Sophie came up with the idea for a foundation when she was a young artist, finding her way; specifically, when she faced the monumental task of procuring a fine instrument at the age of 16.

"It was Karajan who suggested that I should change my Nicola Gagliano to a Strad," Anne-Sophie said. "Back then I was kind of offended, my Gagliano's so beautiful! I never want to change it! But then, what do you know at that age? I got to know some of the great fiddles, and the next problem was, how on Earth was I going to finance that?"

Luckily, the politicians in her hometown in Germany had a commitment to culture, and they helped her to pre-finance the violin.

"That was an enormous help, but I still felt that one day I would build a foundation which would be absolutely perfect, where a musician would be the head of it, knowing what details around the life of a string player that one has to look into," Anne-Sophie said. "It was very clear to me that one day when I would eventually have more time, I would like to try something which would not be out of a specific region but really would embrace the world. So whoever needs help can knock on our door.

"She said she has enjoyed helping pair musicians with the proper instrument, though the final decision must be theirs. They have to match — like a marriage.

"Marriage with an instrument sometimes lasts longer!" she laughed. "But the good thing is you can put it back in the case and close the case; it's never talking back to you!"

She also helps scholars find the proper mentor. "Most of them are on a level where they don't need a day-to-day teacher but there they just need brainstorming, brain-picking..sometimes just sending them off to masterclasses and having a close look on their outcome after the masterclasses is enough. Sometimes very close relationships come about between these teachers and students, that's one of the main focuses, hooking them up with the right mentors. And then the next thing is to find a conductor who will take them under his wing. Not only necessarily to give a lot of concerts, but to grow musically. Christoph Eschenbach, for example, who is wonderful collaborator for my foundation because he is so open-minded towards the young generation and does chamber music with them and really serves as a mentor. That is something that is an important part of that equation."

And then, some scholars need non-musical things. "Just to get them out of their nutshell," she said. For example, one student was obsessed with playing and wanted to play from dawn to dusk. "I told him listen, playing an instrument is not about repeating. On your technical level, it's about understanding where a musical thought comes from and what it is part of, where it grows out, how it evolved. So you have to get away from the instrument! So what did I do? I took him mountain climbing in Austria and rowing on a lake. I just wanted to show him the beauty of Bruckner's landscape."

She also introduced him to a quote in German literature: "Before you go to bed in the evening, you have to ask yourself the question, do you live in order to write, or do you write in order to live?"

"For a musician it's very much that question: is it a calling or is it fortune and fame?" Anne-Sophie said.

Hint: if the answer is that you are doing it for the "fortune and fame," that's the wrong answer!

JANINE JANSEN

Originally published on February 25, 2011

Exhaustion from a heavy performance schedule caused Janine Jansen to take a break from the stage, which lasted from late summer 2010 through the end of that year. We spoke after her return to the concert stage.

Violinist Janine Jansen is back, and if you are lucky enough to be in New York this week, you'll have plenty of opportunity to see her perform: tonight she starts a series of four concerts at Avery Fisher Hall, featuring the Britten Concerto with the New York Philharmonic and Paavo Järvi. On Monday she will play selections from her new album of French works at Le Poisson Rouge with pianist Inon Barnatan.

Exhaustion from several years of a 90-plus-concert-a-year schedule had forced a five-month break on the Dutch violinist last summer and fall, but she was in good spirits on Tuesday, speaking over the phone from the recording studio at Carnegie Hall.

"I'm feeling much better — I'm very happy to be back and playing again," said Janine, who is cutting back to more like 60 or 70 concerts a year. "It was definitely a break that I needed, but I'm fine. I love music, I love being able to perform and bring music to people, and that's what I want to do."

The Benjamin Britten Violin Concerto is a favorite for Janine, who recorded the work in 2009, and the idea of four straight performances excites her.

"We have four performances with this amazing piece," Janine said of this weekend's concerts. "Over the last 12 years, everywhere I would go, I would fight for this piece." She said she probably drove a few conductors and orchestra managers crazy, "They would ask me, 'What do you want to play?'" and her response was always, "'Britten, Britten!' But it's such a great piece, it's one of the greatest for me, and I want to bring it everywhere. I know that nowadays many more violinists are playing it, but it wasn't like that before. It deserves to be played, and it's so nice that, even though the piece may not be as well-known, we can still do four concerts at Avery Fisher Hall. It's a great chance."

Janine is also promoting her newly-released recording of French and French-inspired music, called *Beau Soir* ("Beautiful evening"), a project she had in the works before her period of rest. Named for the Debussy piece by the same name, the album includes all music for violin and piano, in collaboration with pianist Itamar Golan and with new pieces written by Swiss composer Richard Dubugnon.

It was Dubugnon who saw the connection between the pieces she had chosen — the Debussy *Violin Sonata*, Messiaen *Thème et Variations*, the Ravel *Violin Sonata* and short works such as Debussy's *Clair de lune* and Fauré's *Après un rêve*. The thread that connected each piece was the night, thus the music is meant to progress through one "beautiful evening." Dubugnon sought to fill in any gaps with the composition of three new pieces: *La Minute exquise*, about a moonlight moment between two lovers; *Hypnos*, named for the Greek god of sleep; and *Retour à Montfort-l'Amaury*, an homage to Ravel that Dubugnon composed in the home where Maurice Ravel once lived, now the Musée Ravel.

Janine had met Richard Dubugnon a few years ago, when he wrote a violin concerto for her.

"I asked Richard if he would be interested in writing a few short songs for this recording, and I showed him the repertoire that I had in mind," Janine said. "He always has a very clear, bright look at things, and he really made sure that the recording had a theme going through it. He really made those bridges — going through moonlight, going through sleep, dreaming. A nice theme, I think. It adds to the recording."

Her partnership with pianist Itamar Golan has also been important, especially in a recording of French works, where both instruments have equally important roles.

"In this repertoire, especially in the Debussy Sonata, the whole sound world has to be kind of up in the air," Janine said. "It needs this incredible transparency and sound, otherwise, the whole balance in the piece is gone. It's so flexible in its form, in its characters and in its moods. One needs to be able to change and adjust to each other in seconds, to follow each other and to move together in the most flexible way. I think (the Debussy) is probably one of most challenging sonatas in that way."

And then there is that "Blues" movement in the Ravel Sonata, with its sultry slides, with a character part French and part African-American. While it has freedom, the rhythmic elements are pieced together with the precision of a clock.

"It needs to always feel a little bit like it's pulled back, but at the same time it needs to have this incredible edge and rhythm to it — and this bite," Janine said. "One can only find these things by playing together a lot. And now, even after recording, we've been playing it quite a lot in recitals together, and we still get further in that balance, finding flexibility with the control. There's also humor in it. There are moments in concerts where Itamar does something I'm not expecting — coming in slightly late after a rest or something. It makes me smile. It's great when these things happen, when you can surprise each other, but in the most positive way. If you can have fun with it together, you kind of inspire each other."

When I asked Janine if she had anything else in the works, she said that though she has a full schedule again, she is watching how much she has going at one time.

"I think that after this break, at least for the rest of this season, I have really decided I want to focus on coming back and playing concerts again. Not to immediately to dive under and drown. Just take it one step at a time," Janine said. "I think I learned a good lesson from the break I had to take, and I don't want to go back to that place, ever."

NICOLA BENEDETTI

Originally published on March 25, 2011

Certain violin concertos have been recorded many, many times, and the concertos by Max Bruch and Pyotr Tchaikovsky are among them. What can anyone say about these, that would be new? The young Scottish violinist Nicola Benedetti spoke passionately and intelligently about both, reminding me that there is a reason why such works endure. Since this interview, Nicola has released an album of movie-related violin music called The Silver Violin *in early 2013. During the same year, she was appointed* Member of the Order of the British Empire *for services to music and charity. She serves on the board for* Sistema Scotland, *a music education program that is an outgrowth of* El Sistema *in Venezuela.*

I was driving at night when I heard the familiar introduction followed by the long and low "G" that begins the *Violin Concerto* by Max Bruch. The public radio host happened to be featuring Scottish violinist Nicola Benedetti's new recording of the Bruch and Tchaikovsky *Violin Concertos*, recorded with the Czech Philharmonic under conductor Jakub Hruša; I happened to be preparing to speak to Nicola the next day.

Oh the Bruch, why the Bruch? Like many young violinists, I studied it to death back in college — then left it for dead.

But there it was, pouring out of my car speakers — and gorgeously, I must admit. I'd forgotten; this is a beautiful piece. I was picking up my son from his choir practice, so I decided to wait for him in the car and keep listening. I hadn't remembered the peace and stillness of the second movement — it's so soothing, and Nicola inhabits it with ease. My son, age 10, hopped into the car just in time for rollicking chords of the last movement. "Oh I love this music!" he said with the innocent enthusiasm of someone who has never wrestled with the pesky thirds peppered throughout the Finale.

It's not unusual for violinists to come to think of pieces such as the Bruch as a stepping stone, associated with a good deal of drudgery.

"I think that's such a danger with works that are not only popular in the concert platform but are also used as teaching pieces and practicing pieces," said Nicola the next day, speaking to me over the phone from New York. "I don't think (the Bruch) really deserves that sort of position. But on the other hand, it's great that most violin students are exposed to the music at quite a young age."

Nicola, 23, appears rather young herself, but she has already lived a very full experience as a touring and recording soloist. Since winning BBC Young Musician of the Year in 2004, she has performed with orchestras across the globe and made numerous recordings with Deutsche Grammophon, including a 2009 album of showpieces and encores called *Fantasie*, a 2008 recording of Ralph Vaughan Williams' *Lark Ascending* and works by John Tavener; a 2006 recording of the Mendelssohn *Violin Concerto* and new piece written for Nicola by James MacMillan, and a 2006 recording of the Szymanowski *Violin Concerto*, Chausson *Poeme* and more.

Recording the Tchaikovsky and the Bruch concertos — two of the most popular in the literature, was a bit of a heavy decision, she said.

"The recordings are inevitably always measured against all the other recordings of these concertos," Nicola said. "I have a very personal and very specific viewpoint of the two concertos and how they link together and how they differ, but yes, it was something I really had to feel ready to do, and I definitely took my time arriving at that decision."

The Bruch *Concerto* was written in 1866 when the composer was 28, for the violinist Joseph Joachim. Violinists and audiences immediately embraced the piece — even to the point of frustration for Bruch, who lived in the shadow of his immensely popular work (for which he was paid only a small sum and never any royalties) until he was 82. Tchaikovsky's *Violin Concerto*, written some 12 years later when the composer was in middle age, was rejected by critics and even by its dedicatee, Leopold Auer, who pronounced it "unplayable." Auer later came around — so did the critics.

"They are much more contrasting than linking," she said of the Tchaikovsky and Bruch violin concertos. "They're both usually thought of as Romantic concertos, but they are structured very differently. Bruch was quite innovative and fresh, his opening movement being a prelude and the second movement being the longest of the three and definitely the sort of meatiest movement. The last movement is quite heavy and rustic and quite bold.

"Tchaikovsky, structurally, is totally different," Nicola said. "The first movement is really the meat of the concerto, it's very typical format of sonata form, with the recapitulation which literally repeats every single note of the exposition and puts you through your paces, basically, with a coda that's probably more tricky than most codas of most violin concertos. The second movement is so fleeting and light, and just almost a short song. And the last movement is a chase. It's so wild and it's so driven and on the crazy side. So structurally, they are two very, very different concertos."

"But also, characteristically I claim them to be quite opposite, though both represent what it is about Romantic violin music that people love so much and why the Romantic era of violin-playing is so hugely popular," Nicola said. The Bruch *Violin Concerto* has an "openness and sort of optimism; there's so much peace and harmony within the concerto." The second movement, for example, is "emotive but still so optimistic. It's quite rare for a composer to manage that."

"Tchaikovsky is quite the opposite; there's not a moment of rest in the whole piece, as far as I can see," Nicola said. "Even the second subject of the first movement, which is a melody and which is meant to be a real contrast to everything that's come before: within 10 bars it is already searching for something that's never quite reached; it's really unsettled. It couldn't be more contrasting in its character to what the Bruch represents. I think they both show really important values of what the compositional style was of the Romantic era."

Nicola plays the 1723 *Earl Spencer* Strad, on loan from Jonathan Moulds, president of Bank of America for Europe and Asia.

"It think it's been about four and a half years that I've been playing it, the first year of which was a battle of trying to get to know and get to control the instrument," Nicola said. "That's the key of a great violin — it doesn't simply just do exactly what you mean, it adds something and it sort of speaks back to you. It almost becomes a dialogue between you and the instrument. I think that amount of character coming from the violin was something I struggled with a little bit in the beginning, but I really developed the strength to control it."

Nicola was born in Ayrshire, Scotland, of Italian heritage, and began playing the violin because her older sister, Stephanie, had fallen in love with the fiddle and spent four years begging their non-musical parents for lessons.

"So when I was four and she was eight, we began playing together," Nicola said. "But my parents aren't musicians at all, there was no classical music in our family, so it was really due to my sister's perseverance on that front."

She spent five years studying with the Suzuki method before she tried out for the Yehudi Menuhin School, where she began studying with Natasha Boyarskaya, shortly after her 10th birthday.

"I was very lucky that I had a teacher who taught me so much and inspired me from the word go," Nicola said. "She was a Russian violin teacher who was very strict,; she definitely demanded a lot of high-standard practice and work. But I was just so happy in that environment because it was what I'd always wanted." She studied there for about five years.

After leaving the Menuhin school, she started studying with a Polish teacher, Maciej Rakowsky, and things started happening very fast. This was when she entered the BBC Young Musician of the Year competition.

"The competition spans a year's time, so you're auditioning for the first round in May and the final of the competition isn't until May the following year," Nicola said. "A lot can happen in a year, and a lot did happen that year. IMG Artists had come to various performances in the

U.K., and following that, I began working with them."

She began to perform many, many concerts and put out recordings – she had a six-recording contract with Deutsche Grammophon and by the time she was 21 her concerts numbered more than 100 a year. At that point, she decided to step back.

"It was just a re-focus on how I was going to plan my schedule in the future, and it came after a period of time of extreme, intense performances, one after another, when I was tired and felt (I was) sort of catching up with myself rather than really on top of everything," Nicola said. "I wasn't entirely happy with how everything was going and how I felt in general. So it was a decision that came from that experience — and one that I'm very grateful I took. It's something I'm trying to continue all the time: a re-focus on how much I should be performing, what sort of repertoire, and at what time — to make sure that I'm really in control. It's a huge thing, to learn to do, especially for me. I have no close family in the industry who knew about this sort of thing."

There's no handbook on how to be a touring soloist, "but I think a lot of solo violinists do have a sort of network from a very young age, of persons who really understand the industry how it should work," Nicola said. "It's something I really had to learn for myself — which has been great, in some ways. I think it pushed me to learn more, even quicker."

If she had to give advise to a young, aspiring soloist? "Never listen to people giving you examples of other violinists or of other soloists, examples that put you under pressure to feel that you should be capable of a certain amount," Nicola said. "We all have different capacities for how much we can top-perform and how much we can cope with, and I think the key is just to try to learn as quickly as possible about yourself and about what your limits are, and never feel under pressure to live up to other people's expectations."

That said, "for me to give the advice to 'go slowly' would be slightly hypocritical because that's not really what I did the first two years of my performing career. I don't regret taking the options that I did; it gave me so much experience, and I managed to pull through," Nicola said. "But I would say to balance that with a real assessment of how much you feel you can cope with and be slightly more on the cautious side."

Nadja Salerno-Sonnenberg. Photo: Grant Leighton

NADJA SALERNO-SONNENBERG

Originally published on April 28, 2011

Nadja Salerno-Sonnenberg is one of the most vibrant people around — even on the written page!

After some three decades as a soloist, violinist Nadja Salerno-Sonnenberg is learning to "blend."

In 2008, Nadja started a new life as the director of the New Century Chamber Orchestra in San Francisco, thrusting her into the role of concertmaster, conductor, music programmer, and more. Her presence has raised the profile of the group, which took a national tour in February and has recorded two albums since she started with them: *Together* (2009) and *Live: Strauss, Barber and Mahler* (2010).

But don't get the wrong idea. If Nadja's learning to blend, she's not going bland. When you add cayenne to the sauce, the flavor changes, not the pepper. Nadja's always been known for her edge-of-your-seat performances, brimming with passion and energy, and accounts of her performances with New Century attest to the fact that she has brought this ingredient to her new band.

Nadja captured the public spotlight in 1981, when she won the Walter W. Naumburg International Violin Competition, and she went on to perform with orchestras across the globe and make numerous recordings, including many traditional classical works as well as her popular collaborations with the Assad brother guitarists. In 1999, she was the subject of *Speaking in Strings*, a documentary by Paola Di Florio that won a 2000 Academy Award and told the story of Nadja's intense personality as well as her recovery from a career-threatening accident in 1994, in which she cut off the tip of her finger.

I spoke with Nadja over the phone in March, and we talked about her career path with the violin, her recovery from the accident, her long musical relationship with the Assad family, and what it's like to be music director of New Century, after so many years as a soloist.

Laurie: I've been following your career a long time...

Nadja: I've been around a long time!

Laurie: You were born in Rome, right?

Nadja: Yes.

Laurie: How old were you when you took up the violin, and what made you want to do that?

Nadja: Well, I didn't want to do it. It was my mom's decision; I was five years old. My mom played the piano, my older brother was playing all kinds of instruments, my grandfather played, everybody played! Typical Italian family: we'd have people over to eat, and then we would go in the other room, play music and talk. I think someone told my mom, "You should give Nadja something to play, or she's going to get a complex." So my mom bought this violin — very, very cheap, the whole package. At the time, in Rome, one of her friends was moonlighting as a beginning violin teacher, so it was really an excuse for them to see each other, that's how it started. I was five years old.

I improved as a kid that age would. There was not any kind of "Oh my God, this is a prodigy" or anything like that. They saw good rhythm, very good intonation and a natural musicality — things that you can't really take credit for, it's just in your genes. So I think they saw a lot of potential. I think the teacher there did say to my mom, "Look, she could be very good if that's what you want her to pursue. If you do, I would go to the United States."

So the whole family moved here.

Laurie: And how old were you when that happened?

Nadja: I was eight.

My mom didn't know what to do with me or where to go, as far as violin teachers were concerned. She had an old friend who taught at Curtis (Institute), and she called him up for advice. He said, "Bring her in to play for the jury here, and we'll give you good advice, we'll set you on the right path." So that's what she did. She and I went into Curtis, and, I mean, I don't remember a thing. There were a lot of older people there, and she played piano for me. My mom and I played some little baby pieces, and I think they were impressed enough to accept me, I guess on potential alone. They started a preparatory division that year, with one student.

Laurie: You!

Nadja: I was it. Then the next year they held auditions for (the preparatory division), and there were like 15 little kids running around, but I was ruler of the roost by then.

Laurie: I didn't know they'd started it for you. Wow!

Nadja: When I was about 14, I pushed over to, not only another teacher, but another method of teaching: I auditioned for Dorothy DeLay at Juilliard for the pre-college division. I was accepted into pre-college there, and I went every Saturday with everybody else and did the whole day there, and then of course I auditioned for the college and got in. Actually, I never graduated from Juilliard. I won Naumberg in 1981 and I still had two years to complete. So I went back for a year as a regular student, but I didn't do very well so I just dropped out.

Laurie: Well if you're soloing and that kind of thing, I imagine it's hard to keep the studies up.

Nadja: I gotta be honest with you, I'm not a bookworm.

But it became a lot harder, yes, because I did have these concerts to play, and I did have to to prepare for them. It was all so, so new for me. I did not have an inkling of the time-management skills that I now have. So it was difficult for me, and I was falling behind in classes, so I dropped out.

But you know, every time I say that, people say, "Oh, what did it matter? In your field you don't need a degree...." It's all very true; I went on to have a wonderful solo career. But I always felt like I missed out, and I always wished that I had the college degree. I was given an honorary Master's, which is really the way to get a Master's. (Both of us laugh.) Let me tell you, that is the way to do it! So I have something on my wall.

Laurie: Where's that master's from?

Nadja: New Mexico State University.

Laurie: For a long time I've had your recording, called *Ain't Necessarily So*. When I first heard it, I was really moved by the *Leibesleid* – '*Love's Sorrow*.' I read the notes that you'd written, and you talked about your grandmother. I myself was extremely close to my own grandmother, she lived with us, and this was very near my own grandmother's death, when I read your notes, and that inspired me learn the piece. You hinted that your grandmother had a real impact on your character and personality, and I wanted to ask you what you meant by that, how she helped shape who you are.

Nadja: Well what I am as a person, I pretty much owe to my grandmother. My mother was always there, but when I was growing up, she was always a disciplinarian to me, which I'm very grateful for and she is now very grateful for, because I can take care of her! But she had to go to work, in her own defense, and earn a living. We all lived together, as is quite common with European families, so the grandparents lived with us. So when my mom went off to teach at the Philadelphia public school system, it was my grandmother who took care of me and raised me. She is the person I spent the most time with, so I learned what I know about life — and about living – from her. Everything which is personal about me, I learned from my grandmother. And it stayed with me — it stays with me. Being in her presence, I watched how people reacted to my grandmother, how people loved her, why they loved her and how they always wanted to be around her, how she had this power. She was a completely uneducated immigrant. That was a huge influence on my character.

Laurie: There has been so much documented about your injury, how difficult it was, and how it was a time of deep depression...

Nadja: That's good copy for a violinist, you know, when you chop off a finger.

Laurie: I imagine there's another side of it, because here you are. I wondered what kept you going during that difficult period of time and how you kept moving forward.

Nadja: When I look back on it, it happened in 1994. At that time in my career, I was completely overworked. It's funny, because I feel that way now, but now it's what I bring into my own life. Then... the management and the publicists do their thing, and you go for the ride, you go along with the tide of it. I was really starting to hit existential despair about playing, and it was becoming very clear to me, the sacrifices I had to make in order to keep this career on the level that it was. I was overworked and tired and questioning things — and I had this horrible accident. At the time, I thought it was a sign, a really clear sign. Of course, the people who were closest to me were also supporting (that idea), because what do you tell someone who is a solo violinist who lost a finger? You just want to try to re-frame it.

It was shocking. It was a shocking day, and everything that I knew of my life thus far was gone, in less than a second. When I came out of the shock, I realized that I would probably would never play again. What was I going to do? I started thinking in those terms. For a while, it was a little bit exciting. As I said, I was tired. I really knew that I could not continue at that pace.

So I looked into this and looked into that, thinking about different possibilities for my future. Meanwhile, the weeks passed and the months passed. The income wasn't coming in because, of course, I had to cancel everything for quite a bit of time. I started to feel pressure to make money again, to be perfectly honest with you. So I was trying to heal the finger and force a quicker recovery than was happening.

I came up with a way of bandaging the finger, multiple times, with New-Skin, with padding, so that I could actually put it down on the fingerboard without feeling the pain or opening up the incision. I came back and played a number of recitals: I remember I played the Tchaikovsky Concerto on tour. I was able to sort of put the finger down, but certainly with no pressure. I used the finger, in a sense, for runs and fast passages, but to actually put the finger down and vibrato and hold the note? That was out of the question. So basically I had to re-finger all this repertoire for three fingers. I played about four months' worth of concerts doing that...

Laurie: Three-finger Tchaikovsky? That sounds pretty hard!

Nadja: I know, it's hard enough with four fingers!

Laurie: It would be hard with five!

Nadja: You know, things that you look back on, and just think, how did you do that? Why did you do that? Wow.

And it came to pass that I actually missed playing. So I think that the accident was meant to be, and it was a sign, and it was a Godsend, to actually kick me in the ass, to remind me why I play the violin anyhow. I missed it a lot, and when I started playing again, I felt whole again.

Everything's fine, 10 years later. I've healed. But I still try to remember how I missed it, and why I play. I had a 100-percent recovery. Later on, skin was grafted from my toe onto the finger so there wasn't any scar, so it's as if it never happened.

Laurie: That sounds like a really difficult lesson, a difficult way to learn something like that.

Nadja: You ought to learn from everything. It's just an attitude that I believe in. Even if it's just sitting in a pile of crap for a long time, you have to think to yourself, there's something here that I'm going to come away with that's going to be very valuable. I've had a few moments, a few real turning points in my life, and I'm very grateful for them.

Laurie: I have been listening to your CDs: *Originis, Nadja and the Assads*

Live from Brasil (2004); *Tchaikovsky and (Clarice) Assad Concertos* (2004); the first album with the New Century Chamber Orchestra, *Together* (2009) and New Century's new release, *Live: Strauss, Barber and Mahler.*

Many of your albums over the last 10 years have involved collaborations with guitarists Sérgio and Odair Assad, as well as Sergio's older daughter, Clarice Assad, who is a composer. I wondered, how did that relationship come about?

Nadja: That came through Nonesuch records. I had signed a contract to start recording with them, and the Assads were already recording for them. At the time, they were very family-oriented and they wanted their artists to work with each other. So I was introduced to them, and I was blown away by what I was hearing. We came up with a project for the recording company, and that's how that started. The project was hugely successful, and we toured together for about 16 years.

Laurie: It seems like it's a really good combination, what do you think works for you with the Brazilian...

Nadja: It wasn't so much Brazilian, they just happened to be Brazilian. It was the combination of the two guitars and the violin, and Sérgio was a really fantastic arranger. If you have a great arranger, the sky's the limit. One of the first things I ever heard them play, before I knew who they were, was *Rhapsody in Blue* – for two guitars! I thought, wow, that guy can arrange.

For the first project that Nonesuch wanted, they basically gave the three of us carte blanche. My first instinct was to do something Baroque, but Sérgio had another idea in his head. He'd had Gypsy music in his head for a while. So he came up with these extraordinary arrangements of original folk tunes from where the Gypsies traveled, in Eastern Europe. Each one had a little folk tune, and he made these incredible arrangements. This turned out to be a hugely successful album, and then Nonesuch put us on tour with it and the trio became very popular. So at one point, we played two tours a year, just constantly playing together. That was a fantastic partnership.

Laurie: It sounds like a lot of fun, too, the music just sounds fun. I also saw that Clarice (Assad) wrote you a violin concerto, and I wondered if you worked together on that, or if she just did it and gave it to you...

Nadja: We didn't work on it at all together, she just wrote it and gave it to me. She wrote that violin concerto for her masters thesis at University of Michigan, and I said, I'll come out and play the concerto, if it helps you to pass, get an A, whatever it takes. So she gave the piece to me, and I liked it so much. I thought it was an amazing first effort — she had not written for orchestra before. So I recorded it.

Laurie: It does seem like the kind of thing that would be fun for violinists to play.

Nadja: It's a wonderful little piece, and everything about life is timing. At that time, when she presented the piece to me, I had agreed to record the Tchaikovsky *Violin Concerto* with my old colleague Marin Alsop and her orchestra at the time, the Colorado Symphony. We were debating about what the other piece would be, because you need more than just the Tchaikovsky, and we just couldn't agree on the other piece for that album. Then boom, I got the concerto from Clarice, and it was in the same key. I thought, I really like this piece, let's do it. And Marin agreed. So it's timing. It just happened that way, and it was a good break for Clarice as well.

Laurie: You have a whole new life now with the New Century Chamber Orchestra. I was going through the orchestra's blog, and you guys have entirely too much fun, or at least it looks like it!

Nadja: We do have a lot of fun when we're playing, and fun when we're rehearsing. Pretty much everything musically with us is so vibrant and wonderful. The other side of that coin, and it's not a bad side, it's just another side, is building an orchestra in a time when it's pretty much impossible to do that. The challenges that we face, financial and otherwise, are extraordinary right now. Yet, it's working. It's working phenomenally well. I think people are moved by inspiration, and people are moved by results, and if you have a combination of these two things, the loyalty and the momentum is always there. So when we're faced with another challenge, we find a way to meet it and conquer it.

I'm on my third season with the orchestra now, and so I'm lucky to have musicians that believe in me and trust in me. I'm lucky to have a staff that is willing to be molded and I'm lucky to have a board which supports me. It's all about inspiration, and it's result-driven. I just took them on tour, and we just released our second album. That's pretty fabulous, considering the times that we live in, and the structure of this organization. They're seeing results, and everyone is having a very good time, fighting the good fight.

Laurie: What is it like, after you've played as a soloist for so long, to be the director of an ensemble?

Nadja: It's something that I've only recently gotten pretty adjusted to, and I'm in my third season. For one thing, I had no idea what the "music director" job description entailed. I thought that I would rehearse the orchestra, get them ready for concerts, lead them in the concerts and pick out the programs, come up with some recording ideas. I had no idea how much (administration) the job entailed. And then, of course, the job entails much more than any other music director because it's my responsibility to put them on the map. That's why they hired me, and that was what I decided I was going to do. So the job became so much more than I thought it would be: it became my life and my musical purpose. It's great, but it is extremely time-consuming.

Musically-speaking, the job was challenging because here I had to sit in a concertmaster chair, and that's not what I am used to, at all. I just didn't know anything about it! Anything! I would say the hardest thing for me in that position is to blend. Blend, and lead at the same time. It's a challenge because I'm sitting in the concertmaster's chair, therefore I'm a member of the first violin section. I have to play that part, but I have to lead the whole orchestra, there's no conductor. So for about a year and a half, possibly two seasons, when I listened to CDs of our performances, I could hear me, over the rest of the section. I know why: it's because I had more responsibility, I have to lead, and I have to be the strong player. But it's still not right; I have to blend with them.

Another huge challenge for me was respecting what is on the page. As a soloist, you respect it to the point where your ego comes in. That's actually what you should do, as a soloist. So for me, as a soloist, a dotted quarter is whatever I want it to be, but as an orchestra member, it is what it is. So it was hard for me to pull back and respect that.

But it's been an amazing adjustment. If I had to sum up what my life has become: I am a total and complete chameleon. I go from one persona to another, very quickly. Director, first violinist, soloist, label owner...whatever it takes, I become that instantly.

Laurie: What do you think they're learning from you?

Nadja: Good question. I think what I brought was a vibrancy, and certainly it's goal-oriented now.

Laurie: What do you mean by that?

Nadja: I mean, they see that they are becoming more and more known and respected. People are actually saying it's the best string orchestra in the United States, which it absolutely is, but people are saying it now! So I think everybody is seeing that, so that trust is there. But I think musically, what they possibly could be learning — I cannot speak for them — is that every note is important, no matter what that is. It could be accompaniment part, it could be a sustained note that you're holding for 16 measures – it still has vibrancy and importance — and a meaning, within the piece. I think that they maybe get that from me. And then there's a lot of energy. I bring a lot of energy to the group.

Laurie: What do you have on the plate for the future, here?

Nadja: Just to sustain this enormous growth we're going through right now, trying to expand our season to include more sets in one season. There's another tour, an east-coast tour that's being planned for November. Of course, recordings will not stop. Just this growth of this orchestra that nobody really heard of except in the Bay Area now has a wide and wonderful national radio presence and we're playing live all over the country. This makes you, it's funny, you have to go somewhere else to be appreciated at home. So it's a strange rule of the world of entertainment, but it's true. So now this is all coming together beautifully, in a very difficult time.

Laurie: And you live in New York, right? So what's it like, to sort of be "bi-coastal"?

Nadja: What you think it is, you get on a plane.

Laurie: I'd think it might be kind of a pain.

Nadja: It is a pain. For someone who's as busy as I am, not because I loved the show so much and it became such a part of my life, but I very much wish we lived in a Star Trek world, where you could just literally just energize to somewhere else and not have to lose an entire day, flying from the west coast to the east coast.

Laurie: Or even a Harry Potter world; we could "apparate."

Nadja: Yes, Harry Potter, too, you are absolutely right.

Laurie: One last question for my violin geek folks. What kind of violin do you play?

Nadja: I like to joke about it and say: I play a used one. It's Peter Guarnerius, Venice, made in 1721.

Laurie: Nice. Still in love?

Nadja: Yeah, I love the instrument. We had an instant chemistry when I first played it, and as far as the size is concerned, it fits my hand perfectly, and it's been a very good instrument for me. I have to say, as a violinist, I think I am the most not-interested-in-instruments soloist of any soloist I've ever met or encountered or talked to or read about. It's always, "Gotta get the next best violin, I bought this one, I've sort of half-paid it off, I'm going to sell it, I'm moving up, I'm going to get this, I used to like Strads, now I like del Gesus..." For some people, it becomes their life. I can certainly see that, but I found a good instrument, I just stuck with it. There are better instruments out there, there are certainly worse instruments, but I feel fine. It's like a really good marriage, I don't have to look any further.

Judy Kang. Photo: Chuck Willis

JUDY KANG

Originally published on May 10, 2011

What is it like, for a highly-trained classical violinist to drop into the world of popular music — in fact, into one of the most popular bands of all-time? Judy Kang gave us a window into her experience as Lady Gaga's violinist during the pop artist's huge Monster Ball Tour *of 2009-2011. Since this interview, Judy Kang released an album,* Judy Kang, *in March 2013, with her own compositions which draw on both her pop and classical sensibilities.*

One day in 2010, Curtis-trained classical violinist Judy Kang set aside the Strad she was playing and hit the road with a brand-new, hot-pink electric fiddle.

You could say she went gaga. More accurately, you could say she joined Lady Gaga's enormously popular *Monster Ball* tour, playing hundreds of shows for more than a million people in all corners of the globe.

And she didn't exactly leave the classical world behind — even while on tour, she occasionally sneaked away to play a classical gig, for example, the Brahms *Violin Concerto* at Carnegie Hall.

But before roaming the world with a rock band, Kang had already covered the map as a classical musician. Born in Edmonton, Canada, Kang has played in orchestras across the United States, Europe and Asia. In addition to her Bachelor's degree from Curtis, she also has a Master's degree from Juilliard, as well as Artist Diploma from the Manhattan School of Music. When playing classical music, she performs on the 1689 *Baumgartner* Stradivarius, on loan from the Canada Council for the Arts.

What's it like to live in both the classical and pop music worlds? Well, let's start at the beginning:

Laurie: What made you decide to start playing the violin in the first place? How old were you?

Judy: My grandmother had a dream the night before I was born — she saw a baby girl holding a violin. So she told my mom, who never played an instrument but had always wanted to. My mother then naturally had the desire to start me on the violin — but only if I was a girl, according to her. As an infant, I was inclined to stop and listen or dance to classical music, as well as other kinds of music, but in particular classical. I had my first lesson when I was four years old and took private lessons on the Suzuki method.

Laurie: I know that you had been playing as a classical soloist, can you give us some idea how many concerts you had been playing a year, with whom, and what kind of music?

Judy: I performed an average of 50-70 classical concerts a year, with orchestras, in recital, and chamber music. I performed standard repertoire as well as explored other kinds of music. I also performed in music rock venues, and clubs collaborating with bands of all types including indie, rock, hip hop, and jazz. I also performed with my own band, which is a mix of electronic, dub, ambiant, and trip hop.

Laurie: How did you learn about this gig with Lady Gaga?

Judy: It was brought to my attention, through a bandmate, that she was looking to have a violinist.

Laurie: Was there an actual audition process? I'm guessing you didn't have to play (Richard Strauss's difficult orchestral excerpt from) *Don Juan*, so what was it like?

Judy: I did go through an audition process. It was first through her musical director, and I was called back immediately. There were several violinists that auditioned, first in Los Angeles, then they held auditions in New York City. I came to the audition in New York. It was a very last-minute thing — I was told about it two nights before the first audition. I got my outfit together the day before and played the next day.

All the contenders were brought into the room at the same time, and we essentially played in front of each other. I had *Bad Romance* and *Speechless* prepared. I had an outline of what I wanted to present, but of course, as I had expected, I ended up playing in the moment: An improvised solo with the two songs as the themes. It was about three or four minutes, and then my callback was a freestyle. I played some of the *Bad Romance* and went into whatever I felt in the moment — virtuosic lines, and some of her song, *Paparazzi*.

The final audition was the next day at an undisclosed location. Gaga was there along with the Haus of Gaga — her creative team and musical director as well. She hand-picked me out of four finalists. It was an amazing feeling, feeding off of her and her team's energy! I love the freedom I had when I performed for her. In some ways, being able to go in without a set list was amazing. But, the possibilities in that case are so endless that I had to think through what I could give to express a lot of different emotions, moods, and technical virtuosity in less than five minutes. I loved the challenge of it!

Laurie: Tell me a little bit about the commitment you have to make, when you sign up for a show like this: how much of your time is it? Does your whole life revolve around the show for a while? Were you worried about leaving behind your classical-music life? Did you kind of have to even leave behind your whole life? What made you say "yes"?

Judy: Initially, it was a year-long commitment, which then extended into a year-and-a-half-long tour. It is a full-time commitment for the most part, with a few breaks in between, at which time, I had complete freedom to do my own projects. I definitely felt excited because I had always wanted to broaden my horizons through experiencing different types of music in different contexts. I wasn't really worried about leaving the classical music life, because I don't ever feel like I left it behind. I believe there is a purpose in every opportunity given in your life, and it is obviously your choice whether to go through that door, or to pass it up. I felt, at this point in my life, I would have regretted passing it up. I am not necessarily a believer that everything happens for a reason, but I know there is always something to be learned when something new comes along in life.

In a sense, I did leave my whole life behind. I was in New York, and I had concerts scheduled. There were a few factors that made me hesitate to say yes initially, and that was one of them. This was the first (and last) time that I had to back out of the concerts I was scheduled to perform. Fortunately, everyone was so supportive, and in many ways, even more excited for me to have this opportunity. That made me feel more at ease and encouraged. I got a lot of advice from family, friends, mentors, everyone! I prayed a lot, and I didn't commit until a few weeks in. My decision to fully commit was determined by getting to know the people I was going to work with and be with for the next year-plus, how we worked together, how our personalities meshed, and all in all, what my heart was telling me. I felt comfortable right off the bat with them, and I just got more and more excited about working with them.

Laurie: Tell me about your set-up. What kind of electric fiddle do you have? What made you choose the instrument that you have, what were the considerations? Was some of it about the "look"?

Judy: I perform solely on an electric violin by Mark Wood. I have sound effect pedals, as well. I wasn't too knowledgable about electrics, to be honest. I was so fortunate to have had a couple of weeks of rehearsals before going on the road, to research instruments. I made a cold call to Mark Wood after suggestions from colleagues, and he was amazing enough to hand-deliver an instrument to me a couple of days later at the rehearsal studio! I had a five-stringed instrument brought to me. Of course, this was the first time I had ever played a five-string, let alone an electric. It was a blast! I had so much fun discovering new feels, new techniques and new sounds... I even shredded on it to the point where my band guitarists and I were having solo contests for fun because of the similarity of sounds! I decided this was the right violin for the show because of the flexibility of movement I have while performing on it. It looked perfect, and it blended well with the other instruments in the band.

I also enjoyed envisioning of how it would work in the show, collaborating and lending my visual opinions to Mark's designer in order to come up with something very personal and creative. I visualized a shiny hot pink violin, and it came to life through the awesomeness of Mark Wood and company!

Laurie: What were some of the adjustments you had to make, going from playing as a concert soloist to playing in this wildly popular show? Do you have to do much dancing or acting in the show? How is the music different?

Judy: I had about two weeks before our first show to get used to playing on the instrument, moving around, walking, dancing and adjusting sounds. The measurements are also a bit different, as well as the touch. I didn't find it too difficult. A lot of the process was very organic and I learned as I went along. I still feel like I am able to discover new sounds and techniques. I think that is a lifelong process. I definitely am a character in the show, as it tells a story. I think one of my favorite aspects is the ability to dance. I've always loved it, and in a sense, this gave me the opportunity to do two things that I love simultaneously. Stylistically, I didn't feel like it was totally venturing out into new territory, as I had always loved pop music and other styles of music. As long as I can remember, I listened to it, and I think that exposure became engrained in me with regard to the articulations, sounds and rhythms. I essentially am bringing what I do and always have done in the past into the show and of course, am influenced by the music but in very organic ways. It feels very natural to me.

Laurie: One of my students arrived at his lesson, very excited to tell me that he recognized a familiar violin song in a Lady Gaga tune.... so is that you, playing Vittorio Monti's *Czardas* at the beginning of the song, *Alejandro*?

Judy: I play it live solo in her shows and performances.

Laurie: What is your favorite Lady Gaga tune at this point, and for what reason? Do you have a different perspective on pop music after doing this tour?

Judy: It changes, but I think overall, *Bad Romance*, because it is amazing lyrically, instrumentally and stylistically. She sounds amazing, and it's just such a big pop tune. Yet having said that, all of her songs are pretty epic, for the most part. This is a tough one to answer, for sure!

My eyes have definitely been open and perspective broader, as to how I perceive pop music. Being around pop artists, writers and producers in the last year and a half has definitely shown me how intricate the process can be. Working in a band capacity has also helped me see how similar the process of practicing is to chamber music. I see how much the lyrics mean to the artists, and that they do come from a very personal place.

Laurie: Are the fiddle parts fun for this music? Are any of them difficult? In what way?

Judy: They are definitely fun! I think the best part is that there wasn't any sheet music. I pretty much created parts and also borrow from different sounds within the songs. I added some lines to certain songs to enhance the performance in the large venues that we perform in. The challenge I might find is not necessarily in the notes, but in staying consistent rhythmically. It is chamber music. You always have to be listening to each other in the band and staying tight. Something that can be challenging with the hiss of a crowd and moving about the stage as you play.

Laurie: My 13-year-old daughter suggested I ask you: Did you get to wear any really weird costumes for the show? Is it just one costume for the show, or do you have to change throughout? Are the costumes different on different nights? Do the costumes pose any logistical issues?

Judy: Haha! Now that is a good question! I was so excited about our costumes and what they would be like. I knew my character, but I had no idea how that would be manifested. I wear a black, lacy dress, form-fitted, with fishnet stockings, hot pink stiletto boots and lots of bedazzled jewelry! The attire is actually quite comfortable and it is the only dress I wear throughout the show.

Laurie: What is the craziest thing that has happened to you on this tour?

Judy: Too many to even remember! We always say, if we had a reality show, we'd be getting the ratings! Everyone has such an enormous and unique personality. There have been so many amazing, crazy situations, from backstage, to being in our tour bus, to some of the things the fans have done or given to me and my colleagues. I think the craziest moment I had on tour must have been when I was jamming with the Kidz — how Gaga refers to us — at our Christmas party, and I broke my bow. It just snapped. It took me a second to realize it. But, funny enough, I wasn't too upset. I guess it felt very Rock 'n' Roll. I was able to get it repaired and it's almost as good as new!

Laurie: What has been the most memorable moment, performing?

Judy: Lollapalooza was insane! I think the outdoor shows are crazy because of the sense of connection with the audience. It's more raw, and you can see the people clearly. I think it has to do with the open air and not ever knowing what to expect. In that situation, there are so many more magical moments. You have to be prepared for anything that can happen, or for the unknown, and just let things be. You can't rehearse or duplicate those moments. I think in each show, we definitely have an amount of flexibility to be spontaneous. There have been several shows where I jammed on a song without having heard or rehearsed it at all. I love that. It's definitely not the first time I've performed something spontaneously on stage.

Laurie: Do you have any fun stories to share?

Judy: Well, I did a concert on one of my breaks in Toronto. I played a concerto with Sinfonia Toronto. After the performance, I was talking to some people, and one of the audience members introduced herself and said that she had come to the Toronto *Monster Ball* show last summer. She was randomly listening to the classical radio station and heard them mention the concert and my name. So, she recognized me and came to the concert. She said it was the first classical concert she had ever been to and she loved it and enjoyed it.

Laurie: Do you feel you are reaching a different audience, has this work given you any sense of mission?

Judy: I am definitely reaching another audience. I get approached, receive notes and emails from fans saying they are inspired to start playing the violin, or they want to listen to classical music. I also met people who are classical fans while being fans of Gaga. I am so excited to be an artist in this day and age, as I feel that artists are influenced by everything. It is hard to not be exposed to a lot these days with technology. I have always felt a mission to serve through music. To be an ambassador of sorts and an example, and to inspire and motivate each other. I want to also open up people's minds and eyes to the endless possibilities of being an artist.

Laurie: Have you missed the classical repertoire?

Judy: I miss it. Especially when I listen to recordings and practice old rep. I try to stick in as many concerts as I can in between tours. Last May, I was able to take a morning flight out of London to do a Carnegie Hall performance that night and fly back to Manchester for a show the night after. I was even more inspired and refreshed with the diversity of music that I had been performing.

Laurie: How has this experience changed you?

Judy: This is a vast question. I feel I could write a whole book about how this experience has, and continues, to shape me. For the most part, I believe that being around so many different personalities — strong personalities, I might add — has given me the chance to view things in various perspectives regarding so many things in life. I've learned about true compassion and understanding of how people can have different opinions and beliefs yet feel very connected and related. I also learned more about myself as an individual and an artist through all of the things I've experienced. I can't really say that my lifestyle is different, in the sense that my daily routine is pretty much the same. I went in with the desire to build strong relationships and to be a positive influence. I wanted to challenge myself and be challenged in all areas of my life in order to become a better person and creative artist. I feel that being in this environment has exposed me to the realities and the ins and outs of the industry, and in turn, I've become more keen and wise in that area. In so many ways, I've resisted the "showbiz" mentality and believed so strongly that it would just develop organically. And it did, to a certain extent. But, it's about finding the balance between the two. But in the end, I am a firm believer that everything serves a purpose in life and I know that this will only help me to further reach my dreams.

Laurie: What's next for you?

Judy: I've reached the end of the *Monster Ball* tour after an intense and exciting time of traveling around the world to amazing destinations and performing for full arenas of over 20,000 fans every other night. I think a couple weeks of sleep is next on my agenda! Spending time with family and friends, eating home-cooked meals, being in one place for longer than two days....I definitely want to get back to playing chamber music as soon as possible! Reading trios, duos, quartets with friends, getting back to doing some recitals…I am excited about what's to come, which is in some ways is a mystery, but I have some projects planned for the near future. I am excited about recording a new CD, collaborating with some amazing artists, as well as writing a lot of new pieces... I hope to continue working with various artists and conductors. I am always visualizing, always creating new ways for performance and art in my mind. I love teaming up and collaborating with artists who may share similar visions and ideas.

David Garrett. Photo courtesy David Garrett.

DAVID GARRETT

Originally published on June 21, 2012

German violinist David Garrett plays pop shows and is one of the most well-known violinists on the planet. His shows sell out huge venues all over the world, but is he a "sellout"? No way. You can't fake the kind of high regard and commitment he has to classical music, musicians, and acoustic violin.

You might know David Garrett as a showman — someone with a model's good looks who plays rock-n-roll violin in amphitheaters. After all, his last album was called *Rock Symphonies*; he's appeared on all kinds of TV shows, and he wound up with the Guinness World Record for playing *Flight of the Bumblebee* in 60 seconds.

But even if David has found great success and enjoyment covering tunes such as *Smooth Criminal* and performing the occasional stunt, he never has renounced his classical roots.

His new classical recording, *Legacy*, was released in the United States this month and has been climbing the classical charts in Germany. It includes his performance, with the Royal Philharmonic Orchestra conducted by Ion Marin, of the Beethoven *Violin Concerto* with cadenzas by Fritz Kreisler, as well as other works by Kreisler.

David writes in the program notes: "My home has always been classical music...I know of no adventure more thrilling than that of discovering the works of great composers like Bach, Beethoven, Mozart,

Brahms, Tchaikovsky and so many more. It is my hope and my wish that this album will help open the hearts of my listeners to the beauty of classical music."

We spoke over the phone several weeks ago, about his early years as a prodigy, about recovering from injury, about his Guadagnini and Strad violins, and about his attitude that performing should be joyful.

Born in Germany, David started playing the violin at age 4, mostly to be like his brother. "I always thought it was a cool thing to do because my older brother was doing it," David said. "It was typical for me to want to have the same things as he did, from clothes, to games, to the violin."

Unlike his brother, who was forced to learn an instrument, "I actually did want to play in the beginning."

Pop music — which David certainly has embraced today — did not meet with much approval from David's parents during his childhood. "It's not that they said, 'You're not allowed to listen to it,' but it was pretty clearly stated that it's not really something which is a quality product," David said. "I always felt almost embarrassed, at a certain age, listening to it. Of course, that's the most ridiculous thing, but when you're young, your parents have a big influence on you."

David was on that young classical prodigy track: he started winning local competitions at age five and playing in public at age seven. At age 10, he soloed with the Hamburg Philharmonic Orchestra, and he was working with conductors such as Zubin Mehta and Claudio Abbado by age 13. At age 14, he was signed to record for Deutsche Grammophon and proceeded to record Mozart violin concertos, Paganini *24 Caprices*, Beethoven *Spring Sonata*, Bach solo works, and the Tchaikovsky and Conus violin concertos — all by the time he was 17.

It was a lot of success for someone so young, but it was also rather stressful.

"I started having problems with my left arm, when I was about 15 or 16 years old," David said. "I pretty much had it until age 21, so that's almost five years. I would go on stage feeling miserable because I was in pain. I felt I couldn't really emotionally connect with music because physically, I was not free. It was a very difficult time in my life."

He couldn't convince his parents that he should see a doctor about the pain. "My father and my mother did not believe in seeing doctors," he said. "I was complaining, 'It doesn't feel right, I can't really move my hands properly.' But being a classical ballet dancer, my mom is kind of a tough cookie. She always said, 'Mind over matter.'"

Things did not get better, so after three years of pain, he went to the doctor on his own, at age 17. "It was just a combination of really bad stuff: the wrong positioning of the violin; practicing a lot; shoulder and neck problems and that went into the arms; a little bit of tendonitis here and there."

How did he get rid of it? First of all, he changed his daily practice routine to several 20- to 30-minute practice sessions, with breaks in between. "It's actually much smarter than practicing for two or three hours in a row," David said. "I find my brain does not function as well after a half an hour. For me, you have to be 100 percent there, physically and mentally. After 30 to 40 minutes, you kind of start practicing wrong. And there's only one thing which is worse than not practicing: it's practicing wrong!"

He also learned to re-position the violin, and he hit the gym.

"Violin playing is not necessarily the most comfortable and the most natural position, so you have to train your back, your whole body," David said. "You've got to be in shape, to be able to play two-and-a-half-hour shows. There's no way you can do this without physically being quite athletic."

What kind of physical activity has helped?

"I do a little bit of cardio, and mostly weight training, just really to get the right muscle groups," David said. "Of course I'm careful, in the sense that every motion is controlled. I'm not stupidly just pushing pushing pushing, I'm very aware what I do. But I do do the weights, and I push myself hard. I think it's very important that you build up muscle groups; it really helps in the playing. Of course, I'm not going to go extreme and bulk up a lot; that would be counter-productive for playing."

"In the beginning, it feels uncomfortable and you think it's going to ruin your playing," David said. "But that's just because you've never worked those muscles. People give up too quickly. If you do this for three months, you will see a big difference — you're going to be more relaxed.

I even work out on the day of a show. Three hours before, I hit the gym hard; no problems."

And how does David mentally prepare for a show? He doesn't feel that it's so much mentally preparing as it is being fully ready. "You're either ready or you're not ready. Confidence is, in that sense, worked. You prepare yourself — you practice, you make yourself comfortable with the piece, and then there's nothing you can do on the day of the show."

"All practicing is practicing your concentration, practicing performing," he said. "It's very important, not just to practice the piece, but to practice playing music. Then when you're on stage, try to make yourself as comfortable as possible. See the stage as your home, as your friend. Don't see it as something you feel uncomfortable with. And invite people to listen to music. It's a blessing to be playing for people, and you should enjoy it. Anything to do with nerves or not being secure with what you have to do is always going to lead to not performing as well. You have to know that you just play better if you're relaxed. You can't stop mistakes from happening. Of course when you practice and you're well with your concentration, they won't happen. But nerves only get in the way, they will not make it better. Once you realize that, you're not nervous."

In terms of teachers, David has worked with some of the strongest personalities and best players of the last century: Ida Haendel, Isaac Stern, Yehudi Menuhin and Itzhak Perlman. He started taking trips to London to see Ida when he was still very young.

"Ida is such a character," David said. She always insisted that she was not a teacher. "We would just listen to each other — she played a lot for me, I played a lot for her. She always insisted that it's not about doing it her way. She wanted me to realize that she had really worked on her own interpretation. Then she would say, 'I put my thoughts into it, now show me what you want to say with it.' She would never say 'Do it like this,' or 'Do this fingering,' or 'Do this bowing,' or 'Phrase it that way.' It didn't matter if she liked it or didn't like it, but it was very important for her that I think about it for myself."

At age 18, David made a unilateral decision to move to New York to study with Itzhak Perlman at Juilliard. "I was readjusting my violin-playing, because I had been without a teacher for quite some time," David said. "Of course I saw Ida, but it was not very regular. So when I went to Juilliard, for me it was more about adjusting certain things that had gotten a little loose: bow arm technique, being aware of sound."

"You can play beautifully, but if you are not being heard properly through the orchestra, nobody will hear it," David said. "It's all about projecting and really being a serious soloist, and having the right physical position in order to get this sound. So that was what I learned mostly from Perlman."

It was at Juilliard that he won a composition competition in 2003 for a Bach-style fugue, and composition remains an important facet of his playing career, both in crossover and in classical music.

In his new album, "All the Kreisler pieces have been newly arranged by me and my good friend, Franck van der Heijden," Garrett said. Those pieces, which they have set to rich orchestration, include *Praeludium and Allegro*; Kreisler's version of *Variations on a Theme by Paganini* by Rachmaninov; *Caprice Viennois*; *Variations on a Theme of Corelli*; *Romance: Larghetto On A Theme By Carl Maria von Weber*; *Tambourin Chinois*; and *Liebesleid*.

"We even put an organ in the background!" David said. "It kind of works, it really is that period, with that Bach kind of sound. I just felt the chords were so very choral-like, like in a Johann Sebastian Bach chorale, so it fits," David said. "It was really nice, especially with the Corelli, to add some harpsichord. I was trying to go with the same basic idea which Kreisler intended, and just update it a little bit more."

The result, to me, is rather epic, for example, in *Praeludium and Allegro*, a piece that I've never heard accompanied by anything other than a piano.

"Some of the pieces, they work beautifully that way," David said. "Of course, you can't just rewrite everything 'epic,' some pieces you have to just leave in that chamber music mode, there's no way to change that. But if it's possible, I'm of course a fan of making it substantial."

Even when David plays his big-ticket crossover concerts that feature popular music, he believes in hiring a substantial orchestra as well. "If I go on the road on a tour and it's basically me lining up the people, it's normally like 50 to 60 people on stage, which is a good, solid symphony orchestra."

Why not just use a synthesizer for the pops concert?

"Because it sounds better with an orchestra; it sounds alive!" David said. "There's nothing more important than music being alive. You can't manufacture music, it needs to come out of the moment. It's like when you talk: you think in that moment, and you say something which means something to you. That's very important in music. Although we repeat the things, it always has to have conviction. With a synthesizer, it would just be repetitive, and I don't like that."

Also, "I never use anything but a classical violin, and I'll tell you why: I think the sound sucks from an electric violin — for me, personally," David said. "If you know how to play the classical violin properly, the electric violin is not even five percent in comparison. Everything you need is in that instrument, to do any music you desire."

What makes a violin great is its subtlety and range. "The colors, the different dimensions, the phrasing, going from little to everything — these kinds of things, you cannot do with an electric violin. It's just a synthesizer sound, even if you play it live."

For acoustic, classical performances, Garrett uses his Stradivarius, the 1716 *ex-Adolf Busch*. For his crossover concerts he uses his Guadagnini — the instrument that was strapped to his back when he fell down a flight of stairs after a 2008 performance of the Mendelssohn Concerto with the London Philharmonic, at the Barbican Arts Centre. He described the incident last year in the *Sydney Morning Herald*: "It had been a rainy day and the steps leading to the car park were wetter than I realized. Still wearing my flat-soled concert shoes, I lost my footing and took the entire flight on my back in classic slapstick fashion, riding the violin case like a sledge."

It was a devastating loss at the time, but he told me that now, "to be quite honest, it sounds the same because I went to a really, really good restorer and he did such a good job. It looks the same, too; but of course, value-wise, it kind of lost the special value." (He declined to name the New York luthier who restored his Guad to playing condition.)

David said that he sees his crossover shows as an opportunity to connect with young people and give his audiences new ways to think about music.

"I don't need to do educational concerts for the young people because I have so many young people coming to my shows," he said. "Basically, my educational concerts are my real concerts. I always talk about music, always explain what I'm doing, what my influences are, why I arranged something like this. For me, it is part of the show, to educate a little bit. People might see it only as entertainment, but my underlying goal, of course, is always to say something which has substance, which will kind of change the way that they listen to a piece."

Leila Josefowicz. Photo: J Henry Fair

LEILA JOSEFOWICZ AND ESA-PEKKA SALONEN

Originally published on October 16, 2012

Since this interview, violinist Leila Josefowicz and conductor/composer Esa-Pekka Salonen's recording of Salonen's Violin Concerto *was nominated for a 2013 Grammy for Best Classical Instrumental Solo.*

I'll be honest, not all new works for violin thrill me; fairly often I feel no great desire to hear them twice. But the fully modern *Violin Concerto* by Esa-Pekka Salonen grew on me fast. The first recording of the piece, called *Out of Nowhere*, is being released today, and I recently spoke to both Esa-Pekka Salonen and violinist Leila Josefowicz about this concerto and their partnership in creating it.

Written in his final months as Music Director of the Los Angeles Philharmonic, Salonen's *Violin Concerto* was premiered in 2009 by Josefowicz, for whom it was written, with Salonen conducting the LA Phil.

The new recording, *Out of Nowhere*, is named for the notes the two penciled on the first page of the *Violin Concerto*. Indeed, the violin seems to come from nowhere to start the concerto, entering alone in a flurry of notes. That flurry becomes a wash of sound, as the orchestra picks up and echoes the violin's motions in the first movement, called "Mirage." The inner movements are called "Pulse 1" and "Pulse 2." The first "Pulse" is full of harmonics, set to the rhythm of lovers' heartbeats in the dark. The second "Pulse" is noisy and rhythmic, perhaps depicting the chaotic culture clash of LA, complete with a drum kit to amp things up. The last movement, called "Adieu," is slow and emotional. Salonen writes, "For myself, the strongest symbol of what I was going through (during his final months in Los Angeles) is the very last chord of the piece; a new harmonic idea never heard before in the concerto. I saw it as a door to the next part of my life of which I didn't know so much yet, a departure with all the thrills and fears of the unknown." Out of nowhere, into the unknown. It's a piece full of poetry.

It's also a piece born of two hard-working musicians at the top of their game. Salonen, after his graceful departure from the LA Phil, in which he left the orchestra in the good hands of Gustavo Dudamel, remains Conductor Laureate of that orchestra and Principal Conductor and Artistic Advisor for the Philharmonia Orchestra in London. Leila Josefowicz has made a reputation as an interpreter of new works, having also premiered works written for her by Steven Mackey (*A Beautiful Passing*) and Colin Matthews; and having played first performances of Thomas Adès' violin concerto, *Concentric Paths*. She was awarded a MacArthur Foundation Fellowship for her advocacy of modern works and was featured on the cover of October 2012's *The Strad* magazine.

Leila grew up in Los Angeles, during the time when Salonen was Music Director for the LA Phil. Over the years, they performed quite a bit together: chamber music, new music, a choreographed *L'Histoire du Soldat*. They performed the Oliver Knussen violin concerto as well as other major performances. And Salonen attended concerts, such as the one in which she performed the John Adams *Violin Concerto*.

It was Josefowicz who first suggested the collaboration — long before it happened, and before many of their performances together. "I did write him a letter, just saying how much of a fan I am of him, and if he were ever to write me a piece, it would be my biggest dream, and I'd put all my efforts into it…" she said, laughing. "A few years after I wrote my letter, I thought, how else can I show him what effort I would put into a piece, if he were to write me one? And one of the ways in which I did that was to record his piece, *Lachen Verlernt for Solo Violin*, for Warner Classics. It's an 11-minute unaccompanied work, it's very good."

When it came to the *Violin Concerto*, "I knew, I just knew, that if he was going to write something, it would be a big success, and it would be an amazing thing to do with him," she said. "Now, looking back, this has been even more incredible than any of us could have imagined."

Indeed, the concerto was met with critical acclaim from the beginning, and Salonen and Josefowicz have taken it on the road, performing the concerto in Paris, Stockholm, Lisbon, London, Berlin, Chicago, Philadelphia, Boston, Brussels, Luxembourg, Dortmund, Ferrara and New York City. Last year, the piece won the prestigious 2012 Grawemeyer Award for Music Composition.

For Salonen, Josefowicz "was the most fantastic partner in this," he said. "She's pretty much fearless, she has an amazing technique, and she's very tenacious. Very rarely did I get the kind of feedback that this can't be played, or this is too difficult."

Josefowicz did not want Salonen to feel constrained by the limitations of the instrument — or her ability to play it. "One thing I did NOT want him think about, with me, was technique," she said. "I said, look, forget about any rules you knew about the violin."

And he already knew a lot: "I'm not a string player by training, but I know the violin well, obviously, based on the fact that I've been conducting for 30 years, but also I've been married to a professional violinist (Jane Price) for about 20 years," Salonen said. "So whenever I've had violin-related questions in my writing or other works, I just point to my wife and ask, 'How does this work?' When I started writing this piece, I felt I had a fairly good idea about idiomatic violin writing. Of course, I know all the major violin concertos rather intimately as a conductor, so I had this reference as well."

"However, I thought that what I would like to do is to kind of stretch the expression of the violin beyond the normal limits. I thought it would be interesting to have as wide a scope of expression and sound as possible, without going into extended techniques — scratching, and so forth. That's why I wrote the third movement in sort of synthetic disco rock music style…to contrast with the essential lyrical finale of the piece."

Josefowicz encouraged Salonen to write whatever came into his head that would get across his ideas, regardless of the difficulty. "I'm the messenger," she said. "I said that I'd tell him if something was truly physically impossible to play."

And by impossible to play, she meant impossible, not "difficult."

"Those two things are very different," Josefowicz said. "When people said that the Tchaikovsky *Violin Concerto* was 'unplayable,' they meant that it's very difficult. It's not unplayable. So 'unplayable' would be combining some incredibly high note with some low note that couldn't be played together because the G string and the E string can't be played at the same time."

To be sure, we are talking about "playable" for Leila Josefowicz, not necessarily for mere mortals! And even for her, it was a lot of work, in a short period of time. For example, the wickedly fast and intricate first movement. "He got the first movement to me first, thankfully — because that's a big job, with the notes and the memorization. But the other movements were, too. I was on him, every week, in this process, to get me more material. I was very insistent. And he went with me, he was great, absolutely fantastic. I probably had three months before the performance, when I knew it in my mind already. But I never worked harder, in my life. It was a lot of work."

"We were a great team; it was a fantastic example of teamwork and what quality can be accomplished well within a certain time period," she said. "Sometimes, I think this is the way great things are created — it doesn't always take forever, if two people — and especially the composer — have their mind on it."

Their process of collaboration had a 21st-century dimension.

"We did some of the cooperation over Skype, and a lot of it was done over email," Salonen said. "I would send her little scraps of ideas and phrases to play, then she would play them back for me over Skype sometimes. I had sort of a live laboratory going with her."

"There were only a couple times where she said, well look, this really doesn't work very well, and she once had a comment about the form," Salonen said. "I had a different ending for the third movement in my first sketches, and she just instinctively didn't like it. I went back to my studio and I thought, she's absolutely right. I re-wrote the whole thing: the last two minutes or so. It's incredibly valuable to have that sort of feedback. The problem with composing is you're sitting in your studio, alone, and you have no concrete feedback until the first rehearsal. Then, quite often, it's kind of late. You can always correct balance and little instrumental inaccuracies in the course of the rehearsals. But if there's a formal problem, a deeper problem, there's nothing you can do about that, at that point. So I felt really privileged to work with her in this way."

One of the things Josefowicz requested for the *Violin Concerto* was a slow movement. "It was something I requested and will continue to request from composers," she said. "It may be risky, in some ways, for composers to do, because they can't get too fancy. No fireworks, no crazy things going on in the score, but just something very still and very simple.

Josefowicz brought up that idea before Salonen had written one note, he said. "A great player can draw some poetry out of one or two notes, just with a subtle change of tone, color, dynamics and phrasing," Salonen said. "She felt that many modern concertos don't offer that option to the soloist; everything is busy and tightly controlled by the composer, so there's no space for individual interpretation. I have had this kind of feeling myself sometimes, over the years. I've premiered about 400 pieces so far in my life, as a conductor. Some of them have been absolute masterpieces and some of them have been absolute crap, and then you know, (he laughs) a whole lot of stuff in between! So I could relate to this."

"I thought about my own works, and I thought that what was missing was a big slow movement in the sort of tradition of Bruckner, Mahler, Brahms, and Beethoven," he said. "I'm not trying to compare myself with those guys, but in that sort of vein: a long slow movement that becomes the main movement of the piece, as it does in, say, Bruckner's Seventh Symphony or in Beethoven's Seventh. So that the weightiest emotional and expressive material is in the slow movement. That's what I wanted to do in this case, because I had never done it before."

Salonen's slow movement comes at the end of *Violin Concerto*, his heartfelt *Adieu*.

"It was written during the time that it really hit me, that okay, my 17 years (as Music Director of the Los Angeles Philharmonic) is coming to an end, and is this the biggest mistake I've ever made in my life, to leave? Or is it something that makes sense and is organic?" Salonen said. "I think a lot of that somehow went into the *Violin Concerto*. I can't say the bar numbers or anything like that, but when I hear it these days, in my mind it very strongly connects with my last months and weeks in LA. It will always be like that, I think."

"I was very, very positively surprised by the reception, and by the fact that orchestras want to program it around the world," he said. "It's very encouraging, and also, somehow it tells me that the genre of sort of the big, virtuoso instrumental concerto is not over. There's still life in the old horse, and we should keep writing music."

For violinists wishing to take up the concerto, there is a piano reduction of the orchestra part, Salonen said, and the score is almost ready for final print. The concerto has been played by a few other violinists already, including Patricia Kopatchinskajas, Thomas Zehetmair and Pekka Kuusisto. Also, Akiko Suwanai will perform it in February 2013 with Philharmonia Orchestra in Tokyo; and Julia Fischer will perform it with Vienna Philharmonic in May 2013.

"So it's kind of leaving home these days," he laughed, "which is nice, but at the same time it's a rite of passage. It really is out there, no longer in your hands. You lose control over the piece because you're no longer there to guard it! That's a healthy, normal situation, and of course I'm privileged to have all those people play it."

Stanley Ritchie. Photo courtesy Stanley Ritchie

STANLEY RITCHIE

Originally published on November 19, 2012

Members of Violinist.com debate endlessly and passionately about whether or not a person should use a 'shoulder rest' or 'chinrest' to help hold up the violin. Most modern players use both, but back in Bach's days, violinists used neither. Here is where the highly accomplished, informed and beloved Indiana University Professor of Violin, Stanley Ritchie, enters the debate.

Have you been secretly wishing to shed both your shoulder rest and chinrest? Here is your friendly, expert guide: Baroque violinist and Indiana University Professor Stanley Ritchie, in his new book, *Before the Chinrest*.

For me, Professor Ritchie's book read like a novel, fully delivering on its cover's promise to reveal the "mysteries of pre-chinrest technique and style." It has that air of revelation, with each page putting a new historical spin on ideas I've taken for granted my entire musical life. Even if you (like I) have no intention of ditching your chinrest or shoulder rest, the combination of history, practicality and sheer love for Baroque music is both enlightening and inspiring. No skimming; I read it fully, with a pencil in hand, and left it full of marks and notes.

Ritchie argues that he has gained a profound sense of freedom in going without the chinrest and shoulder rest. In fact, that sense of "freedom" is also what made him embrace the Early Music movement, which was just making its way from Europe to the United States when he discovered it in the 1970s through his colleague Albert Fuller, to whom his book is dedicated.

Before he "went Baroque" (I couldn't resist), Ritchie was a successful "modern" violinist. Born in Australia, Ritchie graduated from the Sydney Conservatorium of Music in 1956. He then studied in Paris with Jean Fournier; then in the United States with Joseph Fuchs, Oscar Shumsky and Samuel Kissel. He went on to serve as concertmaster of the New York City Opera in 1963, then associate concertmaster of the Metropolitan Opera from 1965 to 1970. In 1970 he joined the New York Chamber Soloists, then in 1973 played as Assistant Concertmaster of the Vancouver Symphony until 1975, when he became first violinist in the Philadelphia String Quartet (in residence in the University of Washington in Seattle). He joined the Indiana University School of Music in 1982 as professor of violin, and has served in that capacity ever since.

Last month I spoke over the phone with Ritchie about how the Early Music Movement changed his life, about playing without a chinrest or shoulder rest, and about how his book clears up some misconceptions people might have about Period Performance.

Laurie: What made you want to take up the violin in the first place?

Stanley: I was born in New South Wales (Australia), in a farming community where there was no live music of any kind. My mother used to listen to the radio, so I was always listening to classical music — even though it was canned. But she wanted me to have music lessons of some sort. When I was seven, my parents took me to the city for the first time, and as we were walking down the street in the city, I saw a violin in a shop window. I pointed at it and said, "I want that!" They discussed it and said, "Well, it's cheaper than a piano..." So that was it!

I took violin lessons at the local convent, the only place to take violin lessons. I had eight years of ladies, all but one of whom knew nothing about the violin at all!

But why did I take up violin and make it my life? When I graduated from high school, I had a scholarship that would have taken me three years at a university, undergrad and everything. I stood on the grounds of the university with my mother, looking around me, tossing between going there, or to the Conservatorium to take music lessons. I chose the Conservatorium for two reasons: A, I was scared of the university, over-awed by the whole thing. And B, subconsciously, I think, to please my mother! That's how I became a violinist. (He chuckles) Not driven from the age of three to be the greatest violinist in the world!

Laurie: What made you fall for Baroque music?

Stanley: I guess the seed, the germ of it, was planted by a question that always appeared in a written exam we had to take to graduate (from the Sydney Conservatorium of Music): "What is meant by 'style' in music?" And so we thought about it. Whatever we came up with, at least we began to think about it.

Then I came to the United States several years later, in 1959, to the School of Music at Yale. I thought about doing a Master's degree, then decided it wasn't the kind of thing I wanted to do...But one course really got my attention, that was "Performance Practice" — a term that I'd never heard before. I took the course, which was taught by the late David Kraehenbuehl, who was a wonderful, wonderful professor. He really opened my eyes — all of ours — to the difference between certain things we took for granted in performance style, and what might have been the truth.

At that time, I was listening to the music of (Heinrich von) Biber, a late 17th-century German composer whom I'd never heard of before — we all thought violin music started with Corelli! (He laughs)

Ten years later, after I'd finished my studies, and after I'd free-lanced in New York and played with the New York City Opera and the Met, I joined a chamber group called the New York Chamber Soloists. The harpsichordist was Albert Fuller, who had been teaching at Juilliard for 40 years. We were concertizing, and one day, on the way back from an out-of-town performance, I said, "Albert, I'd really like to know more about Baroque music, could we get together and read a sonata or two some time?" And Albert grabbed me and said, "When?" — because nobody had ever asked him that before, no free-lance violinist in New

York at the time would think such a thing. When we got together, he said, "Do you know what they're doing in Europe now? They're tuning their violins a down half-step down, they're putting on gut strings and they're playing with old bows." I said, "Why would they want to do that?" And he said, "Well, why don't you try it?"

So I tried tuning my violin a half-step down. And there I was, using a modern bow on loose strings — it was not the greatest fun I'd ever had. Still, he was very persuasive. I had an old Tyrolean violin in the closet that wasn't being used, and we found someone to convert it back to its original condition. And so, I finally had a Baroque instrument — well, a little hybrid: it was late-17th century instrument, with classical fittings, and borrowed a Dodd bow from Jacques Francais and had Bill Salchow make a copy. This was 1971.

Laurie: Had you taken your chinrest off at this time?

Stanley: Yes. I took it off. I had already managed without my shoulder rest, by putting some sponge or foam rubber or something on the back of the instrument. That gradually condensed over a period of six months. By the end of that time, I didn't need a shoulder rest any more. And then the idea of going without the chinrest came.

I remember meeting Gustav Leonhardt after a year or two of playing Baroque. Of course I was still making a living playing modern violin, because you couldn't playing Baroque violin. He spotted the mark on my neck — and he said, "Ahhh, you mustn't play with a chinrest!"

Laurie: Do you still use a shoulder rest for modern playing?

Stanley: I don't need it. When I'm playing modern violin I hardly even use the chinrest now.

Laurie: There's a raging debate about shoulder rests that happens from time to time on Violinist.com. People get almost moralistic and crazy about it.

Stanley: Not using either, all I can say is this: people use shoulder rests because they feel that they need it. But I had a student who is well over six feet tall, with a long neck, and who is now a very successful concertizing Baroque violinist. He doesn't use a chinrest or a shoulder rest, and what he does is quite amazing. So it must be possible for anybody to do it. As I say, I'm much shorter, I'm a good six to nine inches shorter than that man, and it's probably much more comfortable for me. It depends on the physique of the individual, and also someone's ability to relax: not hold onto the violin or shoulder rest as though it were a clutching blanket. A lot of people raise their shoulder under the instrument, they're so afraid of dropping it, which is exactly what one should not do.

Laurie: It sounds like you have to change your technique to make it work properly.

Stanley: Absolutely, of course.

Laurie: If you ditch your shoulder rest and your chinrest and you don't change the technique...

Stanley:...it's pointless, because the instrument is going to be clamped like a vice. The whole point of playing without the chinrest and keeping your shoulder down is so that the instrument can resonate like a bell, whereas if you raise your shoulder, you're clamping. As long as the instrument is in contact with the shoulder, there is a certain dampening effect.

Laurie: People have all kinds of crazy ideas about the period performance movement. As a pioneer in this movement, what kinds of misconceptions would you like to clear up for people?

Stanley: I, for one, am not a flag-waving evangelist about this. I do it because it feels much more natural to me, and I think that's what it should be about: trying to make music in the most natural way. After all, the period instrument and early instrument movement has reached all the way into the 20th century now: from before Mozart, all the way up to Wagner and Mahler.

One of the misconceptions might be that it's very snobbish or elitist. I wouldn't doubt there are people who are that way, but as a movement, its purpose is far from just trying to be better than everybody, but ideally to find out for oneself how music was approached at the time it was written. Any music. All music.

Then of course, there are all sorts of misconceptions such as: you mustn't vibrate when you play early music. That is utter nonsense.

Laurie: The kind of vibrato that you describe in the book sounds like a really subtle kind of vibrato, but it is vibrato. I guess we can just clear that up right here: Was vibrato used in Baroque music?

Stanley: The misconception about vibrato is that you don't vibrate when you play Baroque music. This is only true in (Baroque) orchestral music; you don't do it in orchestral music. Nor should a cellist who is playing continuo vibrate, because it confuses the pitch, and it makes the music expressive in the wrong way.

But on the other side, there's the idea that constant vibrato is the way to play. I don't know when this idea started — well I have an idea, it was sometime in the '20s when it became more general practice. And that is demonstrably incorrect, stylistically. We have lots of evidence, not only from what Leopold Auer said, but others as well. Besides, in performing parts from the 19th century, you can find where they would vibrate — it was like any other ornament. I always say to people, constant vibrato is similar to trilling all the time. If you trilled on every note, people would think you're crazy. If you vibrated all the time in the 17 and 1800's, people would think you were crazy!

Laurie: So vibrato was more like an ornament.

Stanley: Oh very much so.

Laurie: Plenty of teachers tell their students: the more vibrato, the better. They tell them to develop a continuous vibrato — maybe you need that for the Bruch?

Stanley: One of my colleagues certainly insists on it! He doesn't like to hear the violin played without vibrato. And he's somebody I respect very highly. One person, one musician, we really don't see eye-to-eye on this subject.

Laurie: What made you decide to write this book, to put it all down?

Stanley: It started, actually, with the sets of exercises that are at the back of the book. I had developed those exercises over the years for teaching intonation, and one of my doctoral students decided to use Sibelius to write them out. So at first, I wrote some annotation and started to write a few things down about how to use the exercises — then some ideas about intonation and left-hand technique. And I put it out, desk-published it, as something called *The Violinist's Lefthandbook.*

The next step was writing something for the right hand and exercises for the bow, and I called that *The Violinist's Righthandbook.* Then a few years ago I had a sabbatical, holed up in a nice little village in Northern Italy, and set to work putting it all together and adding and introduction and a chapter or two on interpretation. Essentially, it's a distillation of my teaching methods. It's certainly the direction I've taken my students over the last 30 years. They've taught me; it's what I've learned from them that I've put down in this book.

Laurie: I think people get very intimidated by all the rules of Baroque music. For me, even just thinking of the *Treatise* by Leopold Mozart (specifically *A Treatise on the Fundamental Principles of Violin Playing*, which outlines many rules for violin-playing in great detail) is intimidating. People think: if I play Bach, I don't know what people will say about it, because I don't know if I'm going to follow the rules right.

Stanley: That's one of the side-effects of the whole movement; there's much more interest about the way they played Bach. There's so much more information out there now, than there was when I was a student. If people are at all curious, at least questioning the things they've been taught, there's a lot to find out. Curiosity is what got me into Early Music.

Laurie: It seems to me that it's possible to be pretty free, once you know some of this stuff.

Stanley: Absolutely. It's liberating, that's one emotion I really experienced when I took up Baroque violin. After playing so many years professionally as a violinist, I found playing Baroque violin akin to driving a sports car. I felt physically liberated, and then eventually as I became more used to it, expressively liberated.

As for rules, I think we are saddled with at least as many rules in traditional classical upbringing.

That's one nice thing about 17th-century music — there is no tradition that you can feel you're breaking. Therefore, when we approach music that's new to us, music that is not handed down by the traditional classical establishment, we feel we can experiment, try different ways of interpreting.

I always tell my students, the last thing in the world that I want you to do when you come out of here is be a clone of me. I want you to come out of here finding your own way, asking questions, and putting it all together for yourself. Too often, when I hear people playing, they seem bound to a tradition, to the way their teacher taught them, and lacking spontaneity.

Laurie: Wasn't there a lot of improvisation in Baroque music, anyway?

Stanley: Absolutely. But it's something that's not taught any longer, and sometimes people are even discouraged from doing it, in modern training, which is terrible.

When I first started improvising, I was playing a Corelli Sonata using the 1713 edition's embellishments, which may or may not have been Corelli's. I tried those, and then, after a while, I thought, "I don't like that one — I'm going to change it a little" and, "There's nothing here — why shouldn't there be something similar?" And so on.

But the art of improvising is not something that just happens — it's learned, too. One of the greatest improvisers today is Robert Levin, the pianist, who improvises Mozart concerto cadenzas. He's not improvising in the sense of making it up from nothing. He's tried many things and has a storehouse of different possibilities. As he goes along, he chooses one from here, one from there, and so on, and puts them together. Jazz players' improvisation is a learned skill. They're not just doing it off the top of their head.

I sat in for a couple sessions of Dave Baker's jazz improvisation course (at Indiana University), and it was amazing — it's just very complicated. He's a wonderful teacher, but it was much too fast for me!

There were books on how to improvise, certainly, from the end of the 16th to the beginning of the 17th century, showing you how to get from one note to another, and how many different ways, on one page, you can go, say, from E to F — about 20 different ways to get there.

Laurie: So they were certainly doing it 400 years ago.

Stanley: Oh my gosh, yes!

Laurie: I think we have a misconception about that as well!

Stanley: Sometimes we feel as though we know everything because it's the 21st century. I suggest we've forgotten an awful lot! For example, the 18th century, people could teach us quite a lot about intonation. When you open Francesco Geminiani's *Art of Playing on the Violin*, the second thing he does, after the first page, is chromatic scales! We're raised, as modern players, on equal temperament, and on so-called "expressive" intonation. But, as Geminiani demonstrates, when you play pure intervals, you realize that F-sharp is actually lower than G-flat. A-flat is higher than G-sharp. I talk about this in my book. You can really figure it out pretty easily by using pure intervals.

We have to use pure intervals on the violin. However, to do so, we must play on strings tuned in narrow fifths, we have to. So people are confused because, using "expressive intonation," you're taught to push sharps up and pull flats down — this is what I call horizontal intonation. But when playing in a string quartet or orchestra, this kind of intonation doesn't work. One has to use pure intervals, or vertical intonation, in order to be in tune with other players. Every interval's out of tune on the piano except the octave: as string players we don't have to play that way.

Anyway, the overall misconception that I'm talking about is the idea that people back then didn't know as much as we do.

Laurie: Baroque music can even be kind of dissonant, with some really interesting harmonies.

Stanley: Oh yes, tremendously. Musicians at that time were much more aware of dissonance and consonance and their significance than we are today.

Laurie: In the book, you say that there is no such thing as unaccompanied music.

Stanley: Well absolutely. When you are playing unaccompanied music, you are your own accompanist, and so you're playing the bass-line. In other words, you can extract the bass-line from any unaccompanied piece. This is relevant when we talk about breaking chords, as I do in the book. In the book I talk about different ways players break chords. When you are playing unaccompanied music, you are your own accompanist, and so you're playing the bass-line. If you break the chords before the beat, then the bass note comes before the beat. But the bass IS the beat! How would you feel if your accompanist on the piano were a little bit ahead of you all the time?

Laurie: It sort of puts you out at sea, rhythmically.

Stanley: And when you place the bass note on the beat, it actually makes a chord easier to play: you don't have to rush to get the other notes.

Laurie: The sense of time is a fascinating thing in the Bach unaccompanied. People forget, you're not on the metronome, you're not on the clock.

Stanley: Rubato is something that was talked about by Frescobaldi, in the preface to his *Toccatas,* in 1615. He said you must let the music go forward, then fall back, and wait, and so forth. So the idea of rubato in music is ancient; by the time Bach came around it was at least 100 years old. Rubato is a very Baroque concept, it's not something that happened with Liszt...

Laurie:...or Fritz Kreisler or something.

Stanley: One of the things we lost, we've forgotten in our training, is that it's not only possible and desirable, to be free in this way, but it's also a type of expression. Rubato is a way of making the music more flexible and more natural.

One of the important things that the Early Music movement has done is to raise awareness of the rhetoric, the declamation, and the affect, or emotional message, of each piece — and each part of each piece. For example, let's take Bach. When you're playing the unaccompanied pieces from the original, or from an urtext, there are no expression marks — none is written in. But they're really all there: in the harmony. Yes, there's rubato; yes, there's punctuation; yes, there's hesitation. They're all there, if you are aware of the significance of the harmonies: where something finishes, where something starts. There are places in Bach that are ambiguous, too, which you could read one way or the other. That's the nice thing about much of his music: you don't have to play it the same way twice.

Maxim Vengerov. Photo: Naim Chidiac

MAXIM VENGEROV

Originally published on January 9, 2013

After years as a top violin soloist performing 100+ concerts a year, the Russian violinist Maxim Vengerov announced he was giving up the violin in 2007, at age 32. He'd injured his shoulder, and he also wanted to pursue other interests, like conducting. Happily, his break from the violin lasted only four years, and he was back onstage by 2012, with renewed enthusiasm for the violin and a re-worked technique to prevent injury. We spoke about his return to the violin, and much more.

Maxim Vengerov couldn't be happier to be playing the violin again, after his four-year hiatus from performing, and after the painstaking reinvention of his playing technique following shoulder surgery.

Now 38, Vengerov returns to the concert stage with his world enlarged: more conducting engagements, continuing teaching posts with the Royal Academy of Music in London and International Menuhin Academy of Music in Switzerland, and increased involvement with international violin competitions. During his years away from the violin, he studied conducting, and he also married Olga Gringolts, sister of Ilya Gringolts. (They just celebrated the first birthday of their daughter, Elizabeth.) Vengerov will be in North America this May for the Montreal International Music Competition, which features the violin in 2013. Vengerov will conduct the Orchestre Symphonique de Montréal, accompanying the finalists and then the winners of the competition.

Vengerov was a superstar from the start, beginning his lessons at agefive in Novosibirsk, Russia (still the Soviet Union at the time of his birth) with Galina Tourchaninova, then with the great Zakhar Bron. Soon he was winning major international competitions and awards. At age 10 he made his first recording, then proceeded to record just about everything in the violin repertoire. As a teenager, he got to know both cellist Mstislav Rostropovich and conductor Daniel Barenboim, who became friends and mentors to him. He owns and plays the 1727 *ex-Kreutzer* Stradivarius violin, and he was the subject of the documentary, *Living the Dream*, which received the Gramophone Award for Best Documentary in 2008.

Vengerov stopped playing in 2007, citing both professional malaise and a weightlifting injury to his right shoulder that had plagued him since 2005. This month he releases his first recording in five years: the recording of his comeback recital on April 5, 2012, at Wigmore Hall in London.

During the holidays, I spoke with Vengerov over phone from Lugano, Switzerland, where he was visiting family. We talked about his mentors in music and conducting, Rostropovich and Barenboim; about his return to violin playing, with physical pain as his guide; and about competitions and his new role with Montreal International Music Competition and the Wieniawski competition.

Laurie: I enjoy your playing so much, and your Shostakovich recording, with Rostropovich conducting, is one of my favorites. How different is it to conduct a concerto, than to play one?

Maxim: I can tell you one thing about Maestro Rostropovich: he may not have been regarded as one of the greatest conductors from the technical point of view; but I made seven CDs with him, and I must say, those recordings are my best ones. And I recorded with many other wonderful maestros who were not instrumentalists. I think it was his great musicianship and also understanding of the violin repertoire, of the stringed instruments, that helped us to build an incredible chemistry that I had with no one else. That's why I think I've inherited this love for accompaniment, to accompany young people, my colleagues. I love to not only accompany violin but also piano soloists. For me, it is a great challenge and a great privilege to be on stage with them.

Laurie: I know that two of your mentors were the cellist Mstislav Rostropovich and also the pianist Daniel Barenboim, and both of them are conductors. Did you speak about conducting with them, or mostly about music, or both?

Maxim: Both! Music, conducting, playing with the orchestra...They were my mentors, and sometimes our meetings went far beyond technical issues. Of course, the principal source of our meetings was the music, and what was required to perform Shostakovich, Prokofiev, Tchaikovsky, or Brahms, Sibelius, Nielsen....I've recorded most of my violin repertoire with these two conductors, who were also instrumentalists.

Laurie: What kinds of things did you learn from each of them?

Maxim: Slava (Rostropovich) was like a musical father, he was so close to my heart. Again, it was much more that I learned from him than just music, and musical expression. The thing that struck me was his humanity, and he transformed me into sort of a man of the world. Before meeting him, I was just a talented player that loved playing for audiences. We worked principally on pieces by composers that he had met and that he had friendships with. Those were Shostakovich, Prokofiev, Britten, Walton, Stravinsky. Beyond that, we also recorded Beethoven. One of the interesting things, when I came to play Beethoven for him, he said, "You know what, Maxim, I can just feel that Beethoven is trying to say something to me, because I think if you play it like this, he would love it." I asked him, "How do you absolutely know this, that Beethoven would love it?" and he said, "Because I think even the composer was convinced, even if it wasn't his way. Even if the tempo is slower or faster than he would imagine, he would enjoy it!" For (Slava), it was a matter of being convinced what Shostakovich and Beethoven and Tchaikovsky was, even if he had not met those composers.

For Barenboim, it was a different approach. He would view a piece of music as an instrumentalist, as a pianist, from the harmonic point of view, from the orchestration, coloring. (Barenboim's was) also an amazing view, completely different from Slava. With Slava, it was this instant connection with the composer, with the soul of the composer. He would tell me, you have to imagine you were Shostakovich, or you were Prokofiev, performing the music. One of the most striking and touching things Slava told me was right at the end of his life, when I met him for the last time in the hospital. He told me that when he met me, I played beautiful Tchaikovsky, Prokofiev, and he told me a lot of things about those composers. But Shostakovich, he didn't have to tell me; it was as if I knew this composer when he was alive. And that was the biggest compliment, coming from him.

For Barenboim, the work was written, and that's in the past. He would approach it as if he were re-working and re-writing the whole work from scratch. But I think those were also Slava's qualities, he would take the work and say, "We have to try to reinvent this and make it as if we are doing a world premiere of the Beethoven *Violin Concerto*," which is actually hard to imagine! How many times has the Beethoven *Violin Concerto* been performed, since the concerto was written? But he would still find something very personal, something that is personal to him. I learned a lot from this approach.

Laurie: So what do you feel for you, as a conductor, is the most important thing, when working with a soloist?

Maxim: First of all, one has to reach a harmony with your colleague, the soloist.

Laurie: If you can!

Maxim: If you find no harmony whatsoever with the soloist (he laughs) — that happens sometimes — because sometimes the soloist doesn't want to or cannot, due to the lack of experience or an unwillingness to connect with you.

There are some players that think: here I am, a violinist or pianist, and you're an orchestra conductor, to serve me. It's a normal approach — I don't say this as something negative. It's obvious that if we listen to the recordings of Jascha Heifetz of the most beautiful works by Sibelius, Beethoven — with great conductors, you hear a loud, very present violin sound, and somewhere in the back is an orchestra! (He laughs) That's why I don't say this is bad! It's a matter of upbringing, a matter of habit, how the performer views the music. And some people view it in a sort of horizontal way: a line of the violin, or piano, with accompaniment of orchestra.

Laurie: And so what do you do if the soloist views it that way?

Maxim: Then you just serve your best, to be together and to support the instrumentalist, soloist, and try not to be annoying. For me, to be frank, it's less interesting because it becomes a matter of sport: Can I be together, or can I not be together? You use your professionalism to bring the orchestra at the right (dynamic) level, at the right speed, at the right form of articulation — and this is what I call a good service to the soloist.

Now, when the soloist meets you and says, "This is how I feel," and, "Let's make music together," you discuss a little bit, he or she plays for you, something in the dressing room, and then once you start making music on stage, a harmony has to be reached. You can absolutely disagree with the soloist, but again I should serve the best I can at the moment — and not be passive, but be active in the accompaniment, to bring out the harmonies to stimulate the soloist to play his or her best. The conductor and orchestra, depending on the piece, provide the rhythm, character, harmony, and the spirit of the work.

Laurie: Do you like conducting and playing equally well, or is there one you prefer over the other?

Maxim: It's like saying, I was born in Russia and my mother tongue is Russian. Do I love German, or English, more? I can't say I love Russian less, it's just so different! (He laughs) and I enjoy speaking different languages.

Laurie: How many do you speak, by the way?

Maxim: Well I speak English, fairly good German, not reasonable French. (He laughs) In time, I hope to speak French well! And a bit of others...

For me, violin is my first source of communication with the audience

— no doubt, my first love. But before coming to the violin, I wanted to become a conductor, because my mother was a choir conductor, and I saw her conducting. I sat in on all the rehearsals — I was singing in the choir. She wanted to become a symphonic conductor, but because I started playing, and I needed her to be with me, she quit her job. She didn't develop the symphonic conducting career that she wanted. My father worked in the orchestra as an oboist, so I visited his rehearsals and watched the conductor who was the principal conductor of the Novosibirsk Philharmonic, Arnold Katz. I really loved his example. He was my idol at the time, when I was three and four. He just passed away a few years ago.

Laurie: So you had this in mind, for a long, long time.

Maxim: Yes, I had this in mind, but then I started with the violin and I was sort of stuck with that! (He laughs)

Laurie: You were so good at it, still are!

Maxim: Quite successfully stuck, let's say. And I rather enjoyed that, throughout my years. And then there came a time when I needed to conduct the English Chamber Orchestra, and so I needed to take some lessons. I didn't, and I still don't, believe that somebody with absolutely no knowledge of conducting technique can go in front of orchestra and say, okay, I can play the violin great, now I can conduct! It also requires some time, to learn the language of the musicians. You have to speak their language.

Laurie: Whom did you study with?

Maxim: I studied at that time with Vag Papian, who was my pianist. Vag was a student of a very important teacher in Russia, Ilya Musin, who was a teacher of Valery Gergiev, Semyon Bychkov, Yakov Kreizberg, and many others.

Laurie: What kinds of things did you learn from him?

Maxim: He comes from the Leningrad school of conducting, which provides great technical basic skills for the conductor. For me, that was wonderful to go through, the studies with Vag. I progressed quite quickly, and I was able to conduct chamber orchestras. Then in 2009, I decided to study conducting on a different level, a more serious level, so I would be able to conduct symphony orchestras. At this time I became a student of Maestro Juri Simonov. He comes from another school of conducting, also from Leningrad, from St. Petersburg. His teacher was (Nikolai) Rabinovich. So Rabinovich was a student of Aleksandr Gauk, Gauk was a student of Nikolai Malko. Malko was a student of Felix Mottl (and Mottl was a was a contemporary of Mahler.) So that is the Russian-Germanic school of conducting.

Laurie: A good pedigree!

Maxim: I'm very lucky, because Juri Simonov provided a phenomenal manual technique of conducting that allows me to show quite a lot of things with my hands, without using a lot of verbal expressions.

Laurie: I'm sure you wind up in front of orchestras with musicians who speak many different languages, but we all speak music, right?

Maxim: Yes. What's important is to be able to express yourself and the way you feel about this music, your interpretation, with your gestures. That's why you need to learn the source of communication: conducting technique.

Laurie: There are too many people who get up there and do some kind of ballet that doesn't really convey a lot.

Maxim: It may work in the short-term, because the orchestra is inspired. Also nowadays, orchestras (are so good), they can play even without a conductor. But if one becomes music director, you need a different knowledge.

Laurie: Do you want to become a music director, one day?

Maxim: I'm not sure I would like to become a chief director of an orchestra, I will tell you why: simply for one fact, because I may have to abandon my violin. (A music directorship) is a big job: to spend at least 15 weeks with the orchestra, to learn all this repertoire each year, to do the administration, to discuss the agenda with the orchestra, to advocate for the right soloist...there's a lot of work, being a music director. And it's not only the conducting — conducting takes maybe the least time! That's why, I may look for a guest conducting position, which would require maybe three to five times a year somewhere.

Laurie: A regular guest conductor.

Maxim: Yes, to establish a very good relationship with an orchestra. That is what I think, in time, I will be looking for.

Laurie: Now speaking of abandoning your violin, did you ever really do that during your break from performing, or were you pretty much playing the whole time? Are you happy to be back to performing?

Maxim: First of all, I'm incredibly happy to be back on the violin.

When I couldn't play for four years — it was a very good time for me, actually, because I could study conducting. Otherwise, I never would have been able to devote myself to this learning process. So from this point of view, it was great that I didn't play the violin. Also, it's increased my deeper knowledge in music, not only conducting, but I think I have more colors to my violin playing than before, for the fact that I hear it somehow differently.

Anything we learn and anything we go through in life gives sort of an imprint on your main profession. I can feel now, as a violinist, I'm a different person, and I'm thankful for these four years of time.

But I missed my violin for at least two of the years that I didn't play: the third and fourth years. The first two years were just great — because I had a good rest! But then I said to myself, "Ooh, I really miss it," and I was looking for a way to come back. It wasn't easy, I must say, it wasn't.

Laurie: How did you do it, how did you come back?

Maxim: I came back because I was lucky to find a good surgeon who performed wonderful surgery on me, on my shoulder. And then I had one year of rehabilitation.

Laurie: I wondered if you had to change your violin technique.

Maxim: Not only did I have to change technique, but I wanted to. It was very natural for me to change technique. I feel much more free with the instrument. Because simply, I was putting too much effort into the violin-playing, it was sort of too physical. Now, I use only what's necessary to produce the sound and articulation — whatever I need. Now I don't move too much, whereas before, my movements were sort of like a palm tree!

Laurie: When you rehabilitated, did you work with a doctor, or a violin teacher, or both?

Maxim: Totally alone. I had two criteria: First, music. The final result in music, what I wanted to hear, because I have very strong expectations, always, as to how it has to sound. And the second criteria: it had to be as less-physical as possible. So I wanted to achieve the (musical) results I wanted, with as less effort as possible.

Laurie: Did you play repertoire, did you play scales, how did you do it? I can think of a lot of violinists who would love to improve their physical playing to improve their health, but it's hard to know how.

Maxim: I must say that in this way, I was really lucky, because I had had an operation, and I was still in pain when I got out of the operation. Four months after the operation, I had done a lot of rehab, physical exercises, but I still couldn't play. So I had to work with pain, with quite a lot pain, actually. I had to (address the) matter of relaxation in my playing, otherwise I couldn't sustain playing more than 10 minutes.

Laurie: So the pain kept you from overdoing it.

Maxim: Exactly. So pain was sort of my red light. (He laughs)

Laurie: Pain was your teacher.

Maxim: Yes. If I had pain, that meant I was doing something wrong. It's amazing, actually. I realized that if I am in pain when I'm playing, I had to balance it. (I had to use) force, but just enough to get through. And I had to always increase the amount of playing. I started with 10 minutes, then 15 minutes, then 20, I got to an hour. It was quite a long process.

Then very naturally, I could see that my movements were more refined than before. I had reconstructed everything, including my left hand, and my position of the neck.... Violin-playing, as anything else in life, is not only about being relaxed, but you have to contract your muscles and de-contract. The relaxation after the contraction is very important, you have to be 50-50. So I was working with this balance for a very, very long time, until I felt absolutely at ease, which is now. Now I feel that.

Yes it's true, I could write a book about this.

Laurie: It would be a very interesting book! Inspirational. It's hard to work back from something like that.

Maxim: Actually, I didn't do it totally alone. My father was my mirror all that time. He helped me — he was more of a psychiatrist. (He laughs) But I think now my father can — if you gave him the violin, I think he would start playing now! (He laughs) Although he never touched the violin in his life!

Also, I'm helping a few young people now, who came to me after the operation. I understand their difficulties. I'm actually the one who has gone through it, and I'm a good example for them. Not direct students, but they come to me and I see them regularly.

Laurie: You do teach, though, at the Royal Academy in London, yes?

Maxim: Yes. At the Royal Academy, and at the International Menuhin Academy of Music in Gstaad, Switzerland.

Laurie: I've watched an old masterclass video of you teaching and you look like a fun teacher. Do you enjoy teaching?

Maxim: Yes, although I must say that my style of teaching is different now, due to experiences I've had, and also my conducting experience, and experiences with viola and baroque violin — all of these things add to the package.

Laurie You have also been more involved with competitions — as chairman of the jury for the Wieniawski Competition, and this year you will be working with the Montreal International Music Competition. How did you get involved with the Montreal competition?

Maxim: I've known about the Montreal International Music Competition for quite a long time. It's a wonderful competition, and when the organization approached me, I thought it would be a great honor. Also, with my experience as chairman of the jury for the Wieniawski Competition, I felt this would be wonderful continuation, to be involved with another competition.

Laurie: So you will be both conducting and serving on the jury?

Maxim: We decided that I should not be on the jury after all, because I'm going to conduct in the final round. It's difficult to be on both sides of the fence! (He laughs) So this time I prefer to be with the colleagues, with the young competitors. I know how difficult and challenging it is to perform in front of the jury — not only that, but to compete among other brilliant young musicians. We have a very good committee, so I'm sure the choice will be made wonderfully, and I trust the competition is going to be at the highest level possible.

I'm very excited about conducting all the finalists. Conducting the violin repertoire is one of my favorite things to do, because I do understand the challenges of the concerto, and I know the difficulties of playing with the orchestra. As conductor, I think I can be of some help to the young competitors.

Many people wonder, why do we need to do competitions? Many young people say, maybe if I can learn a couple of concertos, can get a good PR agent, it will just happen for me. Yes, it might, because with today's media possibilities — the Internet, TV, all the promotional activities — you can achieve phenomenal things to promote yourself. But there is something that we forget, by promoting yourself. We sometimes forget about the main reason why we are playing for people. We are playing the greatest compositions — Beethoven, Brahms, Shostakovich, Tchaikovsky — they left for us this great heritage. It's as if people go to museums to see Leonardo da Vinci, the great paintings — we have to deliver these great works, all the concertos, sonatas, chamber music, symphonies, in the best possible way that we can. We have to find very personal approach to them. Every soloist nowadays has to try to say something unique, something personal. Otherwise, if you're playing just another performance of Brahms concerto, why do we need to hear that?

That is the great lesson that Barenboim taught me. I played the Sibelius concerto for him, in a private room with the pianist, and I was very happy about my performance. I felt it was very emotional, good technically — and he didn't say anything. I asked him, "Maestro, don't you like it?" He said, "Yes, I like it. It's great violin-playing. But I want to hear your Sibelius! I didn't hear your Sibelius." I asked him, "What do you mean, my Sibelius?" He said, "Well, take the score, don't play the violin any more. Just study the score. Tomorrow morning, we have the first rehearsal with the orchestra, and I want to really hear your Sibelius, your discovery, based on your new, detailed knowledge of the musical score."

I spent one whole night with the score of the Sibelius, and I totally re-discovered this work. Of course, the first rehearsal was far from perfect, and even my technique started to lose something because I was more busy with the music. So I went a step back, and after rehearsal I was very unhappy. But Barenboim came to me and said, "Well, I am happy that you have started now."

Why do we need competitions? We want to hear every young competitor, to compare their interpretations, their souls, their personalities, how each of them views Beethoven, Mozart, even Paganini — Paganini was a great composer, not only sportsman, as some people view him. And we want to go definitely beyond technique, because in today's society, with all our new technological possibilities, the level of technique has grown. That means the development of the human souls has to be even higher, has to match the technical possibilities.

Laurie: So when you are on a jury, it sounds like you are looking for the kind of thing that Daniel Barenboim was looking for in you.

Maxim: Absolutely. That's why we need competitions. Because we can recognize out of 40-50 players — we want to find the most developed ones, the people who, in their future, will bring something to our audience, will bring something to the music, will add something to the musical world. And beyond that, even those people who do not pass through to the finals, they will have goals, they will have dreams fulfilled because they were at the competition where the atmosphere was incredible, where the level, not only technical but the performing art level, was fantastic. So they go away from the competition with the souvenirs and new challenges.

Laurie: Inspired.

Maxim: Inspired. That's what we need, to inspire young people.

Elmar Oliveira. Photo: Tucker Densley

ELMAR OLIVEIRA

Originally published on April 9, 2013

Elmar Oliveira's career has been going strong for some four decades, and he continues with a full teaching and performance schedule. So I was surprised, when I Googled his name, not to find any interviews with this great violinist on the Internet. Sometimes this is the case for artists whose careers blossomed before the digital age. It was my pleasure and honor to go about rectifying that situation with this interview!

How does a person continue performing, over a four-decade career?

It's all about loving what you do and nurturing a lifelong spirit of curiosity about music and music-making, said Elmar Oliveira, who hit the world stage in 1978 with his gold medal at the Tchaikovsky Competition and continues to perform, record and teach today.

The first violinist to receive an Avery Fisher Prize, Oliveira has a considerable discography, stretching over three decades and ranging from Beethoven to modern composers. He is one of the foremost connoisseurs of the instrument, having likely played more Strads and Guarneris than any other living violinist, but also championing the fine violins made by living makers. Currently he plays the 1729/30 *Stretton* Guarneri del Gesu as well as several contemporary violins.

For his latest project, he's taken up the *Violin Concerto* by Robert Schumann, recorded live with the Atlantic Classical Orchestra, which plays in Vero Beach and Stuart, Florida. The recording includes a conversation between Oliveira and the orchestra's conductor, Stewart Robertson.

It's a slightly unlikely piece. Schumann's *Violin Concerto* has made little headway, in terms of popularity, in the 150 years since its composition in 1853. This is likely because its dedicatee, Joseph Joachim, never performed it publicly. Also, both Clara Schumann, the composer's wife, and Johannes Brahms kept the work secret, declining to publish it along with the composer's other works. Thus the work has remained somewhat obscure and less examined than others of the same era.

Schumann said that the theme of the concerto's second movement was dictated to him by angels; specifically, the spirits of Mendelssohn and Schubert. Composed less than a year before Schumann's suicide attempt and complete descent into madness, the piece seemed, to those closest to him, a product of that madness. That second movement, though, is one of the most divine moments in the piece.

I spoke to Elmar Oliveira over the phone, while he was in Florida, where he winters and teaches at Lynn University. We talked about his career, about teaching and performing, about fine instruments and about the Schumann *Violin Concerto*.

Laurie: Where were you born, and what made you take up the violin?

Elmar: I was born in Connecticut; my family was Portuguese. My parents and both of my brothers were born in Portugal, and I was the first American-born. My father had the incredible love for the violin. He was an amateur; he picked it up on his own. He was an amateur mandolin player first, and then he played the violin. When he was nine years old he heard the violin in church, and the sound never left his being. So it was almost like an obsession, as if no other musical instrument existed except for the violin! (He chuckles)

Laurie: At what age did you decide to play, and what made you want to play?

Elmar: First of all, my brother, John, was a professional violinist, and he was 11 years older than me. He played in the Kansas City Philharmonic at that time, then he played in the Houston Symphony for almost 20 years. He was actually one of my first teachers, and I heard the violin all the time. I probably heard the violin in the womb! If it wasn't my brother practicing, it was the long-playing records being played, or the radio — but the violin was constant in the home. Consequently, I already could whistle and sing all the violin concerti, all the sonatas, all the short pieces — because I had heard them. Actually I started in the public school system, which was a really great thing at that time, and unfortunately we have none of it any more. That was in Naugatuck, Connecticut. I started learning the violin rather late, actually — I was nine years old. I started in the school with a violinist who was a pupil of George Enescu, and was also my brother's first teacher. I developed very, very quickly, once I picked up the instrument. At the end of a year, I played my first recital. I was 10 years old, and I remember I played Brahms *Hungarian Dances*, Mozart *Turkish Violin Concerto*, and all kinds of little short pieces — it was quite something for one year of study.

Things just progressed from there: I won my first competition when I was 14 years old, and I played with the Hartford Symphony on television for that particular competition. Then two years later, I won the Young People's Concerts competition and played with the New York Philharmonic, and it just kept going. The big deal was when I won the Tchaikovsky Competition in 1978.

Laurie: That was a very big deal, not just because it was the Tchaikovsky Competition, which carries so much prestige, but also because of the political environment at that time.

Elmar: The story I heard was that Leonid Kogan, who was the head of the jury at that time, actually had to call (Soviet Communist leader Leonid) Brezhnev and speak with him and say, "You know, there's this American violinist, and I don't think there's any way we're not going to be able to give him a gold medal..." and that's what happened!

Laurie: Wow!

And you have continued to play, to have a successful career for the last 35 years. It doesn't always work that way. Sometimes people burn out pretty young because it takes so much work and dedication. How have you been able to sustain your inspiration?

Elmar: I think it all has to do with the love of the violin, the love of music, and the love of what you're doing. It also has to do with your curiosity about what to do and how to develop as a violinist and as a musician.

Also, I've learned so much over the years from my teaching — not only about how to teach my students: how to get them to play properly, to advance and to try to be artists — but also about my own playing. It's this constant studying, delving into the scores, the composers, the concertos and the sonatas, and having to be able to communicate that to my students. And of course, there are all the different performances over the years. For me, there's never anything boring about it; it's always just constantly demanding: both what it is that you see in the musical score, and what you see in the violin playing.

Laurie: How long have you been teaching?

Elmar: I was in my late 20s when I started teaching. I came back from the Tchaikovsky Competition, and one of the things that I did do was teach. I've taught in various different places: Binghamton University, Cornell University, Manhattan School of Music, SUNY Purchase. I've given master classes all over the place: Curtis, Peabody. And of course now I'm associated with Lynn Conservatory of Music at Lynn University, and it's just really fantastic.

Laurie: You like teaching, obviously. Not all performers do!

Elmar: I could not live without teaching. It's so much a part of my being, of my soul. The thought of getting really gifted students to go to the next level of playing means so much to me; I couldn't live without being able to help young players do that.

Laurie: Something I noticed in your bio for Lynn University: you talked about your teaching philosophy, and you said that you liked to nurture the proper psychological approach to performing. That intrigued me. What is the proper psychological approach to performing? I'm a violinist myself, and I know that I have felt a whole range of feelings when performing.

Elmar: One of the biggest issues is: How do people perceive walking out on stage and playing a concerto with an orchestra, or a recital with a piano? What are they thinking of when they go out there? Of course, everybody is nervous, and how does one deal with nerves? There are so many different issues. The first: where the concentration is, when you are walking out there to perform. If the obsession is with the nervousness, then the concentration is not on the playing, it's not on what you're doing. So one of the key things to do is to learn how to focus on what you're doing, not on your nervousness. Concentrate actually on the playing, be able to start something and, no matter what you're feeling in terms of nervousness, be able to let go of (the nervousness) as quickly as possible and immerse yourself in what you're doing, whether it's concentrating on the musical aspect or the technical aspect. In my case, I feel that there's never a moment in performance where those two things don't go hand-in-hand. So this is what I try to impart in my students. Also, I try to get them to do a lot of performing. If you do it once a year, it's quite different from doing it 20 times a year.

There are just so many issues with the psychological preparation of going out on to a stage and performing, I can only talk about maybe a tenth of the things that you really need to talk about with your students.

Then of course there's the psychological issue about what performance means to an individual student. Some people are only obsessed with "success," and that may be one of the worst things about performing. Because it's not about personal success, or what you achieve and how people perceive of you. It's about the big picture: Where are we all going, with music, with performing? The ultimate goal is to be able to understand what it is that you're playing in a very, very complex way, and to communicate that to your audience.

Laurie: I would think your perception of the audience must have something to do with it, too.

Elmar: I feel that one never plays for one's self. Although one sets particular goals that one wants to achieve for oneself, the ultimate thing in performance is to have the sense that the audience is 150 percent absorbed in what you're doing. Because otherwise, you might as well just play in your living room.

Laurie: Do you remember your first encounter with a really fine instrument, and what that was like?

Elmar: I suppose, the first really great instrument that I played on was the instrument I was loaned to go to the Tchaikovsky Competition, the *Holroyd* Strad — it was a really great instrument. Even before that, I was loaned the *Empress Catherine* Stradivari, to play my New York debut, when I was 19 or 20 years old. That was a great instrument also. When I played on that, of course, my entire sense of playing was very different than playing on a mediocre instrument, or an average instrument.

I'm of the perception that an instrument does not have to be a Stradivari or a Guarneri or a Guadagnini or a Vuillaume to be a fine instrument. It could be made in England, it could be made in Africa, it could be made in China — everything depends on the sound of the violin, what it does for you in a hall, and how it feels in your hand. Those issues are the most important issues. Whether a violin projects in a hall — for a soloist that's a very important thing. Rostropovich used to say, and I think it was absolutely 100 percent on the mark, (his unaccented American English takes on a Russian accent) "I don't care what cello you give me: Give me a loud cello, I put quality in."

There's such a great truth about that. Just think, pianists have to travel and play on whatever piano is available to them. A pianist who has a great sound and knows how to produce great sound could be playing on a mediocre piano; it still sounds great.

Laurie: But there's still a difference. Right?

Elmar: Of course there's a difference. Because a great instrument, in terms of quality and response, can actually enhance your playing. You can learn from your instrument.

Laurie: In what way?

Elmar: Sometimes you have to do certain things on a particular instrument to make it work; whereas on a great instrument, you might do it differently and all of a sudden you realize that something in your technique just stepped up two notches. A great instrument can change the way you approach something. You learn, all of a sudden, something about a particular stroke with the bow, how you do it on a great instrument, very different than how you might do it on a mediocre instrument — and you might have been doing it wrong. So that's how you learn from playing on a great instrument.

Laurie: You have played on a lot of fine instruments — how many Strads have you probably played on in your life?

Elmar: Prior to me, I think maybe Ruggiero Ricci had played the most great instruments anywhere. But I think I finally beat him on that! (He laughs) I've played, performed and recorded on so many instruments — the Bein and Fushi project that I did, the Library of Congress collection — just so many instruments! It's been quite an education and a great experience for me.

Laurie: What do you find they have in common, or they don't? Where there any surprises?

Elmar: I find that they're all different. There are never two instruments that feel or sound exactly the same. The great instruments all have their great qualities, and they all have their drawbacks, as well. It's not like you pick up a great Stradivari or a great Guarneri and all of a sudden your problems are solved. There are things about the instrument that you have to learn to coax out of it.

Laurie: Some people say that sometimes a Strad or a Guarneri is actually harder to play.

Elmar: Sometimes that's true, sure. Therefore ease is not the only thing you should be looking for, when you play a great instrument. There are so many different qualities. Of course, ease is one of the essential things that you would like to have. You'd like an instrument that you could put in your hands and you just play and it feels very comfortable. But there are other issues, like sound and timbre and quality of darkness or lightness of the sound, malleability of the nuance of the sound, whether an instrument can respond to different bow pressures and speeds and all kinds of different things.

Laurie: A number of years ago, you performed with the Pasadena Symphony (in California), and I was playing in the orchestra. I remember that everybody thought you were playing on a fancy instrument, and then you said, "No, it's actually a $12,000 instrument from Salt Lake City!"

Elmar: Right!

Laurie: All the violinists in the orchestra were saying, "What?" and looking at this instrument. So I wanted to ask you what your thoughts are on the current state of violin-making. Are the moderns just as good as the old masters? Is that even a relevant comparison?

Elmar: Here's what I'll say about contemporary makers: I'm perhaps the greatest champion of contemporary violin makers, as far as a player is concerned. Because I've owned so many of them, and I've bought so many of them, and I've supported many of the great modern violin makers, from Joseph Curtin and Gregg Alf at the beginning, through John Young and even the Chinese makers. What I'm finding, in the last 30 years, is that the level of making of contemporary instrument makers is at the highest peak that it's ever been since the Golden Age of violin-making in Cremona (Italy).

Laurie: Why?

Elmar: There are a lot of reasons for that. I think that one of the biggest reasons is that over the last 30 years, all of the big violin-making schools have cropped up and people have been able to go and study and work for two, three or four years, in these school workshops. In that amount of time, the knowledge that we've gathered about violin-making has been so extensive, in terms of the graduations of the great instruments, the varnish, the kinds of wood that were used, the workmanship, how different things were accomplished by the great classical makers, in terms of molds and carving and all kinds of such issues. There's never been a time like this! I think that the fine violin makers that are making instruments today can only be surpassed by the greatest classical makers of Cremona of the 18th century. The people who are making instruments today absolutely do compare to a lot of those makers.

Laurie: And for you, without the question of whether one is better than the other, is there a difference that you can generally talk about between a 300- or 400-year-old instrument and an instrument from today?

Elmar: I think the basic difference is how the instrument sounds under your ear, and if you're a really sensitive player, you're looking for color and nuance in the sound. On certain (modern) instruments, it's closer to the old Italian instrument sound than others, but it's something you have to sort of produce on a new instrument. On an old instrument, a lot of that is automatically there in the sound. I think that this has entirely to do with time. With how much an instrument was played, how much time is given to change, to absorb all the climatic differences that go on. Just imagine that the Stradivaris and Guarneris have been around for more than 300 years, and these instruments are being made last year — they're comparable to some of these instruments that have been around for over 300 years! I think that's one factor that you can never discount that one factor, when you're playing on a new violin: time. Time is so important.

Laurie: Does it help that an instrument has been played on by many people, or by certain people?

Elmar: I'm a firm believer that the instrument takes on the identity of the player, so if it's a really good player playing an instrument, it should sound better going from one player to the next. If there's a bad player in there, you have to get the bad vibrations out. I really believe it!

Laurie: I think to non-violinists, we all sound kooky, but just about every violinist I talk to nods their head in agreement.

Elmar: Absolutely.

Laurie: To turn our attentions to Schumann, what made you decide to dive into this rather complicated concerto by Schumann, and how long have you been playing it?

Elmar: I grew up listening to an old recording that I had of (Henryk)

Szeryng, an old Mercury recording with Antal Doráti. I always had an attraction to this concerto because of that recording. I felt that when this concerto could be played really, really well, it was very successful on a lot of different levels. And the second movement of this concerto is one of the greatest second movements of any Romantic concerto.

Laurie: What makes it so?

Elmar: There's a certain intangible, Romantic, nostalgic quality about it that you can't put your finger on, but it's so beautiful. He described the theme of the second movement as coming to him from the angels, and that's exactly the way I hear it. I feel like it's something that a human being can't really produce. It's got to come from somewhere else. And as kooky as that sounds, I think that most of the great music, of Brahms or Beethoven or Tchaikovsky or Sibelius, I think it does come from somewhere else. Of course, you can analyze it: This was a theme that he developed this way because the tonic goes to the third and blah blah blah — but that doesn't tell you where the inspiration comes from.

Laurie: It was a concerto that I wasn't familiar with, and the second movement almost sounded like Mahler or something to me.

Elmar: I know! First of all, this concerto is the unique language of Schumann. I'm a huge fan of Schumann, but when you go back and you look at the very few works that he wrote for the violin, both sonatas are enigmatic. It's not some kind of music that you can sit down in a concert hall and listen to comfortably, as you would listen to a Brahms symphony. There's always something about it that makes you think, "How did he do this, why did he do this?" That's what attracted me to the concerto.

Laurie: What would you say to the idea that he wrote it that way because he was insane? It was, after all, among the last pieces he wrote before being committed to a sanatorium.

Elmar: I would say *that's* a totally insane idea. He knew very well what he was doing. There were moments when he may not have been so clear, but I feel very strongly that when he wrote this violin concerto, he was in a total state of clarity. Everything seems to work, to me. It's just a question of how much you want to build into it and try to find what it is that works in the piece.

Laurie: If I were wanting to play this piece, what are some of the particular technical challenges that I'd face?

Elmar: It's very un-violinistic; it's much more like piano writing than it is like violin writing. So the challenges are there, first of all, to overcome the technical issues that Schumann writes in the score. For me, they're all solvable. I feel like they're all solvable, but it's not the kind of solvability, if that's a word, that you look at it and it comes to you right away. You have to sit down and look at it and figure out what the best way is to express musically what he wrote in a very un-violinistic way.

Laurie: So this is a challenge.

Elmar: It's a big challenge. Much less in the first movement than in the last movement, but there are sections in the first movement where there are extremely problematic spots for the violin. It doesn't play itself, not by any means.

Laurie: Something you were saying in the conversation that comes with the album is that the last movement is virtuosic, but not in a way that necessarily the audience is going to see it as virtuosic. It's not like Paganini, where everybody drops his jaw and says, 'Look what he's doing!"

Elmar: Absolutely! Yet it's no less difficult than Paganini. In fact, some Paganini is more idiomatic and easier to play than this!

Laurie: Well, Paganini was a violinist! Still, I was reading about this concerto, and has it really been played only as seldomly has they say? Did it really have these long periods of time where no one played it?

Elmar: Yes. It was not played because Joachim nixed it, and Brahms nixed it, and Clara Schumann nixed it, for whatever reasons. My understanding is that Joachim's private performance, with Schumann there, was not good at all. And it's very easy, when the performance is not great, for a violinist to say, "You know what? It's not a great piece." It's very easy to say that.

Laurie: Not my fault, your fault.

Elmar: Exactly.

Laurie: But it sounds like it wasn't even played very much in the 20th century!

Elmar: It's not made its way into the standard repertoire, for whatever reason. I think because it is problematic and so people shy away from it. I think that the violinists that are a little more adventurous don't feel that way. They feel that this is a worthy piece, and I'm going to go ahead with it, I'm going to make it part of my repertoire. A few people have. Gidon Kremer has played it, and Frank Peter Zimmermann and Joshua Bell, but very few and far between.

Laurie: Is it difficult for the orchestra? For example, the syncopation issue in the second movement.

Elmar: That's a challenge. I think the biggest challenge for the orchestra is the ensemble between the orchestra and the violin solo. Because the physical writing is rather mainstream, even for Schumann: you have pretty much the violin doing what it's doing and then in the tuttis the orchestra plays whatever it needs to play. It's not like Brahms Concerto, where you have underlying thematic material in the orchestra and the violin is doing something, it's just mostly violin, tutti, violin, tutti.

You were asking me if I've played this concerto a lot. Actually, this is the first time I've played it. And it's the first time that this orchestra, the Atlantic Classical Orchestra, has recorded a CD, so it's their first CD. And I think that's pretty important because the caliber of the orchestra is very wonderful, yet nobody's heard of it.

Laurie: What made you decide to record it live, instead of in a studio?

Elmar: I love live recording, I just feel that live recording has an element that's very hard to capture in the studio. When you're on the stage and there's the chemistry between the orchestra and the conductor and the audience — I don't think that can be replaced.

Laurie: It's a little more risk and excitement.

Elmar: Absolutely. Everything you hear that's done in the studios these days is note-perfect and everything is together, so you really don't know how people play. For me, even if something isn't perfect, it really gives you a sense of performance, live recording. And I just love that.

Hilary Hahn. Photo: Michael Patrick O'Leary

HILARY HAHN

Originally published on November 11, 2013

Announced in 2011, Hilary Hahn's idea to commission 27 living composers to each write her an encore piece is one of the most forward-looking projects the classical music world has seen in recent years. This interview took place after those pieces had all been written, performed live in concerts all over the world, then recorded by Hilary. It's this kind of experimentation, risk-taking and spirit of collaboration that will keep classical music evolving and relevant for 21st-century audiences.

What started as several dozen cold-calls to composers has now become a major life focus for Hilary Hahn, whose album, *In 27 Pieces: The Hilary Hahn Encores*, is officially released today.

Besides giving life to 27 new, short-length pieces for violin, Hilary's project has done much more: it has provided a sort of tasting menu for both listeners and musicians to sample contemporary classical music by living composers.

And how many flavors might we find? A lot! Other than the fact that these works are all under about five minutes and that they are written for violin and piano, each is strikingly unique. I listened and took notes on all 27 pieces, and my observations varied wildly. Here is a sampling:
"hypnotic and minimalist; rhythmically driving and complex; a tonal, beautiful melody; sirens and Psycho; busy and fast; fly buzzing; bluegrass language; mournful and throbbing; fast syncopation; Eastern and slide-y;

deranged mental patient; melodic, as in a movie score."

The 26 composers that Hilary commissioned in 2011 to each write an encore piece for violin are: Antón García Abril, Franghiz Ali-Zadeh, Lera Auerbach, Richard Barrett, Mason Bates, Tina Davidson, David Del Tredici, Avner Dorman, Du Yun, Søren Nils Eichberg, Christos Hatzis, Jennifer Higdon, James Newton Howard, Bun-Ching Lam, David Lang, Paul Moravec, Nico Muhly, Michiru Oshima, Kala Ramnath, Einojuhani Rautavaara, Max Richter, Somei Satoh, Elliott Sharp, Valentin Silvestrov, Mark-Anthony Turnage, and Gillian Whitehead. Jeff Myers was chosen as the 27th composer through an online contest that attracted more than 400 submissions.

I spoke to Hilary a week ago about her partnership with pianist Cory Smythe in this project; about what it was like to work with so many composers and learn so much new music in such a short time; and about how other violinists can move forward with contemporary music, using these new miniatures as a possible entryway.

We started by talking about the CD release party she held at Greenwich House Music School on Nov. 3. She had many of the composers present for the all-day event, during which there were panel discussions, performances of other works by the composers, a screening of a movie that featured a film score by one composer, and ultimately, a four part-performance, in which which she and pianist Cory Smythe played all 27 encore pieces.

Laurie: Tell me all about your release party, it sounded like such a unique event!

Hilary: There were a lot of composers, and also a lot of different things happening in various rooms, where I heard pieces by the composers that I hadn't heard before, played live. I played all the encores myself, and pianist Cory Smythe, who is on the record, played with me. We performed all of them for the first time in one day, and we played them in record order. That was interesting because we had toured this program over two seasons, but the record mixes those seasons together. It's not like one disc is one season and the other disc is the other season. So we hadn't played a lot of them in those sequences before. It really gave us an overview, physically, of the project, that we hadn't had before.

Laurie: How long did it take to play them all, live?

Hilary: I don't know! (She laughs) We did them in four parts.

Laurie: How many of your composers were there?

Hilary: About 10.

Laurie: That's a pretty good turnout.

Hilary: They're international, so it was nice that so many were able to make it. Not everyone who is in New York was able to make it, and people came from outside of New York as well.

Laurie: I've listened to all of the encores, and as I listened, I noticed the important role of the pianist. How did you choose Cory for this project, and what was it like to do this together? It's just such an immense amount of new music.

Hilary: Each piece had its own trajectory, and while we worked on them simultaneously (to prepare for touring), it really felt like we were focusing on one at a time. The material doesn't really overlap, and I hadn't played a lot of these composers before.

Cory does a lot of new music; he was recommended to me for a concert for which I needed a pianist, and we really hit it off. It just happened that the *Encores* project was contemporary music, and I was working towards that at the time. So it was as if it was meant to be!

He really helped me with understanding how to approach things that you have no idea how to begin with. Not that the pieces were unrecognizable to me, but it was just so much new material, and he works on a lot of new material. While I'd worked (in the past) on one piece at a time, he had experience rehearsing lots of different things at once. So he was able to help me come up with different ways of approaching things when I'd hit a wall. It was really helpful.

He's been such a good collaborator; really dedicated, and he's really made this project possible for me in a practical way, performing it day in and day out. He's been such a part of it.

Laurie: How did you approach each piece? I mean I'm sure each was different, but over doing 27 of them, did you come up with sort of a process? Do you start it with the violin part alone, or do you read it together first, how did it work?

Hilary: I had to start with the violin part alone because I was on the road most of the time. With something that you've never played before, especially a composer you've never played before, you have to familiarize yourself with the patterns and the sequences, sort of the mechanism of how they write for the instrument. So I had to figure out things like bowings and fingerings to start with. Also, I needed to check to see if there was anything that needed to be addressed directly with the composer, before the rehearsal process began. So I would work on it, then I would send some comments to the composer, if I had anything. But mostly, I tried to get it to where I could play it, and then get together with Cory to make sure that it was do-able, that I knew that the piece was in shape in the sense that I wouldn't need to make requests from the composer. Then we could just work on it further. Often we were aiming for a tour, so we had a deadline! (She laughs) We'd work on the deadline.

When you're touring, you don't really have as much luxury of time because you have deadlines all the time. Every week you have a performance coming up, with repertoire that's pre-set. Not every performance is the repertoire that feels most comfortable at the time. So you never quite know what's going to take more time that particular week, and what's going to take the majority of your time the next week. You just try to work on everything and leave enough room so that if something needs more time, you can give it that time.

Laurie: What role did the composer have, in bringing to life these pieces? Did you play these pieces for each composer before you performed them? Were you playing them for composers on Skype, did you wind up doing any changes or revisions together with the composer?

Hilary: I tried in some way to work with the composer on each piece, while still letting the composer write what he or she wanted to write.

The first part was just the commissioning process, what I requested from the composer: to write something between 1 1/2 and five minutes

HILARY HAHN

long, and for it to be for violin and piano. The reason I gave them that time frame was because when you perform something, sometimes you stretch it a little bit, and anything above six or seven minutes is really too long for an encore. I figured, if they wrote for five minutes, it would be fine. And anything under a minute and a half feels too short, but a minute and a half can be a really great length for an encore.

Working with the composers themselves — I spoke with them if I had a question about the violin part, or if I felt like something didn't fit — or it fit in my hand really well, but it might be tricky in general. For example, I have a really big stretch, so I can stretch to certain things that may not be the best solution for everyone who might play the piece in the future. Of course, there are things that people would do more naturally than I would, but I wouldn't think to mention! (She laughs) But those things that I noticed, I tried to bring up, then the composer could decide whether to write that as an optional feature, rewrite it or just leave it. I don't like to tell a composer what to do, I just like to point out what I can see being an issue for a large group of people. If I'm having trouble playing something and I'm having to come up with a solution that's very unorthodox, I know that other people will have to go through the same process. Sometimes that can be challenging to the listeners, because it sounds like something isn't quite right in that spot. But that's kind of my criteria for mentioning something to the composer. Otherwise, if it's an interpretive issue, I try to take that into my own court and take responsibility for that.

As we were rehearsing before the performances, I got to meet and talk with a few of them. If I had a question about how something was written, I did get to meet with these particular composers and ask, "What do you mean, and how to you want me to play it?" before I got too far into playing it a certain way. But that wasn't everyone. Mostly, we prepared for the performances and then started performing the pieces. We got a feel for what the pieces could be, and then sent off rehearsal recordings to the composers — very unprofessional recordings! — but good enough that they could tell if we were doing a wrong note. I wanted to make sure that the composers could catch that, and also they could give input on the interpretation. I was in touch with all of them about

299

that, except for one person who was just pretty much impossible to reach via technology.

If I hadn't managed to reach them before the tours, I made sure to reach them before we recorded, so that going into the sessions, we knew what to do. We wanted to be sure that the composers would be happy, as much as possible.

Laurie: I noticed that you have interviews up on your YouTube channel with 17 of the composers. They provide an interesting perspective. Did you do those interviews after you'd already been playing each composer's piece for a while?

Hilary: I interviewed some of the composers before I received their pieces; and I talked some to along the way, while I was working on their piece. We'd be in touch about something, and I'd say, "Oh, can you hop on Skype for a little bit, and I can record an interview?" Some of them, I still want to interview. It's tricky when you have a lot of different schedules, different time zones and unreliable Internet connections. If it's a bad Internet connection, it's a bad interview! (She laughs) — at least for the people trying to watch it. If I don't know how good my Internet connection is going to be, it's hard to organize something in advance, if say, I'm going to be somewhere for two days. It's actually more complicated than it seems!

Laurie: It looked pretty complicated to me: you're calling from Berlin, they're in New York...

Hilary: It's fun, I alway enjoy the interviews. I like talking with people when they have a different context to express themselves in. You have your normal collaborative conversations, and you have your chilling-out-after-collaborating kinds of conversations. But then when people are speaking to a different audience, and they don't know who exactly is listening, they explain themselves in a different way. You learn different things about them. That's one reason I really like interviewing people; it helps me understand where they're coming from.

Laurie: One thing I thought was really neat about this project, is that it's almost like a little lens through which you can get to know 27 contemporary composers. I wondered what your perspective was, having really lived with all these pieces. For you, is there any conclusion you can make about the state of music composition here and now, based on this big project you've just done?

Hilary: It's hard to generalize. I never wanted it to be a collection of names — it's more of an exhibit, it's more of a showcase of each one, but there are multiple ones. One thing that I really saw illustrated very clearly in the course of this project is how each composer is so individual. They all have their own reasons for creating, they all have their own ways of creating, and they have different interests outside of music, that are also related to the arts, that feed back into how they write. Since I'd worked with a limited number of composers before, I thought that after a while you would start to see some patterns, or types. But I found that there are actually no types. I haven't found any mirroring between any of the composers and how they write and how they create. That's been illuminating for me, and I think that however far you would go in composition, you would find that to be the case.

I don't think the cliques determine the personality. There may be people who are grouped together as a certain school of writing, or people who studied together, but I don't think that means they have similarities in their motivation. I found that really interesting — because you know, with instrumentalists you can kind of generalize the personality types for different instruments, obviously, it's not quite the most accurate...

Laurie: The high-strung violinists, the relaxed, social cellists...

Hilary: ...the bassists who have so many different hobbies — it seems like I know a lot of bassists who repair cars or bake bread! It's not like every one of the instrumentalists in those groups does stuff like that, but you do see a few patterns. But I found, with the composers, there were none of those.

Working on this project, I wanted each piece to have its own character, and I wanted to make sure that no piece would get lost in the group. Getting a feel for the different personalities of the composers helped me to understand how to differentiate the pieces. But in the end, it was the pieces that really determined that.

Laurie: Was there anything in the pieces that surprised you, or required new techniques or funny ways of using the violin?

Hilary: Each piece taught me something, and it was amazing what difference there was for me, between a piece by a composer I'd played before and a piece by a composer I'd never played. When I received Jennifer (Higdon)'s piece and when I received James Newton Howard's piece, (composers I'd worked with before) it was like recognizing a language. I just knew what to do with it, immediately.

With all the others, I had to find my way into the piece, using the composer's musical language in the context of the piece, to start with, and then seeing how the piece develops on tour. What I thought each piece was, is not necessarily what it turned out to be. When you're working on something, you first need to take what's presented to you in the score, and then you need to figure out what really makes it innate for you, in order to be able to bring it across to the audience. I was trying to figure out that innate element in every single one — but with brand-new people, brand-new ways of expressing their thoughts, and perhaps brand-new thoughts, too. So there were definitely things that pushed me in each piece. Sometimes it's hard to specify exactly what. It has very little to do with what you actually see in the music itself, and a lot more to do with how you get to the point where you feel like it's part of you. But there were definitely some techniques that I'd never done before, and it really helped to work on those pieces, to have the performances and to get to where those techniques became familiar to me. They became more ways of expression that I could tap into.

Laurie: Like what kind of techniques?

Hilary: Well, if you look at the score for Richard Barrett's piece (*Shade*) or for Elliott Sharp's piece (*Storm of the Eye*), I had to learn how to do a whole bunch of things. In *Storm of the Eye*, I had to learn how to relate to the instrument the way Elliott relates to the instrument, because he's a performer, so he improvises, he plays multiple instruments. (At the release event), he was performing one of his guitar works, and you could really see the thread of continuity between what he was playing himself, and what he'd written for me to play. But I had to learn how to get there in his piece, and I also found it helpful to talk with him about what he was aiming for with the different effects that he wrote. I realized, he's kind of self-taught, and he's looking for these sounds; then in the course of finding them, he figures out how to write them.

I'm not big into researching everything about a composer before you learn a piece for the first time, because I think it can give you a very particular idea of what you should be doing with a piece before the piece actually speaks to you. That's why, in these cases, I wanted to start with the piece. But then when I met with the composers, asked them questions, and they gave me feedback about what I was doing, that's when I realized what they were going for and what I needed to do in order to align with what they had in mind. So it was a multi-step process.

Technically, I'd say Richard Barrett's piece or Elliott Sharp's piece had the most unfamiliar techniques in them. But also, in Du Yun's writing (*When a Tiger Meets a Rosa Rugosa*), I had to figure out what she meant by some of her markings. And when I worked on Antón García Abril's piece (*Third Sigh*), I entirely got the wrong idea from some of his markings. So I'm glad I had a meeting with him because once he explained to me what he meant, it made perfect sense. But it's hard to guess things.

It also makes you wonder how much you've been guessing wrong about other pieces, where you can't talk to the composer! Everyone thinks they know what they're doing, but is that really what the composer meant by that word? You don't know!

Laurie: It could be that 50 recordings of the Tchaikovsky *Violin Concerto* just all have it wrong!

Hilary: Exactly! And even if the source says something, maybe we don't know what they meant by that expression. We think we know. But it's unbelievable how much variety there can be in the same words. So that was interesting. Then in something like Avner Dorman's piece (*Memory Games*), there's a lot of rhythmic novelty, and it was complicated to put together.

Laurie: That's what I wrote when I heard it, "rhythmically complex"!

Hilary: And it's so fast! So it took a lot of time to put together. And then there's a piece called *Levitation* by Søren Nils Eichberg, and I had to figure out, with those particular forms of phrase he writes, how to relate to that in the longer violin line. Also, it handles differently on violin than it does on piano, but we play overlapping things. So I had to figure out with Cory, what our goals were with those phrases.

Laurie: Listening to that one, I wondered if Eichberg was a pianist, because there was so much in the piano with that piece.

Hilary: Which is nice. I was hoping that people would write things which were substantial for piano. People were all over the place with how they wanted to handle the duo capabilities. By "all over the place," I don't mean in a messy way, I mean in an interesting way. David Lang, for example, wrote this piece (*light moving*) that has the violin pretty much accompanying, and the piano takes the lead on the phrasing. I really liked that aspect of that piece, and that's something new that I got to do.

Every piece has something, a certain approach, that I had to learn.

Laurie: Did it change you as a musician, to learn all these new pieces?

Hilary: I think every piece does, doesn't it? When you work on something that's new, but also when you work on something after working on something else, it changes your context for that piece. I don't know if it changes you as much as it informs you and develops you, just to have that (new) context to draw from. Every time that you have a different exposure to music, you have one more thing you can refer to in your experience. And you have more options, also, with musical ideas, when you're exposed to other people's musical ideas, whether that's through working with a conductor, or working with someone who's improvising, or working with someone who wants you to do a certain thing with the instrument. You just get all these different options in your mind.

Laurie: You have a LOT of options here!

Hilary: It's great!

Laurie: Will the sheet music be available, if people want to play these?

Hilary: There's going to be a complete printed edition, and most will be available digitally, as well.

Laurie: Great. When!?

Hilary: This project is so huge! We're wrapping up the fingerings, bowings and proofreading part of the publishing. It's coming soon! Very soon.

Laurie: What if I were to want to play one of these pieces? That would be, someone who is not a superstar soloist, just kind of your average trained violinist. Which of them is maybe the most idiomatic, or, I hesitate to say "easy," but playable to someone who is just approaching these pieces?

Hilary: I'm going to be kind of annoying with this answer because it's not going to really answer your question! I think that with anything new, you have to want to play it. I don't think it's a matter so much of being able to play it, as it is being interested in it.

So I would suggest that people listen to these pieces, and if they really like a certain piece, then check out the music. Even if it's something that they don't know how to play, or something they think sounds really hard — just to work at something at quarter tempo is really interesting, just to learn how something is put together. I don't play piano very well, but sometimes I'll sit down with something really simple, or even something hard, if I'm trying to figure out a phrase in a sonata. I'll just play it super slowly. But it helps me understand what's in the piece.

My goal, for players, is to show a lot of different composers' work and to have a range of things that would interest people. I hope that people will find things they like, and even if they don't wind up playing a particular piece, they'll explore that composer further. Every one of these composers has a range of pieces that they've written, a range of technically challenging things. I think you can probably find something from a composer that you really like, that you can play, no matter what level you're at, even if it's a slow movement, or if it's played at a moderate tempo.

So I'm not going to suggest a particular piece; I would suggest that people listen and find something that interests or intrigues them. If you are curious or intrigued by something, there's no better way to figure out what it is that intrigues you about it, than to look at it in the applied way: try to play it.

Laurie: One of the pieces I was immediately curious about was the one by Jennifer Higdon (*Echo Dash*); it's so fast and syncopated. I thought, is she just following the pianist, a half-beat behind? Holy cow!

Hilary: We're playing 8ths and 16ths, but they're syncopated. And we have staggered 8th notes — we never have staggered 16ths. We have the 16ths together, and we have triplet 16ths. So it could be played at a slower tempo and be fun. You could definitely play the violin part at a slower tempo, even if you're not super virtuosic, you could probably do it. But the most difficult thing about that piece is keeping track of the rhythm.

Laurie: It seemed so!

Hilary: Even something like the Lang — it's very hard to play, but it's the same thing: it repeats an octave higher in the second half, so you could even treat that as a very slow warm up. Not like an etude, but think about it musically. But you can get it in your fingers. Even if you don't want to play the high one, you can play the low one.

There are ways to work on these pieces, even if they're extremely challenging, so that you learn contemporary music and incorporate it into your daily life, without it being a big deal. Everyone works on pieces that are hard, and it doesn't have to be a piece that you've heard for decades, it can be a newer piece, too. I think sometimes people think of new music as a whole separate category — but it's really not. It's just part of the continuum, and I think we need to treat it as part of the continuum and include things from all different centuries in our daily musical work or exploration.

Laurie: These pieces are a nice entree for both players and listeners. If you're a listener, it can be the kind of thing where you say, "Oh, I've never heard of this Lang, maybe I like his music, I'll go listen to other things by him."

Hilary: Exactly, that was a big hope for me. And also, if you think about it, none of these pieces is extremely long. I think the longest violin part is 10 pages, and the shortest is one page. So you can learn them and work on them over time, and play a whole piece that's contemporary. And with piano, you can have a way to work on it without needing to put together an orchestra or program something for a half an hour. You can chip away at things, work on it with a pianist you know, and get to know it, without it taking up your entire year.

Laurie: I'm looking forward to the book of sheet music coming out for these.

Hilary: It's kind of a trip through possibilities of violin interpretation — interpreting the technique, as well as the ways you can make music with the instrument.

Laurie: I saw your interview with Jennifer Higdon, where she said, "I figured people would write slow pieces." It was interesting she said that, because people wrote pieces all over the map. They aren't all slow pieces, they aren't all fast pieces, there's just everything here, it's crazy.

Hilary: People wrote pieces that were slow pieces, that were fast pieces, that were in between, that were very slow but went fast, that started slow went fast went slow, that started fast went slow went fast, (she laughs) all kinds of combinations! And about half of them were thinking, "What is everyone else going to write? How can I stand out in a way that's different?" And I don't think they could have known what everyone else was going to write, but I think it's an interesting question.

Laurie: An interesting sociological experiment.

Hilary: But you know, they've all been so supportive of the project and of the idea that there are people gathered together, composing for it. I wasn't sure whether the fact that there are multiple composers involved would be frustrating for some of them, but no one had any issue. Everyone was just glad to have everyone else participating. It's been really nice to see that support in the composer community.

ABOUT THE AUTHOR

Laurie Niles was born in Cleveland, Ohio and grew up in Aurora, Colorado. She earned her Bachelor of Music degree from Northwestern University and her Master of Arts in Journalism from Indiana University. After working for five years as a newspaper reporter (for the Bloomington *Herald-Times,* then the *Omaha World-Herald)*, Laurie and her husband, Robert, founded the online musician community Violinist.com in 1996. As editor of Violinist.com, Laurie has written hundreds of articles and interviewed countless violinists and classical musicians. Laurie also has written articles for *The Strad* magazine, *Symphony* magazine and the *American Suzuki Journal*. She lives in Pasadena, California, where she also teaches violin and freelances as a violinist. She and Robert have two children.

17375653R00180

Made in the USA
Middletown, DE
21 January 2015